Edward K. Chatterton

Sailing Ships

The Story of Their Development From the Earliest Times to the Present Day

Edward K. Chatterton

Sailing Ships

The Story of Their Development From the Earliest Times to the Present Day

ISBN/EAN: 9783954273010
Erscheinungsjahr: 2013
Erscheinungsort: Bremen, Deutschland

© maritimepress in Europäischer Hochschulverlag GmbH & Co. KG, Fahrenheitstr. 1, 28359 Bremen. Alle Rechte beim Verlag und bei den jeweiligen Lizenzgebern.

www.maritimepress.de | office@maritimepress.de

A SEVENTEENTH-CENTURY ENGLISH WARSHIP

SAILING SHIPS

THE STORY OF THEIR DEVELOPMENT
FROM THE EARLIEST TIMES
TO THE PRESENT DAY

BY

E. KEBLE CHATTERTON

WITH A HUNDRED AND
THIRTY ILLUSTRATIONS

LONDON
SIDGWICK & JACKSON, LTD.
3 ADAM STREET ADELPHI W.C.

PREFACE.

THIS history of sailing ships has been written primarily for the general reader, in the hope that the sons and daughters of a naval nation, and of an Empire that stretches beyond the seas, may find therein a record of some interest and assistance in enlarging and systematising their ideas on the subject, especially as regards the ships of earlier centuries. It is not necessary to look far—no further than the poster-designs on advertisement-hoardings— to observe the errors into which our artists of to-day are liable to fall owing to lack of historical knowledge in this subject; and to put (for instance) triangular headsails with a rectangular sail on the "bonaventure mizzen-mast" of an early sixteenth-century ship, is an inaccuracy scarcely to be pardoned.

Quite recently one of the chief librarians in one of our biggest national treasure-houses informed me that when an artist, who had been commissioned to illustrate a certain work, came to him for guidance as to the ships of a recent period, he was at a loss where to

PREFACE

lay his hands on a book which should show him what he wished to know by picture and description. Only after much search was the requisite knowledge obtained.

I trust that both the yachtsman and sailorman will find in these pages something of the same exciting pleasure which has been mine in tracing the course of the evolutions through which their ships have passed. Those whose work or amusement it is to acquaint themselves with the sailing ship and her ways, and for lack of time and opportunity are unable to seek out the noble pedigree of what Ruskin truly described as " one of the loveliest things man ever made, and one of the noblest," may care to learn what were the changing conditions which combined to bring about such a highly complex creature as the modern sailing ship. Perhaps at some time when handling a rope, a spar, a tiller or a sail, they may have wondered how it all began ; what were the origins of all those various parts of a ships " furniture "; why some essential portions have scarcely changed ; and how other portions are the outcome of time, experiment, and science. I hope that to neither the amateur nor the professional sailor I shall seem impertinent if I have attempted to tell them something about their ship which they did not know before. But if, on the other hand, I shall have succeeded in increasing their love for the sailing-ship by outlining her career, I trust that this may be allowed to counterbalance the defects which, in a subject of so vast a scope, are hardly to be avoided in spite of considerable care and the generous assistance of many kind friends.

Finally, I make my appeal to the younger generation, to whom ships and the sea have in all times suggested so much that is bound up with adventure and brave deeds. The present moment sees us at a stage in the history of ships when the Royal Navy as a whole, and the Merchant Service almost entirely, have no longer any convenience for sail. There is a dire need in the latter for both officers and men, whilst on shore the conditions of employment are exactly the reverse. Surely it is only by a mutual adjustment of the two that both problems, on sea and land, can possibly be overcome ; and it is only by winning the enthusiasm of the boy who is to become father of the

PREFACE

man that the sailor's love for the sea can be handed on from generation to generation. We have received from our ancestors a splendid heritage, a unique legacy—the mastery of the seas. That legacy brings with it a commensurate responsibility, to retain what our forefathers fought for so dearly. Perhaps to the healthy-minded Anglo-Saxon boy, not yet too *blasé* and civilised to feel no thrill in reading his Marryat, Cook, Ballantyne, Henty, Fenn, or the glorious sea-fights and discoveries in history itself—perhaps to him this book may be of some assistance in visualising the actual ships of each historical period.

I desire to return thanks to many who, from motives of personal friendship or of love for ships, have so readily lent me their assistance in the course of this work. If I have omitted to include the names of any to whom my obligations are due it is from no sense of ingratitude. Especially I am anxious to return thanks to Dr. Wallis Budge and Mr. H. R. Hall of the Egyptian Department of the British Museum, as well as to the officials in other departments of the same institution, particularly those of the Coin Room, the Print Room, the Manuscript Room, Greek and Roman Antiquities, and British and Mediæval Antiquities: to Mr. Clifford Smith of the Victoria and Albert Museum, South Kensington, and to Mr. R. C. Flower of the Public Record Office for assistance in research: to Dr. Hoyle of the Manchester Museum for permission to use photographs of two Egyptian models: to the Board of Education for permission to reproduce photographs of models in the South Kensington Museum: to the Curator of the Royal Naval College Museum, Greenwich, for granting special facilities for studying the collection of models : to the British Consul at Christiania, for assistance in obtaining photographs of Viking ships; to M. Ernest Leroux for permission to use the illustration of the *navis actuaria* found on the Althiburus mosaic : to the Elder Brethren of Trinity House, jointly with Messrs. Cassell and Co., for allowing me to reproduce Phineas Pett's *Royal Prince:* to the Committee of the Royal Victoria Yacht Club, Ryde, for permission to reproduce Messrs. West's photograph of the rare print of the *Alarm*, Fig. 113 : to Captain Roald Amundsen for the plans of the

PREFACE

Gjoa : to the authorities of the British Museum for many illustrations either sketched, photographed, or reproduced from their catalogues: to Lieut.-Colonel A. Leetham, Curator of the Royal United Service Museum, Whitehall, for permission to photograph models and prints: to Captain C. E. Terry for the illustration of the *Santa Maria:* to Mr. A. E. M. Haes for the photograph of the *Oimara:* to Messrs. Camper and Nicholsons, Limited, for the plans of the yacht *Pampas:* to Messrs. White Brothers for the lines of the yacht *Elizabeth:* to Messrs. Fores for the illustrations of the *Xarifa* and *Kestrel:* and to Mr. H. Warington Smyth for the Nugger in Fig. 8, the two illustrations of Scandinavian and Russian ships in Figs. 30 and 31, and the American schooner in Fig. 91. I wish also to acknowledge Mr. Warington Smyth's extreme courtesy in offering to allow me to use any of the other sketches in his delightful book " Mast and Sail in Europe and Asia," and only regret that circumstances prevented my being able to avail myself more fully of so generous an offer.

The illustrations in Figs. 26 and 27 appear by arrangement with Mr. John Murray: Fig. 51 by arrangement with the Clarendon Press, Oxford: and Figs. 30, 31, 87-90, 92, 93, 95, 102, 104, 106, 111, 112, 114, 115, and the Plans, by arrangement with the editor of *The Yachting Monthly.* Thanks are also due to two artists skilled in marine subjects—to Mr. Charles Dixon for his two pictures in colour, at once lively and accurate ; and to Mr. Norman S. Carr, not only for the initial letters of the chapters, but for thirty or more sketches specially drawn for this book.

Finally, I have to express my thanks to Mr. John Masefield, who has been kind enough to read the proofs, while the book was passing through the press, and to give me the benefit of his valuable advice.

E. KEBLE CHATTERTON.

June 1909.

X

LIST OF ILLUSTRATIONS

LIST OF ILLUSTRATIONS

LIST OF ILLUSTRATIONS

LIST OF ILLUSTRATIONS

LIST OF ILLUSTRATIONS

LIST OF ILLUSTRATIONS

PLANS.

(AT END OF VOLUME.)

CHAPTER I.

INTRODUCTORY.

SHORT time ago one of our Naval Museums came into possession of a certain model of a sailing ship. She was a fine vessel, one of the first of the old "wooden walls" to be built in the reign of the late Queen. The Curator wisely determined to have this model fully rigged with all her spars, sails, and gear, just as the original had been in her days of active service. Every detail was correct; every halyard and brace were made of proportionate thickness. Even the right kind of "stuff" was found, after some difficulty, for the cable. An efficient rigger, too, was found, who happened to have served on this same ship.

Finally, when the model was completed the Curator looked at it and said, "*Now* it will be possible for those who come after us to tell exactly how a sailing ship was rigged; in a few years' time there won't be a man alive who will know how to do it."

It is with a similar desire, to preserve all that can be gathered, that an attempt is made in the present book to collect into one continuous narrative the historical data available concerning the evolution of that fast-disappearing object—the sailing ship. With the advent of steam was

A

hoisted the signal for abolishing sail; and although for a long time the famous old clippers put up a keen fight, yet for commercial purposes, when passengers and mails, merchandise and perishable food, had to be hurried from one side of the world to the other without loss of time, it became impossible for a sailing ship, that depended so entirely on the mercy of wind and weather, to compete successfully with the steamship. By 1840, it will be remembered, steamers had commenced crossing the Atlantic, and within the next ten or fifteen years the sailing ship, except for such long voyages as to China, Australia, and other distant countries, was for ever doomed. Perhaps these beautiful creatures, oversparred and under-manned though they are nowadays, will be allowed, in spite of competition and low freights, to remain with us a little longer. It is probable that the introduction of the motor, instead of assisting to complete the departure of sails, will help in their being retained : for it has now been found commercially profitable to instal the internal-combustion engine in ships of a size not exceeding about seven hundred tons. By this means sail can be used in a fair wind, and the motor can take her along in calms, as well as in tolerable weather against a head wind. In entering harbours and leaving there will also be a saving of the charge for a tug. Perhaps when the marine-motor industry has become more perfect it will be possible to fit a sufficiently powerful motor to a 4000-ton barque.

If that should be possible, then it would be indeed welcome news to hear that the sluicing ebb of sailing ships and sailormen had stopped. (For, of course, no one nowadays, except perhaps the lady passenger, would ever think of honouring the marine mechanics on board a liner or battleship with the title of "sailor," whose knowledge of seamanship is so elementary that they can as a rule neither sail a boat nor make a splice, let alone go up aloft.) But at present, when it is difficult to get enough

2

INTRODUCTORY

officers and men for the steam merchant service, it is doubtful if the sailing ship, except in the case of a few deep-sea vessels and the coasters, fishermen, pilots, and yachts round our coasts, will be encouraged to remain with us.

In setting forth whatever may be of interest in the following pages I have, following the example of that illustrious Elizabethan, Richard Hakluyt, taken "infinite cares," travelled many miles from port to port to talk with every kind of sailorman—deep-sea, coaster, or yacht's hand —with fishermen, pilots, shipbuilders, riggers, marine architects, and sail-makers. In addition to this, I have been fortunate in gaining access to libraries containing, in various languages and of both ancient and modern date, invaluable accounts of ships of earlier days. The study of coins (curiously overlooked by some writers on ancient ships) has enabled me to submit some definite knowledge concerning craft of the classical age. The study of old fonts in this country, especially in those churches which were dedicated in the name of St. Nicholas, the patron of sailors, has helped to confirm the otherwise scanty evidence for the period between the tenth and fourteenth centuries. But perhaps the most valuable and interesting material is the illustration of an Egyptian sailing ship of the XII. Dynasty. This model, rigged for sailing up and rowing down the Nile, will be discussed in Chapter II. Hitherto we have had to depend for our knowledge of Egyptian ships on the illustrations found on the tombs. Although in recent years some models of boats have been discovered in these tombs, yet that which I am enabled to reproduce (Figs. 5 and 6) is the only one showing the boat properly rigged that has hitherto been unearthed. This model was discovered in the season of 1906–1907 at Rifeh, by Professor Flinders Petrie, and is the finest example that has yet reached England. It is now in the Manchester Museum, and I am indebted to

SAILING SHIPS

Dr. Hoyle, the Director of the Museum, for his courtesy in enabling me to reproduce this very interesting model here.

Notwithstanding the deplorable fact that there are gaps existing at those critical stages where information would be the most welcome, it is nevertheless possible to construct a fairly continuous narrative of the development of the sailing ship. It will be noticed that in addition to the information to be found in ancient tombs of Egypt we have the evidence of ancient coins, vases, terra-cotta and wooden models, lamps, monuments, excavations in Scandinavia, England, Scotland, Germany. Coming to more modern times, there is the Bayeux Tapestry, with its excellent copy in the South Kensington Museum. We have, too, the pictorial representations on ancient seals and coins of this country. There are some reproductions of ships in old manuscripts; but it is an unfortunate fact that, except in comparatively modern times, it is rare to find the ship commemorated in paintings. Even when it is found, it is often represented with less regard to marine accuracy than to pictorial effect. When one considers the high position both Venice and Genoa occupied during the Middle Ages, alike in respect of art and maritime pursuits, it is difficult to understand why so remarkably few pictures of ships remain to us among the Old Masters. In both religious and secular paintings the ship is conspicuous by its absence. Perhaps it may be that artists had not received sufficient encouragement to paint marine subjects and that the gulf which to-day exists between the landsman and the sailor was equally great then.

However, various painters have seen fit to take the Pilgrimage of St. Ursula as their theme. Memline's celebrated panels on the reliquary of that saint, now in St. John's Hospital, Bruges, are of interest for our purpose, for no fewer than four of the six panels contain pictures of ships belonging to the period of the artist. The date of

4

these miniatures is some time not later than the year 1489. Old printed books of the sixteenth century onwards frequently contain illustrations of ships of the time. Among the books, for instance, presented to the South Kensington Museum on the death of Lady Dilke will be found an interesting illustrated French translation of the Acts of the Apostles. The ships (of mediæval design) illustrating the Voyages of St. Paul are of value as showing the rig and details of the craft contemporary with the artist. These and similar illustrations, excepting always when the artist has become too fantastic and imaginative, are important links in connecting the story of the ships of ancient days with the modern full-rigged ship. Coming down to the seventeenth century, the paintings of the Dutch artists Jan Van de Cappelle, of Willem Van de Velde the younger, Bakhuizen, Ruisdael, and Cuyp give us the most interesting details as to rigging and hull. Claude's picture, in the National Gallery, of the "Embarkation of St. Ursula," painted towards the end of the seventeenth century, shows the high-pooped ship of his own day. Charles Brooking of the eighteenth century, Turner and Clarkson Stanfield of the nineteenth, show us in their pictures many invaluable minutiæ of sailing ships. And even if Ruskin's criticism hold good, that Stanfield's ships never look weather-beaten but "always newly painted and clean," yet for our purpose this is no disadvantage; and it will be appreciated still more in a few years when our descendants go into art galleries to seek out from contemporary paintings the appearance of ships of the Victorian period.

Happily the ships of our day have been perpetuated by such admirable marine artists as Moore, Wyllie, Vicat Cole, Napier Hemy, Dixon, Somerscales, Tuke, and others. But in addition to pictures, we have at hand some hundreds of models of vessels in the South Kensington Museum, the Royal Naval College, Greenwich, the Royal United Service Museum, Whitehall, in the

Louvre, in Continental churches, museums, and arsenals, and in many private collections. Some of these models in Greenwich and South Kensington have been rigged from historical information in the museums themselves. It is impossible to deny the important influence that these wonderful little ships may have on the youthful minds of our nation, which has had the privilege for so many years of being called maritime. But to the student of ships of any age they are the greatest aid in assisting him—far greater, indeed, than pages of description, far greater also than the work of any painter—to realise the vessels that carried our ancestors across the seas. I am as certain that we owe to the Government the greatest thanks for putting these facilities before the public as I am uncertain that the same public appreciates them in the manner they deserve.

From all these sources, then, already enumerated, we are to begin to reconstruct as far as possible the ships of all ages. If we should be accused of arguing at times by inference without actual facts before us, let us be allowed to say this much: there are signs in a ship's lines and rigging which, to the landsman, are devoid of meaning, but to the man who has been wont to handle ships, and perhaps to design and build them, they are full of significance. Generally speaking, to the former a model is a nicely-carved piece of wood, adorned with a maze of complicated strings. Curves of hull, the position of the masts, the amount of sail area aft or forward, go for nothing. To the expert every inch of rope has its definite value, every line of her design speaks of speed or seaworthiness, or of the opposite. The careful balance of sails will show whether she is, to use sailor slang, "as handy as a gimlet" or as hard-mouthed a beast as ever was governed by a rudder. Therefore, if, in looking at the lines and rig of a ship of the Phœnicians, we should say, without being able to quote any historian of antiquity,

6

that she would never go to windward because her sail area was deficient and her draught of water too slight, and assume from this that the Phœnicians always waited for a fair wind or rowed with oars, we must not be accused of proving too much. This is not a matter for the archæologist, but for the practised mariner with some knowledge of the theory of his art. Any sailor, for instance, on looking at a model or illustration of a Burmese junk (see Fig. 1), would tell you at once that her lines and rig are such as would make her useless for going against the wind. He knows this by *inference*. As a *fact*, he learns afterwards that, like the boats of the Egyptians—which she much resembles in general shape, in mast, and in sail—these junks can only sail before the wind (which is usually favourable) in ascending the river Irawadi, and return with the current.

A nation exhibits its characteristics, its exact state of progress and degree of refinement in three things: its art, its literature, and its ships. Indeed we might go so far as to affirm that these last are but a branch of the first. Just as the house was at first merely a thing of utility, becoming in the course of time adorned with carvings and decoration, so the ship, from being the rough, clumsy dugout, with the advance of civilisation becomes adorned at first with animals' heads, with eyes, with a human head, with coloured hull, and at a subsequent stage with sails bearing devices of high artistic merit. Finally, gilded portholes and gilded sterns were added to the ship, so that, to quote the description of Charles I.'s *Sovereign of the Seas*, "she was so gorgeously ornamented with carving and gilding that she seemed to have been designed rather for a vain display of magnificence than for the service of the State."

The development of the ship, then, is parallel to the development of the State. In the rude ages she is a rough creature, remaining more like the tree out of which

7

FIG. 1. BURMESE JUNK.

she is made than a thing of being. In the hands of a nation that has reached a high degree of civilisation, though she is still made of oak from the forest, yet she has lost all resemblance to the tree-trunk. Instead, she has acquired a most wonderful personality of her own. The wood of the tree has become merely the means of expressing the most admirable combination of delicacy and strength, of slender lines and powerful masses.

Thus we must go to the East, the birthplace of civilisation, to trace the beginnings of our subject. We shall for this reason start from Egypt and Phœnicia, and, tracing the development through Greek and Roman times, advance to Northern and Western Europe and further west still to America. And in covering a period of roughly 8000 years, in spite of the enormous difference in time, in nations, in geographical and other conditions, we shall find that no feature is more amazing than the extraordinary spirit of conservatism which has spread itself universally over both ships and their sailors. So remarkable are the examples of this, even under widely opposed conditions, that I have thought it worth while here to submit some of the more important ones as being worthy of special consideration.

First, let us take the shape of the Egyptian ship, from which the Greeks and Romans eventually obtained their shipbuilding ideas. The high poop and the rockered bow with its bold sweep aft have, it is not too much to assert, influenced the whole world's shipping ever since. True, the ancient galleys of the Greeks and Romans possess a straighter keel and a pointed bow. But this was done for a purpose. These galleys were fighting ships; and as the ram had to be placed forward in such a manner that keel, stempost, and strut-frames centred their combined force at the extreme point, the shape of the bow could not follow that of the Egyptians. The keel, too, was flat and straight, because it was the custom of the Greeks and

Romans to haul their galleys ashore nearly every night. Again, we must bear in mind that the Roman or Greek war vessel was primarily a rowing boat and not a sailing ship, and that mast and sail were always lowered before going into battle. Yet, for all that, the Greek vases bearing pictures of war galleys still show the Egyptian stern. But when we come to consider the Greek and Roman merchant ships, we find the Egyptian stern and a modified Egyptian bow unmistakably present. And we must remember that the merchant ships were primarily sailing ships and only used their oars as auxiliaries.

Throughout the ages many of these general lines of the Egyptian ships have been followed. We see them appearing in the prehistoric ships of Norway, in the Viking ships of old, and in the ships of the Baltic to-day. We see this conservatism in the ships of the twelfth, thirteenth, and fourteenth centuries, in the caravels and caracks and galleons of the fifteenth and sixteenth centuries. We see it down to about the time of the *Royal George* in 1746 ; and even since then, when the great sweep from bow up to the extreme height of the poop-deck was modified until it practically disappeared, yet we find traces of it in the forecastle and raised quarter-deck of the modern sailing ship. And to continue the argument one step further, I suppose if you could by sending a current of electricity through one of the Egyptian naval architects, now lying as a mummy in one of our museums, bring him to life, so that you might take him to see the yachts racing during Cowes Week, he would not hesitate to say that such ships as *White Heather II.* and the newest *Shamrock* were based on the designs he had made for his masters under the Twelfth Dynasty. If the reader will take the trouble of comparing the Rifeh model (Figs. 5 and 6) with the lines of the latest British yachts now being built under the new universal rule, and then recollect how many years have passed in the interim, he will not cease to wonder that the same "overhang" at bow and stern is as prevalent on the Solent as it was on the Nile. Whatever else these facts may prove, they certainly show what a high state of civilisation the Egyptian had attained ; more, perhaps, than we realise at present. The naval architects of that time must indeed have lacked as little that we could teach them in design nowadays as—we know from subsequent excavations—the shipbuilders of Viking times could learn from our shipbuilders of to-day.

An additional proof of the wisdom and knowledge of the ancients is to be found in the rig of their ships. The squaresail of the Egyptians was very like that used subsequently by the Greeks and Romans, and afterwards by the Vikings and many of the Norwegian and Russian ships to-day. It survived, moreover, beyond the Middle Ages, the only important difference being that three and sometimes two additional masts were provided with squaresails, with a lateen sail on the mizzen and a sprit sail and sprit topsail forward. Thus, though the headsails of a modern full-rigged ocean ship have been altered during the last hundred and fifty years, yet the arrangement of her lower courses is practically that of the single sail of the Egyptians, omitting for the present certain details which do not alter the method of harnessing the wind as a means of propulsion. They had in these early times learned the value of stretching a sail on yards. They had, besides, understood where to place backstays and a forestay to support the mast, and they had adopted the use of braces to the yards as well as of topping lifts.

The eyes painted on the ships of the Greeks and Romans still survive to-day in the hawse holes on either side of a ship's bow. And this belief of the ancients that by means of these eyes the vessel could see her way was but one article in the general creed still shared by every sailor, amateur and professional alike, that a ship, of all the creations of man, is indeed a living thing. Mr. F. T.

Bullen, in a delightful little essay, has demonstrated the varying ways in which a ship will manifest her personality. In "The Way of the Ship" Mr. Bullen also remarks: "Kipling has done more, perhaps, than any other living writer to point out how certain fabrics of man's construction become invested with individuality of an unmistakable kind, and of course so acute an observer cannot fail to notice how pre-eminently is this the case with ships."

Though you may build two ships on the same yard from the same plans by the same builder, yet their personalities are different. The yachtsmen who elect to have a one-design class know very well that though you may raffle as to the ownership of each ship, yet there will always be one or two of the fleet that will be superior to the rest. But the ancients were before the yachtsmen in discovering that a mere contrivance of wood and metal should have a distinct character of its own.

The decoration of the bow and stern of the ship has existed for many hundreds of years; and though the figurehead was especially prominent during the Middle Ages, it is now fast disappearing both from sailing ships of commerce and from yachts also. On steamers it is hardly ever seen except on the steam yacht. The decorated stern, too, so prevalent up to the eighteenth century, has now vanished; although the final traces of this may be noticed in the old-fashioned architecture to which the modern Royal steam yachts of this country still cling, and in the gold beading which frequently ornaments the name of a steamship under her stern.

In Northern latitudes we find the most extraordinary cases of historical obstinacy; the rig and hull of the Scandinavians have remained practically unaltered for some two or three thousand years. The very word "snekkja," applied to the ancient longships of the Scandinavians, is still used to-day. Moreover, the "bonnet," which was attached to the foot of the sail to give additional area—unlaced, of course, in dirty weather—was used by the Vikings; was adopted from them by the ships of mediæval England; and is still used to-day by the ships of Scandinavia, and in England by the Lowestoft "drifters" that go

FIG. 2. NORWEGIAN "JAEGT."

forth to fish in the North Sea, as well as by the pleasure and trading wherries that sail up and down the Norfolk Broads. Fig. 2 shows a Norwegian "jaegt," with bonnet and bowlines.

The influence of this dogged conservative spirit of the Norwegians is to be seen extending over Great Britain in other ways. No one who has visited the Orkney and Shetland Isles can have failed to have noticed the close similarity between their boats and those of the Norwegian. Until about forty years ago their fishing boat was exactly a Norwegian "yawl," the most obvious descendant from the lines of a Viking ship. Indeed, until about the year 1860 all the larger fishing boats of the Shetlands were imported in boards direct from Norway ready for putting together at Lerwick. The type is still further preserved in the whale-boats that are despatched from the mother ships in various parts of the world to harpoon the cachalot. And, not to weary the reader with yet more examples of the great influence which these Viking ships have had on the naval architecture of our country, it is interesting to remark that the latest fashion in yacht design is the so-called " canoe-stern" or " double-ender." This, of course, derives its inspiration from the Norwegian ships of the present day ; and, as we have already said, they in their turn have conservatively held to the models of their ancestors. Whether, as some have thought, the Viking " double-ender" can trace a direct descent from the ships of Egypt is a point that we must defer to another chapter.

Next to the squaresail rig, none has survived so persistently as the lateen. I think that in all probability it was adapted, a few centuries before the introduction of Christianity, from the Egyptian squaresail. Its very appearance and the corner of the world in which it is found as the prevailing rig both suggest that. It is reasonable to assume that in the course of years, when the more experienced Easterns began to discover the art of sailing against the wind and to find that the rig of the Nile boats was not suitable for this, there would be evolved a modification of the Egyptian sail to allow of tacking. This, probably, was the origin of the lateen sail of the dhow. It is of extreme antiquity, and has endured with but little alteration from the time of Alexander the Great, about 350 B.C. The prevalence of this kind of rig in the Red Sea, the Indian Ocean, off the East Coast of Africa, especially as far south as Zanzibar, is well known. The fact that it is still found everywhere up and down the Mediterranean, on the Nile and on Swiss lakes, shows how firmly established did this lateen rig become in the course of time. As we shall see, at a subsequent stage

14

the lateen sail was adopted by our mediæval ships for the mizzen, and this continued right down till the close of the eighteenth century. It will assist us to realise this conservatism if we remember that the ships of St. Paul's time were of a similar kind to these Eastern ships of which we are now speaking. Let me here be allowed to quote again from an author who has sailed in every sea and been preserved to tell us in so many charming records what many others have seen but not troubled to notice. In a further essay on " The Sea in the New Testament " Mr. Bullen, referring to the ships in which St. Paul voyaged, remarks :

"On the East African coast, even to this day, we find precisely the same kind of vessels, the same primitive ideas of navigation, the same absence of even the most elementary notions of comfort, the same touching faith in its being always fine weather as evinced by the absence of any precautions against a storm.

"Such a vessel as this [i.e., St. Paul's] carried one huge sail bent to a yard resembling a gigantic fishing-rod, whose butt, when the sail was set, came nearly down to the deck, while the tapering end soared many feet above the mast-head. As it was the work of all hands to hoist it, and the operation took a long time, when once it was hoisted it was kept so if possible, and the nimble sailors, with their almost prehensile toes, climbed by the scanty rigging and, clinging to the yard, gave the sail a bungling furl." Again, referring to the sailors' activities on the ship in which St. Paul was sailing, Mr. Bullen goes on : " They sounded and got twenty fathoms, and in a little while found the water had shoaled to fifteen. Then they performed a piece of seamanship which may be continually seen in execution on the East African coast to-day—they let their anchors down to their full scope of cable and prayed for daylight. The Arabs do it in fair weather or foul—lower the sail, slack down the anchor, and go to sleep. She will bring up before she hits anything." I have received a like

15

testimony from one who has also cruised in those parts within recent years.

The prevalence of the fighting top has been maintained from the time of the Egyptians down to the present day. To mention but a few instances, the fighting top is seen in a battleship of Rameses III. (about B.C. 1200), and it is found on ancient seals of the thirteenth century of the present era, and so on, of course, through the Middle Ages to our latest battleships.

From the times of the Egyptians the stern was always reserved for the owner or captain and officers. This custom was that of the Greeks, the Romans, the Vikings, and the English right down to the building of H.M.S. *Dreadnought* a short while ago, when the longstanding practice of the officers being quartered aft and the men forward was for the first time broken, to the satisfaction, I understand, of neither officers nor men. There has always been a sense of reverence on the part of the sailor for the poop-deck, and though in the Merchant Service many of the old ways have recently disappeared, yet the custom in the Navy, of "saluting the deck" in honour of the Sovereign is, of course, well known. In ancient illustrations we see the place of honour always placed aft.

Finally we must needs refer to the extraordinary longevity of the Mediterranean galley. Adapted from the Egyptians by the Greeks and afterwards the Romans, it flourished, especially in the Adriatic, up to the sixteenth century in a modified form, and only the advent of steam finally closed its career. Even now the gondola will be recognised as bearing a family likeness, and the prow of the latter still shows the survival of the spear-heads which were used in the manœuvre of ramming.

These, then, are some of the characteristics that have been persistent during the course of development of the sailing ship. Each national design and each nation's rig are the survival of all that has been found to be the best for that particular locality. The more ships a nation builds, the more they sail to other ports—seeing other kinds of ships, comparing them with their own, and adopting whatever is worth while—so much the faster does the ship improve. This, indeed, has been the custom throughout the history of the English nation. When she sent her ships to the Mediterranean at the time of the Crusades, her sailors returned home with new ideas. Thus, the ships in which Richard, with his large fleet, voyaged to Palestine in 1190 would be still of the Viking type. Only a hundred and thirty years had elapsed since William the Conqueror landed in similar boats, as we know from the Bayeux tapestry. When Richard was in the Mediterranean he was joined by a number of galleys. It is not assuming too much to say that an exchange of visits would be made between the crews of the respective ships. The difference in ships would most certainly be criticised, for of all people who inhabit this planet, none are more critical of each other's possessions than sailormen. The Mediterranean inhabitants, having reached civilisation earlier than the dwellers of Northern Europe, and having had the advantage of living nearer, both historically and geographically, to the first builders of ships, would no doubt have been far in advance of the shipbuilders of Northern Europe. Therefore, it is fairly certain that the English returned from the Crusades knowing far more of maritime matters than when they had set out. At any rate, it is significant that the illustrations of ships of the date of 1238, or about fifty years after Richard set forth to the East, show the Viking-like ship greatly modified. The beginnings of the stern-castle and fore-castle and of fighting top are now seen. It seems to me highly probable that the idea for these was obtained from the galleys, still influenced in their architecture by the methods of fighting adopted by the Greeks and the Romans.

SAILING SHIPS

The English nation, more than perhaps any other, has been characterised not so much by her inventiveness as by her skill in adapting other nations' ideas. The present age of electricity and other inventions illustrates the general truth of this statement. Thus, her ships of to-day are the result of continually improving on the designs of other nations. From Norway she got her first sailing ships; from the Mediterranean she assuredly derived considerable knowledge in maritime matters generally. Certainly from Spain she learned much of the art of navigation, of rigging and of shipbuilding. From the French, as we go down through time, she acquired a vast increase of her knowledge of ship-designing and shipbuilding. Not the least of this was the importance to a vessel of fine lines. The Dutch taught us a good deal of seamanship and tactics, as we know from Pepys's Diary. Finally, about the year 1850, after the American clippers had raced all our big ships of the mercantile marine off the ocean, England learned to build clippers equally fast and superior in strength, and so regained the sea-carrying trade she had lost. In yacht designing also she has learned much from American architects, as the Germans within the last few years have learned from us.

Sailing ships are the links which bind country to country, continent to continent. They have been at once the means of spreading civilisation and war. It is a fact that the number of new ships to be built increases proportionately as the trade of a country prospers, and one of the first signs of bad trade is the decrease in the shipbuilder's orders. But, good trade or bad trade, peace or war, there will always be a summons in the sea which cannot be resisted. It summoned the Egyptians to sail to the land of Punt to fetch incense and gold. It summoned the Phœnicians across the Bay of Biscay to the tin mines of Cornwall. It called the Vikings to coast along the Baltic shores for pillage and piracy. It called the

18

INTRODUCTORY

Elizabethans to set forth from Bristol and London in order to find new trade routes, new markets for their goods, fresh sources of their imports. It calls some for trade, some for piracy, some for mere adventure, as in the case of the yachtsman of to-day. It seduces ships from the safety of snug harbours only to be tossed about by the billows of a trackless expanse. The sea ever has been, ever is, and ever will be, uncertain, fickle, unkind. In spite of the fact that for 8000 years and more shipbuilders, designers, and seamen have by experience and invention sought every possible means to overcome its terrors and to tame its fury ; in spite of the fact that these men have never succeeded in getting the upper hand, yet the call of the sea will ever be obeyed. When once she has fascinated you, when once you have consented to her cry and got the salt into your veins, you become as much the slave of the sea as any Roman underling that pulled at the oar of an ancient galley. The sea calls you ; you hoist up your sails, and come.

CHAPTER II.

THE earliest information that we can find about the sailing ship comes, of course, from Egypt: for although the first signs of the dawn of culture were seen in Babylonia, yet that is an inland country and not a maritime region. Notwithstanding the fact that to the east of the Syro-Arabian desert there flow the navigable rivers of the Tigris and Euphrates, and granting that it is only reasonable to suppose that the earliest inhabitants on the banks of these important streams did actually engage in the building of some sort of boat or ship, yet we are not in a position to make any statement from definite evidence. The age of the Babylonian civilisation is exceedingly remote, and long prior to that of the Egyptians, but that is the most that we can say. What their rowing or sailing craft were like—who knows? The discoveries made in this, the most historic corner of the world, by Layard and his successors have told us something about the craft that breasted the waters of the Tigris, but this information belongs to no period earlier than 700 or 900 B.C. Whether subsequent discoveries may lift up the curtain that hides from our view the remains, or at least the crude designs, of the first objects that were ever propelled by wood or sail is entirely a matter of uncertainty.

EARLY EGYPTIAN SHIPS

Of one thing we may rest assured—that Babylonia was in a comparatively high state of civilisation about six thousand years before the Christian era. For at about this date from the East came Babylonian settlers, who found their way towards the setting sun and, finally halting to the North-West of the Red Sea, colonised the region on either side of the Nile. Here, then, they arrived from Babylonia, not a barbarian wild tribe, but, as we know from the most learned Egyptologists, a highly civilised people, possessing great ability in certain arts and of definite intellectual development. It would be only natural that a band of emigrants that had been living by the banks of the Tigris or Euphrates should eventually settle by a river. An Englishman who has lived all his life on the lower reaches of the Thames, is far more likely to fix his habitation on the shores of a colonial river than to trek inland and ultimately " bring up " in the middle of a grazing country. The new inhabitants of the land that we know by the name of Egypt would feel themselves at home by its river. Whatever knowledge they had possessed of boat building in Babylonia they carried with them across the Arabian desert and put into practice along the banks of the Nile. The accompanying illustration (Fig. 3) will show to what ability these colonisers or their immediate successors had attained. Here will be noticed the earliest form of sailing ship in existence. The mast, the square sail, the high bow and the curve of the hull are to us of the highest possible interest as showing the first beginnings of the modern full-rigged ship or yacht, This illustration has been taken from an amphora found in Upper Egypt and now in the British Museum. The date ascribed to it by the ablest Egyptologists is that of the Pre-Dynastic period, which for the sake of clearness we may regard as about 6000 B.C.

On other vases of this period, some of which may also be seen in the British Museum, are to be found curious crescent-shaped designs that have been sometimes taken for primitive ships by previous writers. Even to the most imaginative it must have been difficult to have given these curious drawings the right to be called boats. The extraordinary erections on what would be the deck, have

Fig. 3. Egyptian Ship of about 6000 b.c.

not any right to be called masts or sails. To any one with the slightest practical knowledge of boats and their ways, it is amusing to find that even these primitive ideas should have been thought to depict any kind of river craft. But I have been enabled to discuss this matter with such eminent Egyptologists as Dr. Wallis Budge, the Keeper of the Egyptian and Assyrian Antiquities in the British Museum, and Mr. H. R. Hall, both of whom are of the opinion that these designs do not represent ships at all. Dr. Budge suggests that they represent "zarebas," a word that became very familiar to English people during Kitchener's campaign in Egypt. In that case, the structures that have been mistaken for masts would represent erections to frighten away enemies or wild beasts. Another theory is that the series of straight lines below what was taken for the ship's hull, and which were wrongly supposed to represent waves, are perhaps the piles on which the dwelling is built. I have, therefore, omitted such designs as not bearing on the subject of sailing ships.

Starting with a definite illustration before us of a sailing boat of about 8000 years ago, our mind naturally wanders back to the period when the first boat was ever made. Picture, if you will, the prehistoric man standing by the banks of the Tigris or Euphrates gazing in utter helplessness and awe at the liquid mass gurgling on its way to the Persian Gulf. He sees the fishes able to swim beneath its surface and the waterfowl to float above. Then when his mind has reached a sufficiently developed state to permit of his being able to reason, he begins to wonder if he—the superior to fish and fowl—could also be supported in the water until he has reached the other side of the river on which he has as yet never set foot. So, on a day, greatly daring, he entrusts his body to the flowing stream, and at length discovers that by certain exercises he is able to float and swim across to the other side. A new accomplishment has been made, a new world has been opened out to him. When he gets back home he begins to reason still further. How can he carry himself, his family, his goods to the other side? One day, perhaps, while hewing down a tree for his hut, a branch falls into the water. Behold! it possesses the ability of the water-fowl—it floats. So he hews down the trunk itself, sits across it, and for sport, launches off from the bank. Lo! the trunk supports both its own weight and his.

Thus encouraged, his primitive mind sets slowly to work. "If I get a bigger trunk and hollow it out, it will carry me, my family and my property across to the other shore." So having turned the trunk into a boat, he makes of the branch a punting-pole, At a later stage he puts on a cross-piece to one end of the pole and thus propels himself by paddling, until this in turn becomes an oar.

Since human nature differs but little from age to age, and its chief tendency is ever to proceed along the route of least resistance, he begins to seek some means of motion without work. His descendants improve upon the tree-trunk until it has become more shapely and less clumsy. Then while returning home one evening, tired out with paddling and hunting, he rests on his paddle for a moment! Yet still his boat moves. He holds up the blade of his paddle and the canoe moves a little faster. He stands up, and, the larger the space that is exposed to the wind blowing in the direction in which he is travelling, the more quickly still does the little ship run on. Next day he brings with him a stick which he erects in the boat. That will save him standing. To the stick he makes fast a hide and spreading it to the wind sails faster than anything he has ever seen float on the water.

This is all very well in following winds: he can get along, too, when the wind is abeam, although he has to keep helping her with his paddle—such a lot of lee-way does she make; but every time the breeze gets ahead as he winds round the reaches of the Tigris he has to lower the sail and mast. This is too much for him. His mind is not able to conceive of such a manœuvre of tacking: how could a boat possibly go against the wind? It is unthinkable. He would be a fool to try and reason otherwise against a law of nature. Not, indeed, until thousands of years after him is tacking invented. The Egyptians at any rate did not understand it. Their ships were built for sailing up and rowing down the Nile, and there is abundant evidence to show the mast lowered down on to the top of the after cabin and the oarsmen propelling the boat with the stream.

EARLY EGYPTIAN SHIPS

The prehistoric man has thus made almost the same kind of boat that the savage or half-civilised race makes to day. The American Indian, the Negro and the undeveloped Asiatic races cannot create any boat superior to the dug-out, because their lack of intelligence is a fatal barrier. But just as the first inventors of flying machines have begun by studying the action of birds on the wing, so in navigation as in aviation. The early boatbuilders who followed the rough dug-out gave a shape to their ships that was derived from the creatures of the water. If the reader will look at the " bows " and underbody of a fish he will see how the general lines of the ship began. If, too, he will look at the stern and "counter" of the duck and swan he will easily notice the resemblance to the overhang of the early Egyptian boats. This is not so fanciful as may appear at first sight. The ancients certainly were affected by the waterfowl in their designing of ships, and the graceful neck of the swan was a regular decoration for the stern of the later Roman ships. It is but common-sense that when man is about to study the method of navigating water or air, he should begin by copying from the creatures that spend their whole time in this activity.

For the development of the art of shipbuilding, few countries could be found as suitable as Egypt. Surrounded on the East by the Red Sea, and by the Mediterranean on the North, it had the additional blessing of a long navigable river running through its midst. Of inestimable value to any country as this is, the equable and dry climate of Egypt, the peacefulness of the waters of the Nile, the absence of storms and the rarity of calms combined with the fact that, at any rate, during the winter and early spring months, the gentle north wind blew up the river with the regularity of a trade wind, so enabling the ships to sail against the stream without the aid of oars—these were just the conditions that many another nation might have longed for. Very different, indeed, were the circumstances which had to be wrestled with in the case of the first shipbuilders and sailormen of Northern Europe. It is but natural, therefore, that the Egyptians became great sailors and builders: we should have been surprised had the reverse been the case.

In earlier times our sources of Egyptian history were limited almost entirely to what could be derived from ancient Greek and Roman writers. Nor was this of anything but a vague and unreliable character. Happily within our own time this has been supplemented, to an enormous degree, by Egyptian exploration. The first beginnings of this are found in the scientific study of Egyptian monuments, which began about the middle of the nineteenth century. The foundation for the interpretation of hieroglyphic inscriptions was laid in the Rosetta Stone, now fortunately in the British Museum. Discovered at the close of the eighteenth century, its bilingual writing in Egyptian and Greek paved the way for future scholars. Englishmen, German, French and American students have since engaged in the fascinating pursuit of systematically and with scrupulous care, excavating the temples and palaces of the older civilisation that lived on the banks of the Nile thousands of years before the Incarnation. Encouraged alike by the settled state of political affairs in Egypt, and by the support granted in the interests of research by the Egyptian and European Governments, the excavation and preservation of these unique monuments have gone steadily on from year to year. It is from the annual reports of these exploration societies, as well as from the explorers themselves, that we are able to present the details of the Egyptian sailing ships.

It would have been strange if a nation with such a vast waterway, and living in such close proximity to the Mediterranean and Red Seas, should not have left behind some memorials of her shipping. Happily we have no need for disappointment, for the information surviving to us is of two kinds. Firstly, we have the wall-pictures of the ancient buildings, which show almost everything that a picture could tell of a ship and her rigging. These wonderful illustrations have been faithfully copied on the spot. But besides these, within recent years have been unearthed most interesting little wooden model boats. These are of two kinds, those made in the form of a funeral bark, and those which are models of the actual ships that sailed up the Nile at the time they were made. In the former the dead man is seen lying under a canopy or open deck-house with or without rowers. These funeral barks, not being sailing boats, are only of interest in pursuing our present subject as showing us the general lines and shape of the hull, together with the steering and rowing arrangements.

It is the models of sailing ships that demand our attention. These were placed in the tombs with the intention of providing the deceased with the means of sailing about on the streams of the underworld. Very touching is the care of the ancients that man's most beautiful creation—his ship—should not be separated from him even in death. (We shall see, later on, a similar devotion expressed in the burial of the Vikings.) Models of houses and of granaries, with curious little men working away, so that the departed should not be lacking for food while he sailed about the underworld, are also found. Some of these models of ships, granaries and soul-houses are to be seen in the British Museum and the South Kensington Collection. The reader who is interested in the subject will find additional information in the fascinating book by Professor Flinders Petrie.* Each boat was provided with masts and sails and elaborately decorated

* "Gizeh and Rifeh," by W. M. Flinders Petrie, London, 1907. (Double volume.)

steering oars. Dr. Budge, in his guide to the Third and Fourth Egyptian Rooms of the British Museum, points out that another religious idea was connected with these boats, namely, the conception of the boat of the Sun-god, called the "Boat of the Million of Years," in which the souls of the beatified were believed to travel nightly in the train of the Sun-god as he passed through the underworld from West to East.

The Egyptians thought that by a use of words of magical power, the models placed in the tombs, whether of boats or houses or granaries, could be transformed into ghostly representations of their originals on earth. "The boat," adds Dr. Budge, "was considered to be such a necessary adjunct to the comfort of the deceased in the next world, that special chapters of the Book of the Dead were compiled for the purpose of supplying him with the words of power necessary to enable him to obtain it. Thus, 'Tell us our name,' say the oar-rests: and the deceased answers, 'Pillars of the Underworld is your name.' 'Tell me my name,' saith the Hold: 'Aker' is thy name. 'Tell me my name,' saith the Sail: 'Nut,' (*i.e.*, heaven) is thy name," &c.*

But let us make a survey of the development of the Egyptian ship from the time prior to the Dynasties until the third or fourth century before the Christian era. Ancient Egyptian history has been divided by scholars into three periods—the Old Kingdom, the Intermediate, and the New Kingdom. These again have been subdivided into Dynasties, of which the First to the Tenth are covered by the Old Kingdom, the Eleventh to the Seventeenth, by the Intermediate, and the Eighteenth to the Twentieth, by the New Kingdom. Afterwards the various Foreign Dynasties of Mercenaries formed the Twenty-second to the Twenty-fifth. The Twenty-sixth

* "A Guide to the Third and Fourth Egyptian Rooms, British Museum," London, 1904.

was the time of the Restoration, the Twenty-seventh to the Thirty-first represented the time of the Persians. This will assist us in following the changes that came about in the ships with the progress of time.

We have already drawn attention to the illustration of a ship, or rather sailing boat, in Fig. 3, belonging to that remote period anterior to the Dynasties. There can be no possible doubt as to her being intended by the artist, who painted this design on the amphora, for a sailing vessel of some kind, though the mast and square-sail are set much further forward than is found later in Egyptian ships. There is a figure-head on the extreme point of the sternpost. Below is a small platform, possibly for the look-out man whom we see later in Egyptian ships armed with a pole for taking soundings. Right aft is a small cabin for the owner or distinguished traveller. Probably she was a decked ship and steered by one or more oars from the quarter. The reader will notice a great similarity between the stern of this vessel and that of the Boeotian sailing boat shown in Fig. 11.

From the earliest times up to about the year 3000 B.C., the Egyptian craft are less ships than boats. The sailing boats of the third dynasty are decked and fitted with a lowering mast, which when not in use is lifted bodily out of its sockets and rests on the roof of the after cabin. The boat was then propelled by paddles, with a look-out man forward, the steersmen aft, and the commander amidships armed with a thong-stick to urge the rowers on. The sailing boats of the fourth and fifth dynasties become gradually bigger and more seaworthy, but the mast and rigging show only slight advance. The former, from the third dynasty to the eleventh, is in the shape of the letter A. It fits into grooves either in the deck or the side of the ship, and at first has no backstays or shrouds. Being a double mast these are not necessary. The sail at this period is deep and narrow, reaching from the top of the mast down to the deck, being fitted with both yard and boom. Braces are attached to the ends of the yards but no sheets are shown. During the fourth and fifth dynasties, while the A-shaped mast remains, backstays are added, sometimes numbering as many as nine or ten (see Fig. 4). These

FIG. 4. EGYPTIAN SHIP OF THE FIFTH DYNASTY.

would become essential as the ship grew larger and her gear heavier. These backstays lead from roughly three-quarters of the way up the mast down to the spot about a quarter of the ship's length forward of the stern. An additional stay from the top of the mast to the extremity of the stern is also frequently shown. Two or three men are seen steering with paddles, standing on the overhanging counter. On big ships the steersmen number as many as five, and the paddlers with their faces turned in the direction in which the ship was proceeding are shown to be twenty-two or twenty-three on each side. The fact that only one man is shown sitting aft holding a brace in each hand, must be an additional proof of the gentleness of the northerly wind on the Nile and the absence of squalls. No cleats are shown, and in anything much above a zephyr his weight and strength must have been sorely tried. The forestay, the enormous overhang both at bow and stern, the look-out man forward with his pole for taking soundings of the Nile, and possibly for tilting the ship's head off whenever she got aground—an experience that is far from rare on the Nile even to-day—the presence of the commander with his thong-stick, are still shown in the ships of the fourth and fifth dynasties.

As showing the wonderful influence which Egyptian ships of this period exercised on the rig of the Far East, and even of the Far North East, let me be permitted to call attention to the Burmese Junk in Fig. 1. I will ask the reader to note very carefully her A-shaped mast, her squaresail, her steering paddle at the side, and most important of all the general sweep of the lines of her hull, coming right up from the overhanging bow to the raised overhanging poop. This is the Burmese junk of to-day, which, like the Egyptian ships of old, finds the prevailing wind favourable for sailing up against the river Irawadi, and when returning down the stream, lowers her sail and rows down with the current. Between the Chinese and Burmese junks of to-day and the Egyptian ships of about six thousand years ago there are so many points of similarity that we are not surprised when we remember that the Chinese, like the Egyptians, derived their earliest culture from Babylonia, and that India—using the name in its widest geographical sense to include Burma—is mainly, as to its culture at least, an offshoot from the Chinese. Until quite recently, China remained in the same state of development for four thousand years. If that was so with her arts and life generally, it has been especially so in the case of her sailing craft. I am not contending that the Chinese junk is identical with the ancient Egyptian ship, but I submit that between the two there is such close similarity as to show a common influence and a remarkable persistence in type.

But whilst engaged in this present work, I became interested in a half-civilised tribe called the Koryak, dwelling around the sea of Okhotsk, in the North West Pacific. Here, in this remote corner of undeveloped Siberia, they have remained practically forgotten by the rest of the world, except for a few occasional visits from the land side by the Cossacks, and from the shore side by the American whalers. Recently, thanks to the Russians, a few have begun to embrace Christianity, but for the most part, they remain in their primitive state with habits too repulsive to mention. Naturally, since (as we have already pointed out) a nation exhibits its state of progress in its art, its literature and its ships, we are not surprised to find that the Koryak craft have, at any rate in respect of rigging, several highly important similarities to the Egyptian ship of the fourth and fifth dynasties. Thus, besides copying the ancients in steering with an oar, the fore-end of the prow of their sailing boats terminates in a fork through which the harpoon-line is passed, this fork being sometimes carved with a human face which they believe will serve as a protector of the boat. Instead of rowlocks they have, like the early Egyptians, thong-loops, through which the oar or paddle is inserted. Their sail, too, is a rectangular shape of dressed, reindeer skins sewed together. But it is their mast that is especially like the Egyptians and Burmese. The following description, written by a member of the Jesup Expedition which recently visited the Koryaks, is notable:

" Instead of a mast, they employ a more primitive contrivance. Three long poles are tied together at one end with a thong which passes through drill-holes, and are set up in the manner of a tripod. On one side, the whole length of the sail is sewed to a yard, the middle of which is slung from the top of the tripod by means of a stout thong. The tripod is set up in the middle of the boat by tying both ends of one of the poles to the ribs on one side of the boat, while the third pole is fastened on the other side of the boat. The sail can revolve around the top of the tripod, and is set in the direction required by the wind, by means of braces and sheets made of thong, which are fastened to the rails."*

Lacking the civilisation of the ancient Egyptians, wanting, too, no doubt the wood wherewith to build their boats, the Koryaks' sailing craft are made of seal skins. But there can be little doubt that their rigging is of European rather than of Asiatic origin. Possibly it came from Egypt to India and China and so further north to the Sea of Okhotsk. At any rate, although the Egyptian ships we have been considering had a double and not a treble mast, yet it must not be supposed that the latter did not exist, for Mr. Villiers Stuart, some years ago, found on the walls of a tomb belonging to the Sixth Dynasty at Gebel Abu Faida, the painting of a boat with a treble mast made of three spars arranged like the edges of a triangular pyramid.

After about the period of the fifth Dynasty the sail, instead of being deep and narrow, becomes wide and shallow. Instead of the several steersmen with their paddles at the stern, we have one large oar in the centre of the stern, resting on a large wooden fork and worked by one steersman by means of a lanyard. If the reader will refer to Figs. 5 and 6, he will see this quite clearly. These are the interesting little models already alluded to as having been discovered by Professor Flinders Petrie, and which are now in the Manchester Museum. This most instructive "find" was made by the British School of Archæology in the season of 1906-7 at Rifeh, whilst

* "The Jesup North Pacific Expedition," vol. vi. part ii., "The Koryak"; see pp. 534-538. By W. Jochelson, New York, 1908.

excavating the tomb of the sons of an Egyptian Prince belonging to the Twelfth Dynasty. In the coffins were these two excellent little ships, the one, as will be seen, with her mast and yards, braces, topping lifts and halyards for sailing up the Nile; while the other ship shews very clearly the mast lowered in a tabernacle on to the cabin, the foot of the mast being balanced by the weight of a stone—exactly the practice of the Norfolk wherries of to-day, saving that instead of stone lead is used. The steersmen will be noticed and the highly decorated blade of the steering oar. Unfortunately, before being photographed, the oar in Fig. 5 has been placed too high. It should, of course, have been dropped lower beneath the water line. Notice, too, that the rowers sit now with their backs to the bow. Paddles have been dispensed with, and finding that so much more power could be obtained by putting the whole weight on to the oar, rowing has been taken to instead of paddling. The little figure with a cloak round his shoulders in the bows (Fig. 6), is the look-out man.

In Fig. 5, the look-out man with his pole is also seen forward; the crew are gathered round the mast to haul at the halyards, and get in the sheets and braces; for now that the sail does not reach right down to the deck, sheets have become indispensable. It will also be remarked that the boom has been introduced to make the sail set better. The amount of sheer given to the boat is enormous, although the curve-in of the top of the stern is exceedingly attractive. Assuming that the dimensions of the model are proportionate she must have had precious little grip of the water, and if, when on an expedition to the land of Punt, the Egyptians ever encountered a beam wind, their ships must have made a terrible lot of leeway. For even a light breeze, coming at right-angles to those overhanging bows with no great draught amidships, would drive her head right off the wind. The steersman would naturally stand to leeward, to get a pull on his steering-thong or

34

lanyard in order to luff her up, and prevent her sagging too much to leeward. At a later date, when, as we shall see, an oar was used each side for steering in place of only one at the extreme stern, the helmsman stood on the lee side and worked the lee steering oar. By reason of its size, this would have some of the effects of the lee-boards on a Thames Barge or Dutchman.

Although these two models are the finest tomb group that have yet reached England, yet others have been found at Sakkara, and elsewhere, sometimes with a hull painted yellow and a cabin with an awning painted to imitate leather, in which the proprietor, more carefully made and of better wood than his sailors, sat with his box by his side. Another boat model was of light papyrus with flower-shaped prow and stern. It was painted green, and carried a light shelter under which the owner usually stood.*

These ships of the Twelfth Dynasty have an additional interest for us, since they belong to the time when Egypt was enjoying the fullest prosperity, and had reached its highest degree of civilisation in its capital of Thebes. But it is in the illustrations of ships afforded by excavations in connection with the Temple of Deir-el-Bahari that we find the most detailed information. The south wall of the middle terrace of this building is most informative, depicting as it does the naval expedition to the land of Punt. In Egyptian history various expeditions are mentioned to Punt. One occurred as early as the fifth Dynasty, for it is recorded in a tomb of a dynasty later. During the eleventh Dynasty, a similar expedition was made under Sankh-kara, and Ramases III. also sent an expedition. These last two voyages are said to have started from a harbour on the Red Sea which was reached from Koptos, probably the modern Kosseir, and to have returned there.

* See "The Egypt Exploration Fund: Archæological Report, 1906–1907."

SAILING SHIPS

Although it is now thought by some Egyptologists that Queen Hatshopsitu did not send an expedition to Punt, but that she was only copying the expedition of the eleventh Dynasty, and that these Punt reliefs are merely replicas of other reliefs still to be discovered in the older temple, depicting an expedition under Nebkheruna, yet it is a doubtful point and by no means settled by critics.

But supposing these are the ships of the Egyptian Queen of the eighteenth Dynasty, they are seen with fifteen oarsmen a side, whilst two look-out men are standing forward in a kind of open-work forecastle. The general shape of the ship by now has become considerably modified. Whilst there is still considerable overhang both at bow and stern, yet she is long on the waterline. The bow resembles nothing so much as that of a modern gondola. There is a beautiful line sweeping up aft to a raised poop with an ornamentation curving gracefully in-board to another open-work castle or cabin. These illustrations of the eighteenth Dynasty show how thoroughly the Egyptians had mastered the art of ship-building. When a ship is sailing on the sea, she is thrown up by the motion of the waters till she rests pivoted on the crest of a wave. The middle of the ship is thus supported, but the bow and stern, not being waterborne, have a tendency to droop while the centre of the ship tends to bulge up. This is technically known among naval architects as " hogging." In the case of ships with an enormous over-hang, unsupported by water, such as was the case of the Egyptian ships and is now the fashion with our modern yachts, this hogging would need to be guarded against. Only recently the writer saw on the south coast a modern yacht with no beam but considerable length and overhang. She had been badly built and the " hogging " was very noticeable a little forward of amidships. Her skipper gave her a very bad name altogether.

In the Hatshopsitu ships we see the " hogging " strain

FIG. 5. MODEL OF AN EGYPTIAN SHIP OF THE TWELFTH DYNASTY.

guarded against by a powerful truss of thick rope. This truss leads from forward, sometimes being bound round—undergirding—the prow: sometimes it is made fast inside, perhaps to the deck or to the floors. It then leads aft, being stretched on forked posts until it reaches the mast, where it is wound round in a sort of clove-hitch, and then continues aft again been stretched on other forked posts until it is finally girded round the counter. This truss was as large as a man's waist, and has been calculated by Commander T. M. Barber of the United States' Navy to have been able to withstand a strain of over 300 tons.[*]

The manner of steering from the centre of the stern with one oar has given way to that of using an oar on each quarter. Each oar rests on a forked post rising above the head of the steersman who works the oar with a thong loop. As already pointed out, it is noticeable that he uses the lee steering oar always. It is probable that going to the land of Punt, the prevailing North wind favoured them. But returning, if the wind was foul, they would have to row. Even had they understood the art of tacking at this time they would have had some difficulty. As far as one can gather from the look of a ship of this kind, as soon as ever the lee oar was pushed over so that she came up into the wind, she would get into stays and not pay off on to the other tack except with the aid of the oarsmen.

In these Punt pictures, too, will be noticed the fact that the rowers have their oars in thongs instead of the later invention—pins or rowlocks. These ships were certainly decked, but that was probably only down the centre, for though we see the ship crowded with all sorts of merchandise, yet the rowers' bodies are only visible from the knees upwards. They were probably placed on a lower platform.

[*] "The Tomb of Hatshopsitu," p. 30, by Edouard Naville, London, 1906.

SAILING SHIPS

Just as in the course of time the double and treble mast gave way to the single spar, and the deep, narrow sail to the broad, shallow square-sail, so later, about the year 1250 B.C., we find that the boom was discarded, and therefore at any rate, by now, sheets must have been introduced. But before we pass from Hatshopsitu's ships (about 1600 B.C.) let us examine the sail of that time. So much confusion exists in the mind of many who see occasional pictures of these early vessels that it may be well to make an effort to clear this matter up. The yard was of two pieces lashed together in the middle; the same statement applies to the boom. Pulleys not being yet invented, the two halyards that raised the yard, led through two empty squares formed by a frame-work of wood acting as fair-leads. These halyards led aft, and being belayed well abaft the mast were used as powerful stays to the latter. Let it be understood at once that the boom remained fixed, being lashed to the mast by thongs. From the top of the mast below the yard depended a series of topping lifts about seventeen in number. These coming out from the mast at varying angles spread over the whole length of the boom, and took the weight of the latter, supporting also the sail and yard when lowered. Contrary to the subsequent practice of the Greeks and Romans, the yard was the spar that was raised or lowered by the halyards. Thus, when sail was struck the two halyards would be slacked off, the yard would descend on to the boom, the sail would be rolled up while the topping-lifts would hold the entire weight. The two braces, leading down not quite from the extremities of the yard, a single sheet made fast a little forward of the middle of the boom, a forestay and also a single backstay were also used, but side rigging never.

From about the year 1250 B.C. onwards, the sail was no longer furled by slacking away the halyards, but, having dispensed with the boom, brails of about four in number
38

usually hung from the yard which was now not lowered but a fixture. Consequently on coming to an anchorage the brails would be used for furling the sail to the yard— still standing owing to the weight and consequent exertion needed to hoist it again. This, then, remained the accepted rig of the Phœnicians, Greeks and Romans for over a thousand years as we shall see from the evidence of coins and vases.

The importance of the various expeditions of the Egyptians to Punt cannot be over-estimated. They are the earliest attempt at organising a fleet of powerful ships to voyage far away from home waters. Exactly where Punt was situated it is not possible to say, because the name was given to various regions at different times. Sometimes it is the modern Somaliland, or the shore opposite: at other times it is somewhere in a more southerly direction. But wherever Punt may have been, it was either to the East or South of Egypt. The real motive of these expeditions was to increase the commerce of Egypt, to open up trade with the neighbouring countries, and especially to obtain incense for the burials of the Egyptians. Such commodities as ivory, leopard skins, ostrich feathers and gold were also brought back.

I am indebted for much information with reference to these expeditions to a most interesting publication of the Egypt Exploration Fund,* and to the work of a German scholar.† In the illustrations of the Punt expedition as depicted in Hatshopsitu's Temple, we see five ships arriving. Two have struck sail and are moored. The first ship has sent out a small boat which is fastened by ropes to a tree on the shore, while bags and amphora, probably containing food and drink, are being unloaded to

* "Egypt Exploration Fund: The Temple of Deir-el-Bahari," by Edouard Naville.

† "The Fleet of an Egyptian Queen," by Dr. Johannes Duemichen. Leipzig, 1868.

present to the chief of Punt. The other three ships are coming up with sail set, showing us the most interesting details as to their rigging. On one of them the pilot is seen giving the command " To the port side." There is an inscription annexed to this illustration, which, as stated above, can now be deciphered. It reads thus :—" These are the ships, which the wind brought along with it." And again, " The voyage on the sea, the attainment of the longed-for aim in the holy land, the happy arrival of the Egyptian soldiers in the land of Punt, according to the arrangement of the divine Prince Amon, Lord of the terrestrial thrones in Thebes, in order to bring to him the treasures of the whole land in such quantities as will satisfy him."

We see, too, the ships being loaded with the produce of Punt. The Egyptians are bringing the cargo across a gangway from the shore to the ship. There are bags of incense and gold, ebony, tusks of elephants, skins of panthers, frankincense trees piled up in confusion on the ships' decks. Monkeys, too, have been obtained, which have been truthfully depicted as amusing themselves by walking along the truss. Any one who has ever taken a monkey on board a sailing ship knows that the first thing he does is to run up the rigging. It is a small point this, but it shows that the artist was anxious to be truthful and exact in his details.

The hieroglyphic inscription accompanying this illustration is virtually the bill of lading. It gives a detailed and accurate account of all the articles destined for transport. The translation of this according to Dr. Duemichen is : " The loading of the ships of transport with a great quantity of the magnificent products of Arabia, with all kinds of precious woods of the holy land, with heaps of incense-resin, with verdant incense trees, with ebony, with pure ivory, with gold and silver from the land of Amu, with the (odorous) Tepes wood and the Kassiarind, with Aham-incense and Mestemrouge, with Anau-monkeys,

Kop-monkeys, and Tesem-animals, with skins of leopards of the South, with women and children. Never has a transport (been made) like this one by any king since the creation of the world."

Finally (see Fig. 7) we are shown three vessels of the fleet returning to Thebes richly laden. The accompanying inscription in this case reads: " The excursion was completed satisfactorily; happy arrival at Thebes to the joy of the Egyptian soldiers. The (Arabian and Ethiopian) princes, after they had arrived in this country, bring with them costly things of the land of Arabia, such as had never yet been brought that could be compared with what they brought, by any of the Egyptian kings, for the supreme majesty of this god Amon-Ra, Lord of the terrestrial thrones."

" If the expedition really landed at Thebes," says Dr. Edouard Naville, "we must suppose that at that time, long before Ramases II., who is said to have made a canal from the Nile to the Red Sea, there was an arm of the Nile forming a communication with the sea, which extended much farther north than it does now." *

When we remember the splendour and gaiety of the court at Thebes, the many gorgeous festivals that were held on the water, the Egyptians' love of pleasure and their intense joy in living, we are neither surprised to learn of the great fêtes that celebrated the safe return of these voyagers, nor of the fact that a company of royal dancers accompanied the ships to enliven the navigation with song and dance. That the Egyptians dearly loved their ships and set them in high honour cannot be disputed. Besides burying them in the tombs of their rulers, there were times when sacred boats were carried out of the temples on the occasion of high festivals and dragged along by sledges.

Professor Maspero † believes that the navigation of the

* "Egypt Exploration Fund: The Temple of Deir-el-Bahari," p. 16.
† "The Dawn of Civilisation — Egypt," by Professor Maspero, London, 1894.

SAILING SHIPS

Red Sea by the Egyptians was far more frequent than is usually imagined, and the same kinds of vessels in which they coasted along the Mediterranean from the mouth of the Nile to the southern coast of Syria, conveyed them also, by following the coast of Africa, as far as the straits of Bab-el-Mandeb. These ships were, of course, somewhat bigger and more able than the Nile boats, though they were built on the same model. They were clinker-built with narrow sharp stem and stern, with enormous sheer rising from forward to the high stern. They were not open boats but decked, and we find hieroglyphics denoting the pilot's orders " Pull the oar," " To the port side." Heavier, bigger, with more freeboard and no hold, the Egyptian merchant ships, crowded with their cargo and a complement of fifty sailors, pilots, and passengers, barely afforded room for working the ship properly. The length of ships of the size that went to Punt has been thought to be about sixty-five feet, or much smaller than such modern yachts as " Shamrock " and " Nyria."

We have already mentioned the wonderful influence the rig of the Egyptians exercised to the eastward, but though the old squaresail rig has gone from Egypt, yet to-day we can still see very similar boats and almost the same rig on the Orange Laut of the Malay West Coast. The overhanging bow and stern, the great sheer from forward to the high poop, the large single squaresail, now converted practically into a lug-sail, are still there to keep alive the memory of the ships of the Dynasties.

I have already referred in the previous chapter to the lateen sail having been adapted from the Egyptian rig a few centuries before the Christian era. But it is probable that between the squaresail rig and the lateen there was just one intermediate stage. By tilting the yard at a different angle to the mast, instead of it being at right angles, so that the foot came down lower, and the peak of the sail was pointed higher, it would be found that the ship would hold

42

a better wind. This is amply borne out by the Egyptian "Nugger" (see Fig. 8), which is still in use on the Nile above the second cataract, and is being replaced only very slowly by the lateen. There is a relief on a sarcophagus found in the precincts of the Vatican, and now in the

FIG. 8. AN EGYPTIAN NUGGER.

Lateran Museum, which certainly resembles the "Nugger" in its transition from the squaresail to the lateen. (The date of this is about 200 A.D.). The only important difference is that the Vatican relief shows a topsail added. Finally, discarding the boom altogether, the lateen sail comes with the foot of the sail lower still, and consequently the peak much higher, being but an exaggerated form of our modern lug-sail so prevalent in sailing dinghies. This remains, as we have pointed out above, as the characteristic sail of the Mediterranean, the Nile and Red Sea.

Before we close this chapter one must refer to the

vexed question as to when the ancients discovered that wonderful art of sailing against the wind—tacking. In the absence of any definite knowledge, I hold the opinion that this first came into practice on the Nile about the time the nugger, or dhow was introduced as the rig for sailing boats. My reasons for this supposition are: firstly, the squaresail being more suitable for the open sea and making passages of some length, it would be a country having a navigable river that would be likely to discover such a rig as would enable them to sail with the stream *against* the prevailing northerly wind; secondly, arguing on the theory (which has many adherents) that the dhow came in about the time of the death of Alexander the Great who revolutionised at least one corner of Egypt, leaving behind his name to the port of Alexandria as an eternal memorial, I hold that the invention of this dhow rig made the ship to come very close to the wind—far closer than the old-fashioned squaresail of the earlier Egyptians. Realising, when coming down with the stream, that they could go so near to the wind when approaching the right bank, why—surely it must have occurred to such highly developed minds—could they not do the same when zigzagging across to the left shore? At first, no doubt, they pulled her head round with their oars, until, perhaps, on one occasion, she carried so much way from the last shore that she came round of her own accord—shook herself for a moment, as she hung for a short time in stays—and then paid off on the other tack. After that, the whole art of going to windward was revealed. My third reason is based on the fact that the Saxons, who settled around the mouth of the Elbe and subjugated the Thuringians after the death of Alexander the Great, did possess this knowledge of tacking.

Unless it were with the intention of tacking, it is difficult to see why the dhow, or nugger rig should have prevailed. But we do know that this form of sail was

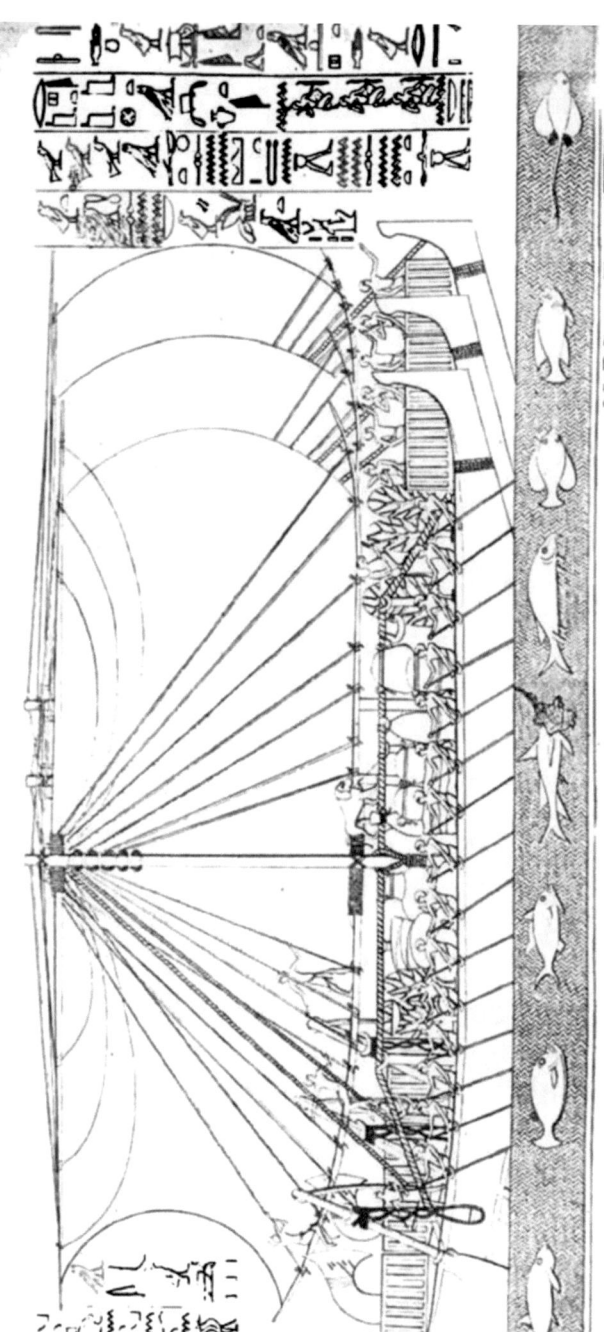

FIG. 7. EGYPTIAN SHIP (IN THE TEMPLE OF DEIR-EL-BAHARI).

extant about the time of Alexander; therefore, tacking must be at least as old as the death of Alexander in the fourth century B.C. A squaresail-ship whether ancient or modern will go no nearer the wind than seven points, whereas the fore-and-after will sail as close as five. This, as soon as the fact was fully realised on the Nile, would hasten that day when tacking was first found out.

Egypt, after flourishing so mightily for so many hundreds of years, had its decline not less than its rise. Just as the earlier Egyptian sculptures are superior to the later ones in sincerity and fidelity, becoming subsequently more stiff and formal, so her shipping eventually deteriorated, and the mastery of the seas passed into the hands of the Phœnicians.

CHAPTER III.

ANCIENT SHIPS OF PHŒNICIA, GREECE, AND ROME.[*]

IT is almost impossible to exaggerate the potent influence exercised by the Phœnicians, as successors of the Egyptians, in being the maritime nation of the world. Happy in their origin by the Persian Gulf, fortunate, too, in having had the Egyptians before them, and so benefiting by the knowledge and experience of the latter, they had developed and prospered through the centuries parallel with the Dynastic peoples. Much that we should wish to know about the Phœnicians is wanting, but we have more than adequate material for the means of realising something of the range and intensity of their sway.

Migrating, like the first Egyptians, westward, they had settled around the Levant, to the north of Palestine. Already, in prehistoric days, they had expanded still further westward into Greece, founding Thebes in Bœotia,

[*] For some valuable matter regarding Greek and Roman ships I wish to acknowledge my indebtedness to the following, especially the first two of these:

"Ancient Ships" by Cecil Torr, Cambridge, 1894.

"Dictionnaire des Antiquités Grecques et Romaines," by Ch. Darembreg (Article under "Navis," by Cecil Torr), Paris, 1905.

"A Companion to Greek Studies," by L. Whibley, Cambridge, 1905. (See article on "Ships," by A. B. Cook, p. 475 et seq.)

and teaching the barbarian inhabitants of that country the elements of civilisation. Everywhere in the ancient world, from remote ages until a century or two before the Incarnation, Phœnician ships were as numerous in the waters of the Mediterranean, as British vessels in all parts of the world are to-day. Possessing a genius for trade, a keen love for the sea and for travel, they had the complete mastery of the commerce and fisheries of the Ægean Sea, until as late as the eighth century B.C. They dragged up from the waters its shell fish to make purple dies; they burrowed into the earth to extract silver; they opened up commerce wherever it was possible, exchanging such products of the East as woven fabrics and highly-wrought metal work. They built factories on islands and promontories, and gave to the towns along the coast-line—especially of the eastern side of Greece—Phœnician names. Troubling but little about inland situations, they made their strong settlements to be their island homes.

Although eventually the Phœnicians were driven out of the Ægean, yet their effect on the inhabitants of Greece was a lasting one. As Greece had received from the Phœnicians her first culture, so she had adopted their religion and their species of ships. We shall see, presently, how very similar the ships of the Greeks and Phœnicians were. But before proceeding thus far, let us remember that, though the Phœnicians were developing while the Egyptians were declining, yet, indubitably, they owed a vast amount to the civilisation of the latter. Why the Phœnicians, more than any other people, were influenced by the Egyptians is not hard to understand if we realise that they alone were allowed to trade to the mouths of the Nile. The Egyptians guarded their kingdom inviolate against all other merchants of the Mediterranean, although Achaian pirates from the North at times swept down to the Nile Delta. Not until the Twenty-Sixth

Dynasty, when Egypt was reunited, and again made a strong kingdom, were the Milesian and other Greek traders allowed to begin commercial operations with the land of the Pharaohs.

Broadly speaking, the Phœnician ships were identical with those of about the time of Ramases III. (1200 B.C.). The fixed yard, the absence of boom, the brails suspending from the yard, the sweep of the lines aft to the overhanging stern, the double steering oar—these characteristics, which in the last chapter we left with the Egyptians, are all seen in the ships of the Phœnicians. The chief noticeable difference is that the latter have altered the bow so that she has a ram. It was the Phœnicians, too, who invented the bireme and trireme in order that speed might be obtained through increasing the height without adding to the length of the ship. The ships become somewhat larger than those of the Egyptians, for the reason that they have to voyage much further afield. Consequently the sail is sometimes found bigger, too, and instead of four brails, six is the usual number seen. The Phœnician bireme had as many as eleven or twelve rowers each side, sails being only used in a fair wind, but never at all in battle. In addition to its crew of seamen, a Phœnician trireme often carried thirty marines, sometimes of a nation different from the Phœnicians.

Right to the end, even when decline had at last taken the place of a rise, the Phœnicians remained good sailormen. Whenever a superior foe overcame them, they were used by their new master with deadly effect against his next enemy. We have an instance of this in the fifth century B.C., when, Phœnicia and Cyprus having been defeated by Cambyses, the latter utilised the strong Phœnician fleet against Amasis, the Egyptian king. And again, in the following century, when Xerxes had enforced the most rigorous conscription, and every maritime people in his dominions had been compelled to put forth its full strength, we find it recorded that the most trustworthy portion of the fleet, far superior to the Egyptians, was composed of ships of the Phœnician cities, the kings of Tyre and Sidon appearing in person, each at the head of his own contingent. Other things being equal, that side was usually victorious which had the Phœnicians with them. For the Phœnicians had the instinct of sailormen; they knew how to build and design their ships to withstand a fight; they had the ships, they had the men, and, what was more important still, they knew how to use both.

But the Phœnicians were more than mere traders or fighters: they were the world's greatest explorers—until the fifteenth and sixteenth centuries of our era. It was they who voyaged out of the Mediterranean across the turbulent Bay of Biscay to Cornwall and perhaps Ireland. I am of the firm opinion that they also continued their travels further eastward across the North Sea: we will deal with that, however, in the next chapter. At any rate about the beginning of the sixth century B.C. they circumnavigated Africa, obeying the orders of Neco, an Egyptian king, "who"—to continue in Hakluyt's Elizabethan English—"(for trial's sake) sent a fleet of Phœnicians downe the Red sea: who setting forth in the Autumne and sailing Southward till they had the Sunne at noonetide upon their sterbourd (that is to say, having crossed the Æquinoctial and the Southerne tropique) after a long Navigation, directed their course to the North, and in the space of 3. yeeres environed all Africk, passing home through the Gaditan streites, and arriving in Egypt." *

It was the Phœnicians, too, who with the Israelites in the time of Solomon sailed down the Red Sea to Eastern

* "The Principal Navigations, Voyages, Traffiques and Discoveries of the English Nation," by Richard Hakluyt. Preface to the second edition.

Africa, Persia, and Beluchistan. Some, indeed, have thought that the Phœnicians sailed out of the Mediterranean and keeping their course to the westward were the first to discover America. Whether this is true or not is a matter for dispute, but it is quite possible. I have seen a little seven-ton cutter yacht that came across on her own bottom, and she is not half the size of the old Phœnician ships. Nor had she a few dozen galley slaves on board to pull at the oars: still less the room wherein to stow them.* There is, then, nothing at all improbable in the Phœnicians having gone so far afield. They were not pressed for time, and could afford to wait till the weather suited them. Given a fair wind they could not have had better shaped canvas for the voyage than theirs. Every sailor will tell you that there is nothing to beat the squaresail for ocean passages, and those who have tried the fore-and-aft rig for deep-sea sailing have lived to wish they had had a rectangular sail set across the mast, so as to avoid the fear of gybing as in a fore-and-after. Lord Brassey, when, in the famous race across the Atlantic in 1905, he commanded his own yacht the *Sunbeam*, afterwards endorsed these opinions about the respective merits of the square-sail and of the fore-and-aft rig.

Moreover, the Phœnicians had ample brails for reefing. True, the ship would roll considerably with so shallow a keel, but her length would be of some assistance, and no doubt the skipper would see to it that the crew steadied her with their oars.

Either from the Egyptians or the Phœnicians—but almost certainly from the latter—the people down the east coast of Africa learnt the art of navigation pretty

* Even still more wonderful and more to the point, as having sailed to the entrance of the Mediterranean, is the passage of the *Columbia II.*, a tiny ship only 19 feet long with 6 feet beam. Navigated solely by Capt. Eisenbram, she sailed from Boston, U.S.A., to Gibraltar, encountering severe weather on the way, in 100 days. (See the *Times* newspaper of November 21, 1903.)

thoroughly, for we know from Hakluyt that when, at the end of the fifteenth century of our era, Vasco da Gama doubled the Cape of Good Hope and called at the East African ports, he found that the arts of navigation were as well understood by the Eastern seamen as by himself. This would seem to imply that these Africans had years ago reached the state of advancement in sailing a ship already possessed by the more civilised parts of the world.

Our evidence as to the actual shape and rig of the Phœnician craft is of two kinds. Firstly, thanks to the discoveries of the late Sir Austin Layard and his successors, we have one or two representations of ships. One of these is a rowing boat pure and simple, very tubby, and obviously never intended to be used with a sail. Secondly, we have the evidence of coins of the towns of Phœnicia. I have been so fortunate as to be able to reproduce two of the latter, both being of Sidon.

With regard to the first class, these date back to a period of about 700 B.C. On a relief belonging to the Palace of Sennacherib found near Nineveh, and now in the British Museum, and also on a relief of the Palace of Khorsabad, built by King Sargon, there are depicted ancient Phœnician ships. This latter is now in the Louvre. But these reliefs do not tell us very much, though they are of assistance if read in conjunction with the coins. The upper deck of the ship from the Sennacherib Palace was reserved for the combatants while fighting, and for persons of quality when making a passage. We see the latter reclining in the sunshine, and the lookout man in the bows. A mast with forestay, braces and sail furled to the yard, would be also on the top deck, but these would be of no considerable size. A row of shields ran round as a protection against the enemy's darts, and the stem ended in a powerful ram. At least seventeen oarsmen in two banks on each side worked

51

the ship, while a couple of steering oars, after the manner of the Egyptians, kept her on her course. This was a bireme for war purposes.

But the ship depicted in the Palace of Khorsabad, while not showing any sail, indicates very clearly a mast with stays leading fore and aft to the bow (which ends in a horse's head) and to the stern. The shape of this craft, if it was anything like the Phœnician ships, which came to Northern Europe, would certainly seem to prove that the Phœnicians continued their voyage further east to Norway; for here, with the high tapering stern and bow, and the decoration of the latter, is what

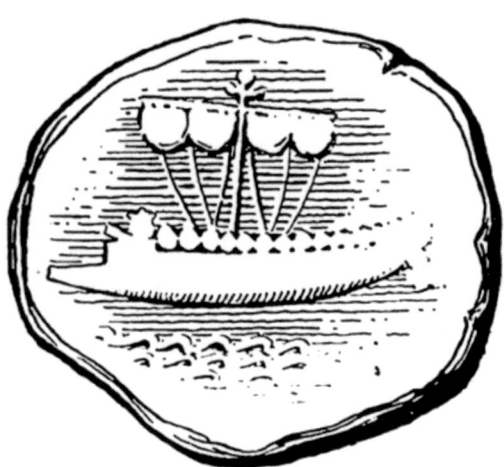

Fig. 9. Phœnician Ship.
From a coin of Sidon, c. 450 B.C.

could very easily be taken for the early design of the Viking ships. She is entirely different from the Egyptian type of ship, though she has evidently been based on the latter.

Passing now to the two coins of Sidon, these are both probably of about the year 450 B.C. Fig. 9 is from a coin in the British Museum. It is a little indistinct, but the Egyptian stern is still seen, though the ram, as already referred to, is at the bows. The double steering oars are faintly visible, though the long line of shields, which survived well into the middle ages, is clearly defined. The curve of the keel-line is very beautiful, and she must have been very fast, as indeed we know from historians similar shaped vessels in Greece were. Although such a ship was of great length, yet by reason of the curve of the

52

keel, having the greatest depth amidships, and because of the design of the stern, she would probably steer pretty easily. This, of course, was essential in the naval manœuvres that were undertaken in fights. As to the sails, if the reader has already followed us in the previous chapter, these call for but little explanation again. The yard is ordinarily kept fixed. The sails hang apparently in two sections like so many curtains, being divided at the mast. The same peculiarity is to be seen in the Irrawadi junks referred to previously.

For shortening sail in a blow, or for stowing when coming to anchor, the six brails seen depending from the yard would be wound round the sail, once or twice, by sending a couple of men to the top of the yard, the crew below throwing up the rope to be passed round sail and yard. It was a clumsy method, but it sufficed. The reader may remember that the Dutchmen have used this principle since the sixteenth century, and the Thames barge of to-day still follows the general idea. The only real difference is that in the Dutchman and Thames barge, being fore-and-aft rigged, the brail comes horizontally— at right angles to the mast—instead of vertically, and parallel to the mast, whilst, of course, going aloft is un-necessary. Even this Dutch brailing system was derived from that used by the lateen sails of the Mediterranean. (See the mizzen of the *Santa Maria*, in Fig. 45.) In detail, too, there is a slight difference, for the modern ships we are mentioning have a ring, or fair-lead, for the brail to come through, one end being fastened to the sail, the standing part passing through the ring on the leach of the sail and so back to the mast.

What we have said regarding this illustration is applic-able also to Fig. 10. But happily this shows us some important details in the stern. First, the staff with crescent-top denotes that she was the admiral's flag-ship. The curved-line immediately below represents part of the structure called the *aphlaston* (ἀ+φλαζω = I crush). This was placed as a protection for the ship against the terrible damage that might be done by the enemy charging into her and ramming her. A still better example of this detail will be noticed in Fig. 14. One can easily trace this as having come from the Egyptian ships of the eighteenth dynasty that went to Punt. Immediately below this, in Fig. 10 again, and hanging down, may be either a protection against the enemy or, as will be seen in the ship of Odysseus (Fig. 16), a kind of decoration resembling some rich carpet, to ornament

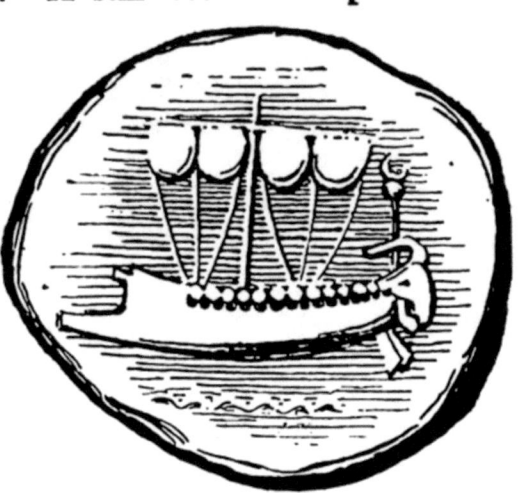

Fig. 10. Phœnician Ship.
From a coin of Sidon, c. 450 B.C.

the stern where the admiral was located in authority. This second Phœnician illustration is from a coin in the Hunterian Collection, Glasgow.

It has been said that some of the larger Phœnician ships were as long as 300 feet, though this statement needs to be taken with caution. At any rate, it is accurate to describe them as being long, straight, narrow, and flat-bottomed, and as carrying sometimes as many as fifty oarsmen. Although the crescent shape had for so long a time been almost a convention for the design of the ship, yet the nation that could found so important and prosperous a colony as Carthage, and that built ships both for Egyptians and Persians, would not be likely to be held down too tightly by custom where their own clever genius and invaluable practical experience taught them

54

otherwise. By completely modifying the bow as it had been customary in the Egyptian ships, the Phœnicians started a new fashion in naval architecture which, permeating through Greek and Roman history, is still found in the galleys of the Adriatic as late as the eighteenth century of our era. Those bows, with or without the ram, even on a Maltese sailing galley, show their ancient Phœnician ancestry in an undeniable manner.

Our information regarding ancient Greek and Roman ships is derived from the following sources : the writings of Homer, Herodotus, Thucydides, Cicero, Cæsar, Tacitus, Xenophon, Lucian, Pliny, Livy, Æschylus, Aristophanes, Euripides, Plutarch, Sophocles, and others ; the inventories of the Athenian arsenals of the fourth century B.C. ; ancient Greek vases ; reliefs discovered in Southern Europe at various periods ; monuments and tombs ; mosaics found in North Africa, ancient coins ; the Voyages of St. Paul ; and finally ancient remains such as fibulæ, terra-cotta models, and earthenware lamps.

From these diverse channels of information we find that the Phœnicians who invented the bireme and the trireme, who had adopted the Egyptian stern and rigging for their ships, handed these features on to the Greeks, and they, in turn, to the Romans. The earliest Greek ships were afloat in the thirteenth century B.C., and by about the year 800 B.C. maritime matters had taken the greatest hold on the dwellers in the Greek peninsula and the western coasts of Asia Minor. The fierce race for wealth which to-day we see going on in America had its precedent in the eighth century before the Christian era in the north-eastern corner of the Mediterranean. Very quickly the contestants found that the shortest route to affluence was *viâ* the sea. Indeed, following the example of their first teachers, the Phœnicians, so zealously did they keep to their ships that the Milesian sea-traders formed a party in the State known as "the men never off' the water." In the seventh century, if not earlier, the Greeks were prosperously fishing in the Black Sea; and though the dangers of rounding Mount Athos in the Ægean were in those days to some extent analogous to the perils which a sailing ship to-day suffers in doubling Cape Horn, yet in the fourth century B.C., Xerxes, rather than risk a series of shipwrecks to his fleet in the stormy seas at the foot of this mountain, had the sandy isthmus connecting the mainland pierced with a canal.

Greece lacked the advantage to be found in a Tigris, a Euphrates, or Nile. Her rivers are so short, and their descent to the sea so rapid, that navigation was utterly impossible. But for what she missed in rivers she was amply compensated in respect of the peculiar formation of the coast. Endowed with the same blessing that makes the west coast of Scotland so attractive (but happily without the drawback of the Atlantic immediately outside the lochs), Greece had her delightful inlets and arms of the seas running far up into the land. The peaceful waters of the Grecian archipelago, the mildness of its climate, the absence of tides, the comparative smoothness of the water—except for occasional squalls with a nasty short sea—these were factors every bit as encouraging for the art of navigation as ever the conditions that smiled on the Egyptians. In some respects they were more stimulating in proportion as the sea makes a better sailor than even the biggest river. Add to this that there was at hand an ample supply of good wood and that the southern shores of the Euxine were rich not merely in timber but in iron, copper and red-lead. Could the shipbuilder's paradise possibly be more complete?

There was just one drawback from which, as it seems to me, the nations on the Mediterranean compared with the inhabitants of Northern Europe have always suffered: even till to-day, or at any rate up to the introduction of steam, the tendency of the Mediterraneans has been to build sailing boats rather than sailing ships. The very conditions that prompted naval architecture at all limited their scope. I mean, of course, that whereas along the coasts washed by the Baltic, the North Sea and the English Channel, the sea-farers had either to build a ship or nothing, the case in the Mediterranean was different. The treacherous waters of the North Sea or Baltic, the existence of dangerous sand banks and rushing tides, were an unfair match for delicately designed craft accustomed to sun-speckled seas. Although the Viking craft had their full complement of rowers, yet they were far abler ships than the over-oared boats of Greece and those of the early days of Rome. Right down to the time of the Spanish Armada, and after, the tendency was ever for the galley or galleass—the *rowed* ship rather than the *sailing* ship—to linger as long as possible, whereas in the North the reverse has been the case. I attribute the prevalence of the " galley " type of craft to two causes—the geographical conditions of Southern Europe and the abundance of slaves. When any amount of physical rowing power could be got with such ease and absence of expense, it was not likely that the sailing ship, *per se*, would advance. I think there can be no doubt at all that this condition of affairs kept back both the rig and design of shipping for very many years. The Southerner's first aim was to create a craft that would be fast ; the Northerner's object was to have a ship that would be seaworthy. The difference between being able to ride out a gale and that of being able to manœuvre with all possible despatch in comparatively sheltered waters, will be found to be the basis of the characteristic features that separate the craft of Northern and Southern Europe.

In Fig. 11 we have some indication of a Greek sailing ship or boat of about the eighth century, when, as we have just said, there existed the great passion for the sea as a means to wealth. This illustration has been sketched from a Bœotian fibula, made of bronze, and now in the British Museum. The boat has not the appearance of being particularly seaworthy, although it is perfectly clear that she is a sailing craft. The *aphlaston* already alluded to will be noticed at the stern. The bow shows the Phœnician influence with its ram-like features, and this characteristic continued to exist with similar prominence till at any rate the beginning of the Christian era. Opinions differ as to whether the teeth-like projections at bow and stern are just the extending horizontal timbers. Per-

FIG. 11. GREEK SHIP.
From Bœotian fibula of the eighth century B.C.

sonally, I believe they are separate fixtures with bronze or iron tips, those at the bow for preventing the ram going too far into the enemy's ship ; those at the stern affording a protection against being rammed by the enemy. The fore-stay leads down to what is apparently a primitive fore-castle, and the man in the stern is standing on a platform, but so crude is the draughtsmanship that it would be un-safe to affirm that this was raised as high as the forecastle. Some have thought that this stern arrangement may denote a latticed cabin, but this seems doubtful. However, it is quite clear that the skipper is either steering or rowing with his foot as the primitive gondolier, while his mate is busy

58

as the look-out. The design at the top of the mast has been thought to be a lantern, but it might also be a flag.

Although not shown in this example, many of the early Greek ships had two forestays and a backstay. The mast was supported at its foot by a prop, and when

Fig. 12. Greek War Galley.
From a vase, c. 500 B.C.

lowered it lay aft in a rest, being raised and lowered by means of the forestays, like the custom of the Thames barge and the Norfolk wherry-man. Fig. 12 represents a war-galley taken from a Greek vase of about 500 B.C. It will be found in the Second Vase Room of the British Museum. The sail (ἱστίον) will be seen hanging from the yard, together with the brails as already described. The two halyards come down on either side of the mast. We should presume that, having the brails, the Greek ships were accustomed to reefing: but we have actual evidence from the expression used by Aristophanes " ἄκροισι χρῆσθαι ἱστίοις," "to keep the sails close-reefed." Similarly Euripides has the phrase " ἄκροισι λαίφους κρασπέδοις,"

SAILING SHIPS

" under close-reefed sails " (lit. " with the outermost edges of the sail "). The reefing method is better shown in Fig. 13. If it came on to blow two hands would be sent aloft to go out along the yard. The brails one by one would be thrown up to the men, who would pass each brail one or thrice round the yard, according to the number of reefs required to be taken in. Fig. 13 shows a ship close-reefed. That this is no fanciful picture will be seen by the reader who cares to compare the relief on the tomb of Naevoleja Tyche at Pompei,* on which will be noticed one man on deck getting ready the brails to throw them up, while two other members of the crew are already out on the yard, and two more still are climbing up the rigging to help them, probably by taking up the ends of the brails.

Each yard was composed of two spars lashed together as in the Maltese galley and Japanese junk of to-day. The Latin word for a yard was always used in the plural—*antennæ*—to signify the two parts lashed in one. The boar's head—a very favourite symbol for this purpose in early ships—will be noticed at the bow of the war-galley in Fig. 12. Above it is the forecastle, and running thence astern is a flying deck, in order that the fighting men might not hinder the work of the rowers. The two banks of oars will be immediately noticed. Astern sits the steersman with his two steering-oars. That which hangs from the stern below is the gangway for going aboard The crew either hauled their ships ashore at night, or, laying out anchors from the bows seaward, carried stern ropes ashore to a rock. The gangway shown was lowered to the land side, and the crew came aboard from aft. The reader who is familiar with the Yorkshire cobble and the method adopted for beaching by the fishermen on the coast above the Humber will find additional interest in this.

* An illustration of this will be found in " Pompeji in Leben und Kunst," by August Mau, Leipzig, 1908.

PHŒNICIA, GREECE, AND ROME

The ship in Fig. 13 is a merchantman. The gangways are very noticeable. So also is the Egyptian stern with the steering oars. Amidships will be seen the wattled screens or washboards, acting as bulwarks for keeping out the spray. A similar arrangement was customary on the

FIG. 13. GREEK MERCHANTMAN.
From a vase, c. 500 B.C.

Viking ships, and remains to this day on Norwegian ships of that kind. At the stern of both this ship and that of the previous figure will be noticed an ornament resembling some plant. Perhaps to us moderns the most striking feature of the ship is her beautiful bow: indeed, had one not seen the actual vase, one might easily have said that the design was taken from a modern schooner bow. There are so many points about this merchant ship that attract us in looking at her that we wonder, not unnaturally, if we have advanced so much after all during these fourteen hundred years since she was designed, for such a bow and such a stern would win applause in any port.

The war-galleys were called longships, and the merchant

vessels roundships. This aptly describes the chief difference which separated them. Whilst the former were essentially rowing-ships, depending on oars only as auxiliaries, the merchant ship was primarily a sailing vessel. Nevertheless she carried twenty oars, not so much for progression as for turning the ship's head off the wind, and perhaps for getting under way and in entering harbour. These trading ships were generally built throughout of pine, while the war galleys were of fir, cypress, cedar, or pine, according to the nature of the forests at hand. The merchantmen had keels of pine, but were provided with false keels of oak when they had to be hauled ashore or put on a slip for repairs or other reasons. It was the custom, however, to keep the merchant ships afloat. We have already pointed out that the galleys, on the contrary, were usually hauled ashore at night, and since the friction of their keels would tend to split the wood it was customary for these latter to be of oak. The masts and yards and oars were of fir or pine. The timber for the keel was selected with especial care, as indeed with so much hard wear and tear it was necessary. Among other woods that were also used may be mentioned plane, acacia, ash, elm, mulberry and lime—these being employed especially for the interior of the hull. Alder, poplar and timber of a balsam tree were used also. Like the Koryaks and the very earliest inhabitants of Northern Europe, in some outlandish districts of the Mediterranean the sides of the ship were of leather instead of wood, but this would be only in cases where the inhabitants were still unlearned or there was a scarcity of timber.

The ancients did not allow the timber to season thoroughly, because it would become thereby too stiff to bend. Steaming boxes apparently had not come into use in shipbuilding. However, after the tree was felled it was allowed some time for drying, and then, when the ship was built, some time elapsed for the wood to settle. The seams were caulked with tow and other packing, being fixed with tar or wax, the underbody of the ship being coated with wax, tar, or a combined mixture, the wax being melted over a fire until soft enough to be laid on with a brush. Seven kinds of paint were used, viz., purple, violet, yellow, blue, two kinds of white, and green for pirates in order that their resemblance to the colour of the waves might make them less conspicuous. As we shall see in Fig. 21, elaborate designs were painted along the sides, but this appears to have been a later custom. The latest discoveries in Northern Africa show this decoration round the side to be very frequent about the second century of the Christian era. Earlier Greek ships had only patches of colour on the bows, blue or purple, or vermilion ; the rest of the hull was painted with black tar like many of the coasters and fishing smacks of to-day. The painting on the bows was probably to facilitate the recognition of the direction taken by a vessel. Ships were not copper-bottomed, but sometimes a sheathing of lead with layers of tarred sail cloth interposed between was affixed to the hull.

Nails of bronze and iron, and pegs of wood were used for fastening the planking, the thickness of the latter varying from $2\frac{1}{4}$ to $5\frac{1}{4}$ inches. In order to fortify the warships against the terrible shock of ramming, she had to be strengthened by wales running longitudinally around her sides. Fig. 14 shows the stern of a Greek ship of about the fifth century B.C. The wales or strengthening timbers just mentioned will be easily seen. Fig. 15 exhibits another example of the boar's-head bow. These two illustrations are taken from a coin of Phaselis, in Lycia, now preserved in the British Museum. The *aphlaston* will be immediately recognised in Fig. 14.

Like the Egyptian ships, these ancient vessels were also provided with a stout cable—the ὑπόζωμα in Greek, *tormentum* in Latin. The spur for ramming was shod with metal—iron or copper—and was at first placed below the water line, but subsequently came above it. The space between the oar-ports was probably about three feet, each oarsman occupying about five feet of room in width. A galley having thirty-one seats for rowing would have about seventeen feet of beam. The draught of these

FIG. 14. STERN OF A GREEK
.SHIP (c. 600 B.C.).

FIG. 15. BOAR'S-HEAD BOW OF A
GREEK SHIP (c. 600 B.C.).

warships was nevertheless very small—perhaps not more than four or five feet.

The old method of naval warfare consisted in getting right up to the enemy and engaging him alongside in a hand-to-hand fight, spears and bows and arrows being used. There is an Etruscan vase in the British Museum of the sixth century, which shows this admirably. At a later date this method was altered in favour of ramming. The ship would bear down on the enemy, and an endeavour would be made to come up to him in such a way as to break off all his oars at one side, thereby partially disabling him. But if the enemy were smart enough, he would be able to go on rowing until the critical moment, when with great dexterity, he would suddenly shorten his oars inwards. We have also referred to the protection of the stern against the wicked onslaught of the ram, but the ship ramming, lest her spur should penetrate too far into the enemy's stern and so break off, had usually, above, a

64

head which acted as a convenient buffer. But we must not forget that sails and mast were lowered before battle, since the galley was much more handy under oars alone. The excitement of a whole week's bumping races on the Isis must be regarded as very slow compared to the strenuous plashing of oars, the shouts of the combatants, and the ensuing thud and splintering of timbers that characterised a Mediterranean engagement.

The reader will find in Fig. 16 one of the finest specimens of a Greek sailing galley with one bank of oars. It is taken from a vase in the Third Room in the British Museum, the date being about 500 B.C. As many as eight brails are shown here. The number of these gradually became so great that we find in the Athenian inventories of the fourth century B.C. that the rigging of a trireme and quadrireme included eighteen brails. No doubt, as time went on, it was found more convenient to be able to brail the sail up at closer intervals. In the present illustration the sail is furled right up to the yard and the rowers are doing all the work. Before passing on to another point we must not fail to notice the fighting bridge or forecastle, the shape of the blades of the oars, and the decoration of the stern previously alluded to. A capital instance here is afforded us of the ever watchful eye which we mentioned in our introductory chapter as being a notable feature of the ancient ship. It is worth while remarking, as showing the extent of this practice, that a representation of an eye is still to be found as a distinguishing attribute on the Portuguese fishing boats to-day.

At the very first, on the Greek as on the Egyptian ships, thongs were used for rowlocks, but subsequently holes were left, as seen in the illustration, for the oars to be passed through. Because the mast had to be taken down before battle, the war galleys were not fully decked all over, Amidships she was open, but, as we have already seen, bridges or gangways extended fore and aft on either side

E

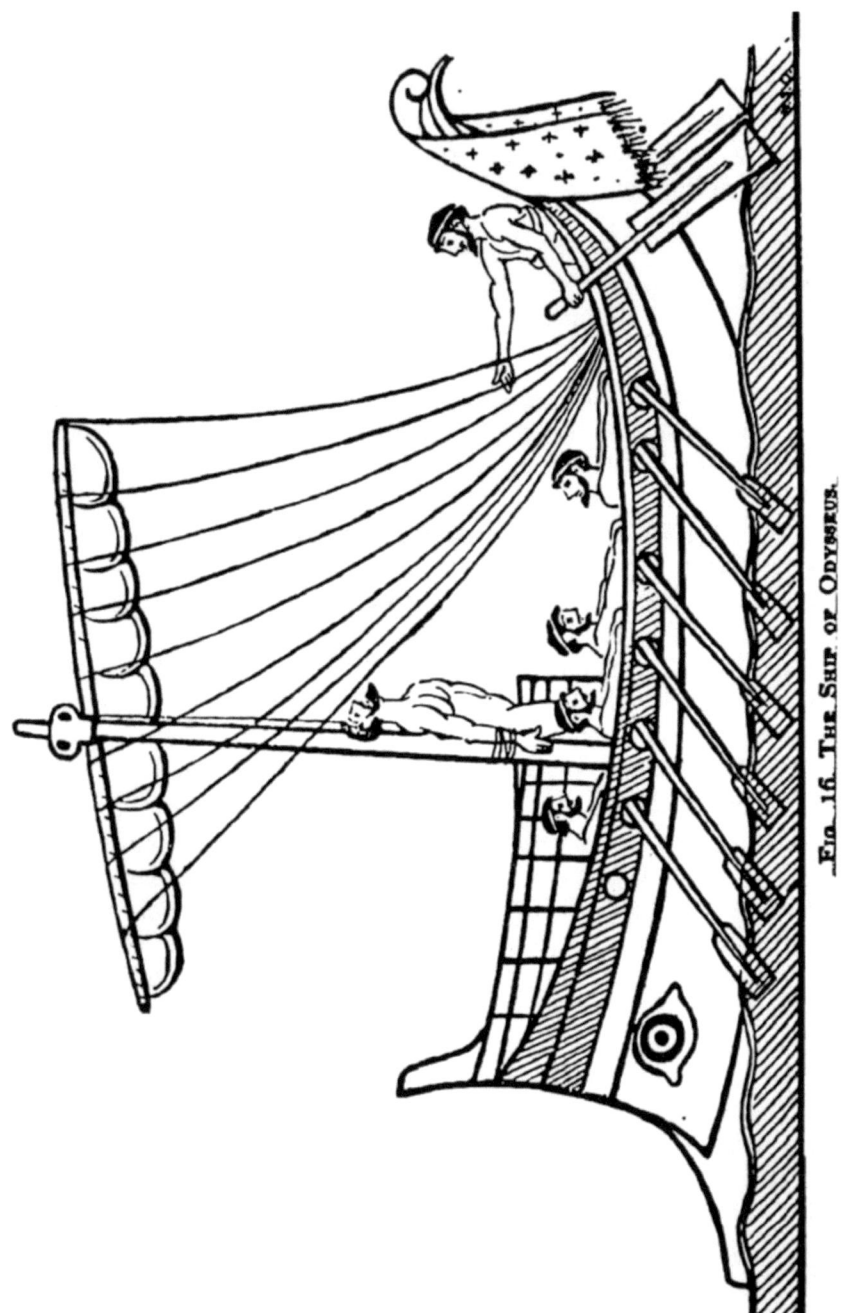

FIG. 16. THE SHIP OF ODYSSEUS.

of the mast, so that the fighting crew should in no way interfere with the oarsmen. Partial decks were also found at bow and stern. Even in the time of Cæsar, we find that completely covered vessels were not in general use. These flying bridges were placed on supports and then covered with planks as shown in Fig. 12, leaving the intermediate hold undecked. The sail was made of several pieces of white canvas or cloth. Not infrequently they were coloured, a black sail being a universal sign of mourning, while a purple or vermilion denoted the ship of an admiral or sovereign. Just as pirates were wont to paint their ships the colour of the sea, so in the time of war, on board scout-ships, both sails and ropes were dyed of that hue. One can easily understand that with the powerful rays of the southern sun their disguise would have been effectual.

Ropes were made of twisted ox-hide, or fibres of the papyrus plant. This was the usual practice for many years also in other parts of Europe. The edges of the sail were bound with hide, the skins of hyena and seal being especially used for this purpose, as the sailors believed this would keep off lightning. The Koryaks, also, still employ seal-hide for sails and ropes. Later on, windlasses were introduced for working the halyards and cables of the larger ships. After the crew had gone aboard the galley, and everything was ready for getting under way, the gangway would be slung from the stern, and three poles would be used for pushing off from the shore. It is interesting to remark that the word used for this pole by Homer— κοντός—is still found in the word "quant," given to a long pole for pushing the Norfolk wherries in calms along the banks.

The vessel shown in Fig. 17 is a terra-cotta model of a merchant ship. The socket for the mast will easily be seen. The high stern aft must not be supposed to have been raised to such an altitude solely for the convenience of the steersman. The greatest foe that the merchantman had to contend with was the pirate who swept down and robbed him of his cargo. Therefore, to obtain some protection, these traders were usually fitted with turrets of great height, by means of which missiles could be hurled down

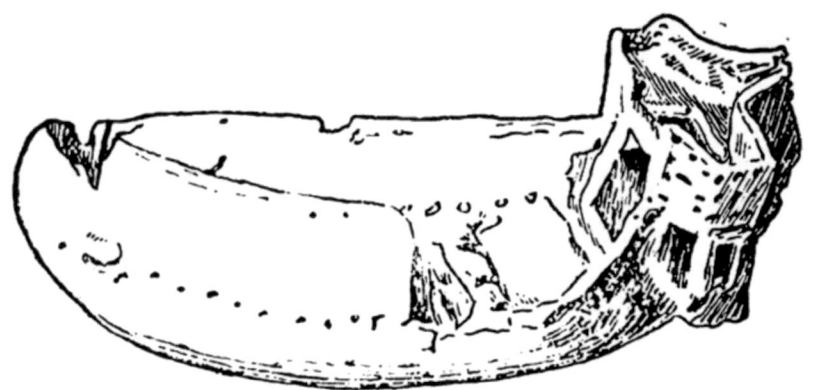

Fig. 17. Terra-cotta Model of Greek Ship of the Sixth Century b.c.

on to the enemy below. It is possible that the side "castles" shown were also used as some protection for the steersmen, one standing in each with the protection of a roof over him. Probably, too, on these occasions the score of oars would be brought out in order to manœuvre quickly. A merchant ship sometimes carried as many as eight of these turrets (two in the bows, two in the stern and four amidships). They were easily movable and were known to have reached to a height of twenty feet. The model here shown belongs to the sixth century b.c. It will be noticed that she has a very flat bottom, but this would be a convenience whenever she had to be beached, for there were only two sailing seasons—in the spring, and in the months between midsummer and autumn. After the setting of the Pleiads, the ship was beached and a stone fence built around her to keep off wind and weather. This custom, then, would somewhat modify ier lines below the waterline. It was, further, the custom to pull the plug out when laying up for the winter, so that the water should not rot the bottom. Tackle and sail and steering oars were carefully stored at home until the fair weather returned once more. These were the customs as far back as 700 B.C.

The model we have just alluded to was found in Cyprus, and is now in the British Museum. Many others similar to this have also been found. There is an amusing legend that Kinyras, king of Cyprus, having promised to send fifty ships to help the Greeks against Troy, sent only one, but she carried forty-nine others of terra-cotta manned by terra-cotta figures.

Although the Phœnicians probably must be credited with the honour of having invented the trireme, a ship with a triple arrangement of oars, yet the Greeks were responsible for having developed the use of this to a considerable extent, especially after the fifth century B.C. Eventually the word "trireme" denoted not necessarily that she had this triple arrangement, but became a generic expression for warships. We have in later history similar instances of the same designation remaining to a ship even when she has entirely altered the right to her previous definition. Thus the galleass, which was essentially a rowing vessel, frequently bore the same name during the Middle Ages, even when she was a sailing ship proper. A similar instance may be found in the different meanings which the words "barge," "wherry," "yawl," "cutter," and "barque" denote at different times.

Triremes had two kinds of sails and two kinds of masts, but before battle the larger sail and the larger mast were always put ashore. Such enormous yards and masts would be very much in the way on boats of this kind. Regarding the arrangement of the oars of the trireme much controversy has been raised. The theories of thirty or more banks of oars have now been pretty well dismissed.

The amount of freeboard that this would have given to a ship must necessarily have been colossal, and militated against the very object they had in view, viz., handiness. It is highly probable that the crew consisted of two hundred rowers, sixty-two on the highest tier, fifty-four on the middle and fifty-four on the lowest, in addition to thirty fighting men stationed on the highest deck. The upper oars would thus pass over what we now call the gunwale, the second and third rows being through port holes. Even when very large numbers of oarsmen are mentioned, we must not suppose that there were so many lines of rowers as that; several men were needed to each oar. Considering their weight and the size of later ships, this would seem to be very necessary.

Before we pass from the subject of the trireme, it is not without interest to mention that in the year 1861 Napoleon III. had constructed a trireme 39 metres in length and $5\frac{1}{2}$ metres in beam. She carried 130 oarsmen, who were placed two by two. Of these forty-four were on the first row, the same number on the second, and forty-two on the top. Like her ancestors she had a three-fold spur, a rostrum, and two steering oars. But to us a far more important piece of information lies in the fact that she was actually experimented with on the sea at Cherbourg in good weather. It was found that she bore out all that had ever been written by the ancient historians concerning her: for she was both very fast and could be manœuvred with great ease.* According to the ancients, a trireme could average as much as seven and a half knots an hour, covering one hundred and ten during a day. The merchant ship was going at a good pace when she reeled off her five knots an hour. Her average was about sixty

---

* A model of this ship is to be seen in the Louvre. See "Musée Rétrospectif de la Classe 33. Matériel de la Navigation de Commerce à l'Exposition Universelle Internationale de 1900, à Paris. Rapport du Comité d'Installation."

knots in a day: but during a whole day and night, with a favourable wind, she was capable of doing as much as a hundred and thirty. Comparing this speed with the craft of to-day, it may be worth noting that the average day's run of a moderate-sized coaster would work out at a hundred or hundred and twenty knots. The speed of the ships of the Mediterranean was not slow, then, though they would appear ridiculous if compared with some of the marvellous passages made by the famous old clippers of the second half of the nineteenth century of our era.

The navigation employed by the Greeks was that of coasting from port to port, from one headland across a bay to another. There was no such thing, of course, as being able to lay a compass course from one point to another out of sight. The system of buoyage was also non-existent, but there were lighthouses, as we know from designs on ancient pottery and reliefs. On certain points of the land the Greeks erected high towers, the most ancient of these being at the entrance to the Ægean Sea —about 800 B.C. Later, about the period of 300 B.C., a tower was raised on the island of Pharos, near Alexandria. At its summit two wooden fires were kept burning constantly, so that the flame by night and the smoke by day might aid the primitive navigators. In the fourth century B.C., however, Pytheas, by means of an instrument called the *gnomon*, which indicated the height of the sun by the direction of the shadow cast on a flat surface, determined the day of the summer solstice, to which the greatest height of the sun corresponds. He thus succeeded in fixing the latitude of Marseilles.

We have already mentioned that when a galley was cleared for action she sent her big spars and sails ashore. One set of double halyards of course served for these, the larger sails and spars being no doubt for fair weather when near the shelter of the land. Mr. Torr in his excellent little book,* which is a mine of information, the result of considerable classical research, gives the name of *akation* to the smaller gear—mast, sail and yard included. He mentions the very interesting fact that the expression "hoisting the akation" became synonymous with "running away" from the enemy. Aris-

tophanes made use of the phrase in a play produced in 411 B.C.

The names *dolon* in 201 B.C. and *artemon* found mentioned about 100 B.C., were also used to indicate the smaller masts and sails. We shall refer to this latter again presently. Anchors are supposed to have been among the inventions of Anacharsis. In the earliest times they were, as one would expect, merely a heavy weight of stone. Then they were made of iron, and later on of lead. Fig. 18 shows that

FIG. 18. A COIN OF APOLLONIA, SHOWING SHAPE OF ANCHOR.

the shape was a cross between a modern "mushroom" anchor and the ordinary one in everyday use. The triangular space at the crown was used for bending on a tripping line. The illustration is of a coin found in Apollonia (in Thrace), and now in the British Museum. The date is about 420 B.C. Two anchors were carried by galleys, and three or four by merchantmen. Even in those days the mariners understood the usefulness of marking the position of their anchors with cork floats. The cables were of chain and of rope. Flags and lights were used on the admiral's ship, three being allowed for the latter and one for galleys.

The illustration in Fig. 19 has been taken from De Baïf's book,† not so much because it gives a representative

* "Ancient Ships," by Cecil Torr, Cambridge, 1894.
† "Lazari Bayfii annotationes . . . de re navali." Paris, 1536.

picture of what a Roman warship was like, as for the fact
that the various parts of the ship may by this means be

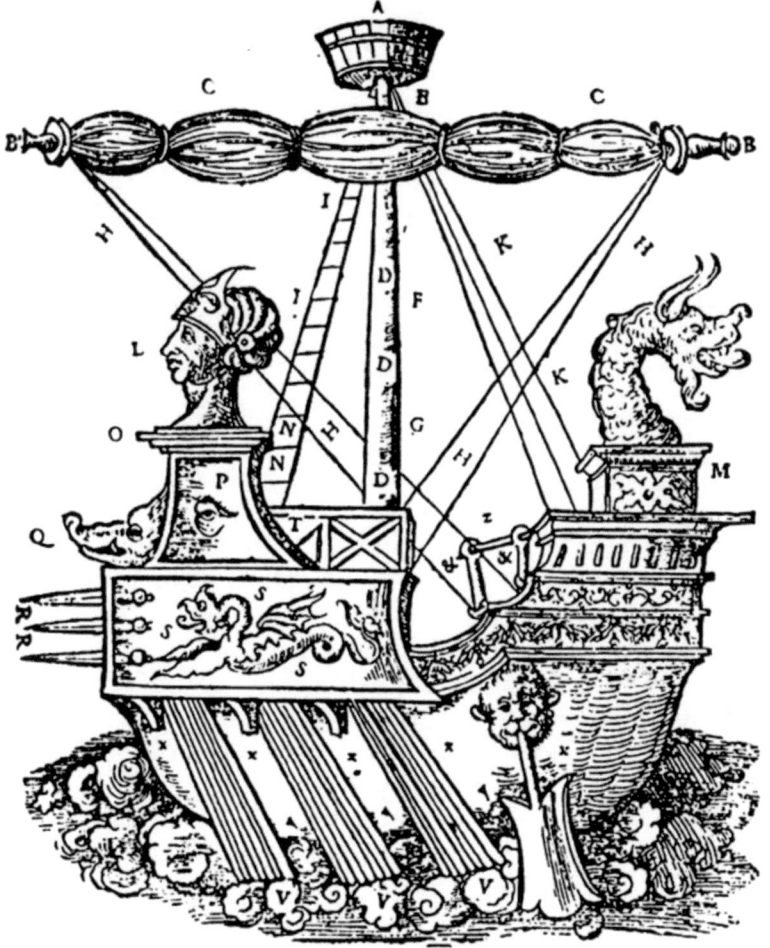

FIG. 19. A ROMAN WARSHIP.

made somewhat clearer than if we had an ancient relief
before us. I have, up till now, throughout this chapter,
included Roman vessels under the description given to the
Greek ships, there being for a long time but little difference.

73

In Fig. 19, A is the fighting top; BB are the ends or "horns" of the sail yards; CC are the *antennæ* or yards; D is the mast; E is the *carchesium* or upper part of the mast to which the halyards led; F is the *trachelus*, being half way up the mast; G is the *pterna* or heel of the mast; HH are the *opiſcri funcs* or braces; 1 is a rope—*calos* (ladder); KK are the backstays; L is the figurehead, the *parasemon* or distinguishing mark, so that in a fleet of ships, each alike as to rig and size, this would be very necessary; M is the stern; N is the turret or forecastle already discussed above; O is the prow; P is the all-vigilant eye which the ship was supposed to possess; Q is the *rostrum*, beak or boar's head, while R is the *rostrum tridens* with its three-toothed ram; S is the *epotides* or cathead whence the anchor was let down. The word is used by Euripides and Thucydides. T is the *katastroma* or flying deck, that the marines might be able to fight without hindering the rowers; V, of course, shows the oars, X the hull; Y is the *dryochus* which properly means one of the trestles or props on which the keel for a new ship is laid; Z is the *clavus* or handle of the tiller; "&" refers to the tiller itself.

Fig. 20 is also taken from De Baif, and is reproduced here not as being an accurate representation of a Roman sailing ship, but because it well illustrates by its exaggeration several points not easily discernible in other reproductions. The inclined mast in the bows carries the artemon sail, but it is out of all proportion. A is the steersman; BB are the oarsmen; C is the πρῳράτης, or in Latin *proreta*—the look-out man; D represents the beak —τα ἀκρωτήρια, the extremities of the ship; E is the θρόνος, or seat of authority for the steersman. (Compare a similarity in the illustration of Furttenbach's galley, in Fig. 58.)

Coming now to the ships of much later date, the dimensions were sometimes pushed to vast extremes.

Exulting as we rightly are in these days of magnificent liners of immense tonnage and luxurious comfort, it seems astounding that the ancients, when they had embraced self-indulgence whole-heartedly and set forth to throw away their fine energies in wasteful and extravagant pleasures, should at so early a date have built mammoth ships fitted with the most luxurious deck-houses, with bronze baths and marbled rooms, with paintings and statues and mosaics in their

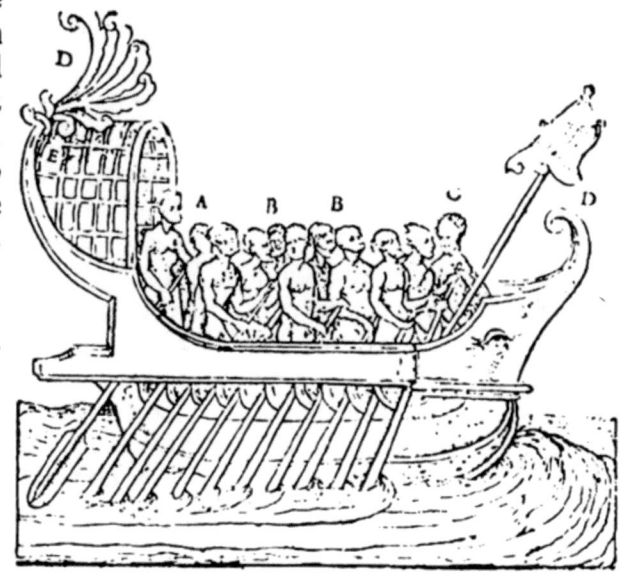

Fig. 20. Roman Ship.

sumptuous saloons, with libraries and covered walks along the decks, ornamented with rows of vines and fruit trees planted in flower-pots. Even the ample luxury and the small trees on the decks of the *Mauretania* have not yet reached to such excesses of civilisation. Throughout the third century B.C., several of these monstrosities were built by the kings of Sicily, Macedonia, Alexandria and Asia. The size of one of these " floating palaces " (to use here aptly a much abused expression) may be gathered from the dimensions of one of them, which was 280 cubits long, 38 cubits wide, while the stem rose to a height of 48 cubits above the water. Nevertheless, her draught, in spite of so much top-hamper, did not exceed 4 cubits, and she carried seven rams, was fitted with a double and stern, and had no less than four steering paddles.

Could we but see some of these ancient mammoth ships, could we but wander through their saloons looking up at the wonderful statuary, marvelling at the spaciousness of the tiled galleries, how interesting it would be! How we should thrill with delight at being once more transported into the ships of Roman times! Of course, you will say, such a thing is impossible. Even if representations are preserved on tomb or mosaic of contemporary ships it would be ridiculous to expect that the ships themselves should still exist. But we all know that truth is sometimes wonderfully romantic, and in the history of ships there are some amazing surprises always ready for our attention. Let us say at once, then, that two of these floating palaces of the time of Caligula are in existence to-day in Italy. Their details are interesting to the highest degree, and the following account, based, as will be seen, on actual experiences of those who have been into the ships, agrees with the historical descriptions already referred to. For the valuable particulars of these two ships of Caligula, I am indebted to Mr. St. Clair Baddeley and to Señor Malfatti.*

Caligula possessed that overpowering passion for water and ships which throughout the world's history has always manifested itself in explorer or privateer, yachtsman, or whomsoever else. Suetonius † says that this megalo-

---

* See "Caligula's Galleys in the Lake of Nemi," by St. Clair Baddeley, article in the *Nineteenth Century and After*, March, 1909; also "Le Navi Romane del Lago di Nemi," by V. Malfatti, Rome, 1905, which gives an interesting account, with illustrations, of the finding of these galleys, as well as an excellent plan of one of the ships of Caligula as far as she has been explored. She has a rounded stern and pointed bow. An ingenious pictorial effort is made to reconstruct the galley afresh. The book contains photographs of the floats, showing the shape of the boat, and of some of the chief relics recovered in 1895.

† "Life of Caligula," xxxvii.

maniac had built two galleys with ten banks of oars, each having a poop that blazed with jewels and sails that were parti-coloured. These "galleys" were fitted with baths, galleries, saloons, and supplied with a great variety of growing trees and vines. In one of these ships, Caligula was wont to sail in the daytime along the coast of Campania, feasting amidst dancing and concerts of music.

Now, in the northern end of the Lake of Nemi, not far from the Campanian coast, there still lie to this day, at right angles to each other, two such galleys as Suetonius describes. Recent research beneath the water has revealed much that is invaluable to us in the study of the sailing ship. From the inscriptions on several lengths of lead piping laid for the purpose of supplying the galleys with water, and which have been brought up by divers, it is proved that these belonged to Caligula, and that therefore they are of the remote period of 37–41 A.D. And this date has been further corroborated by the discovery of tiles and bronze sculptures found on board.

The history of the efforts to make these galleys speak to us from the depths of their watery grave is almost as interesting as their very existence. During the fifteenth century, owing to the fact that fishermen on the lake frequently in their nets drew ashore objects of wood and bronze, divers were sent below and discovered the undoubted existence of a ship of some sort. At last ropes were made fast and endeavours were made to draw the vessel to shallow water, but these efforts were only crowned with the unfortunate result of breaking off part of the stem. However, the nails were found to be of bronze, whilst in length some were as much as a cubit. The wood was discovered to be larch, and the vessel to be sheathed with lead, covering a stiff lining of woollen-cloth padding fastened on by bronze studs. It is important to note that the ancients in 37 A.D. had the good sense to realise what

77

Sir Philip Howard, and other naval authorities in the time of Charles II., did not discover until the year 1682, that lead sheathing round a ship, used with iron nails, was bound to set up corrosion.*

Further operations on Lake Nemi were suspended until the year 1535, when an expert went below to the ship again. A large amount of her wood was brought to the surface, and was found to consist of pine and cypress, as well as the larch previously noticed. The pegs were of oak, and many bronze nails in perfect preservation were rescued from the deep. These, said the diver, fastened the plate of lead to the hull of the ship. There was also a lining of linen between the lead and the timber, whilst within the ship were pavements of tiles two feet square, and segments of red marble and enamel. He also makes reference to the rooms of this watery palace. As to her size, this was found to be about 450 feet long, and about 192 broad, whilst the height from keel to deck was about 51 feet.

Various attempts were made in 1827 by means of a diving bell, but no success resulted, and it was not until September of 1905 that a fresh search was made by divers, when both galleys were located at a depth of thirty feet of water. "By attaching long cords with corks to the galleys, the divers," says Mr. Baddeley, "sketched out in outlines on the surface the shape of the vessels." The length of the other vessel was found to be 90 feet by 26 feet beam. The decks were paved with elaborate mosaic work in porphyry, green serpentine and *rosso antico*, intermingled with richly-coloured enamel. The bulwarks were found to be cast in solid bronze and to have been once gilded, for traces of the latter were manifest. From the other vessel lying nearer in-shore, the divers brought up various beautiful sculptures. The outer edge of the vessel is covered with cloth smeared with pitch,

* See p. 245.

and over this occur folds of thin sheet lead, doubled over and fastened down upon it with copper nails.

It is thought that these galleys were designed by their builder Caligula in imitation of those he used along the Campanian coast which, though sailing ships, were rather of the nature of floating villas. As to their purpose, it is probable that they were connected with the worship of Virbius and of Diana. There, then, at the bottom of Lake Nemi, these two galleys lie—still in existence, though owing to their long immersion and the depth of the water their ultimate recovery is extremely doubtful.

Among the many interesting items of marine information which we are enabled to gather from the voyages of St. Paul, we find * that the lead-line was in use, for we are told that " they sounded and found it twenty fathoms : and when they had gone a little further they sounded again and found it fifteen fathoms." Also they " were in all in the ship two hundred threescore and sixteen souls," so she was a vessel of considerable size. Then in the morning, having espied a snug little creek with a good shore for beaching, " when they had slipped their anchors they left them in the sea, at the same time loosing the rudder bands, hoisted up the artemon, and made towards the beach." They had, no doubt long previously, learned the action which has saved many hundreds of ships, at all times of the world's history, from foundering, by detaching the cable from the ship and not waiting to heave up the anchor. Moreover, they had found a nice beach under their lee, so the artemon or fore-sail was hoisted up the small foremast, and she would be able to make the beach without too much way on, and without the enormous amount of work that would have been necessary had the mainsail been set —a proceeding, considering the weather about, that they were not anxious to attempt. " Artemon " is the word used in the Greek of the New Testament : the translation

* Acts xxvii.

of this as "mainsail" in the authorised version is of course quite wrong. The later ships were fitted with a mainsail and mast, but also a small foremast tilted at an angle of perhaps twenty-three degrees projected out from the bows, on which another small square sail was set. This was the artemon or foresail, and it would be in just such a manœuvre as this, or for giving the ship a sheer when getting up the cable or when coming into port even in fine weather, that this headsail would be found of the greatest use. We must not forget that this kind of foremast and foresail continued right till the beginning of the nineteenth century on all full-rigged ships, in the form of bowsprit and sprit-sail, until the triangular headsails with which we are so familiar nowadays came in. Finally, before we leave the voyages of St. Paul, we must not omit to notice the reference to the statement that after the anchors had been slipped they *loosed the rudder bands*. Instead of leaving the rudders to get foul of the stern cables when they had put out the four anchors, or to run the risk of being dashed to pieces by the waves, the ropes extending from the stern to the extremities of the steering oars would be hauled up so that the blades were quite clear of the water. It was a similar operation to a Thames barge hauling up her leeboards. Therefore, having cast off their anchors and being under way again, the rudder-ropes would necessarily be lowered. The same method of "rudder-bands" obtained among the Vikings. If the reader will turn to Fig. 29, of the Gogstad Viking ship, he will readily appreciate this point.

I am not going to enter here into any discussion as to the authorship of the Acts of the Apostles, but whoever he may have been had an accurate knowledge of the ships of his time, for we are able to see just the same kind of ship as St. Paul's in a merchantman of about the year 50 A.D. and another of seventeen years later. The artemon mast and sail are well shown. It was, of course, the

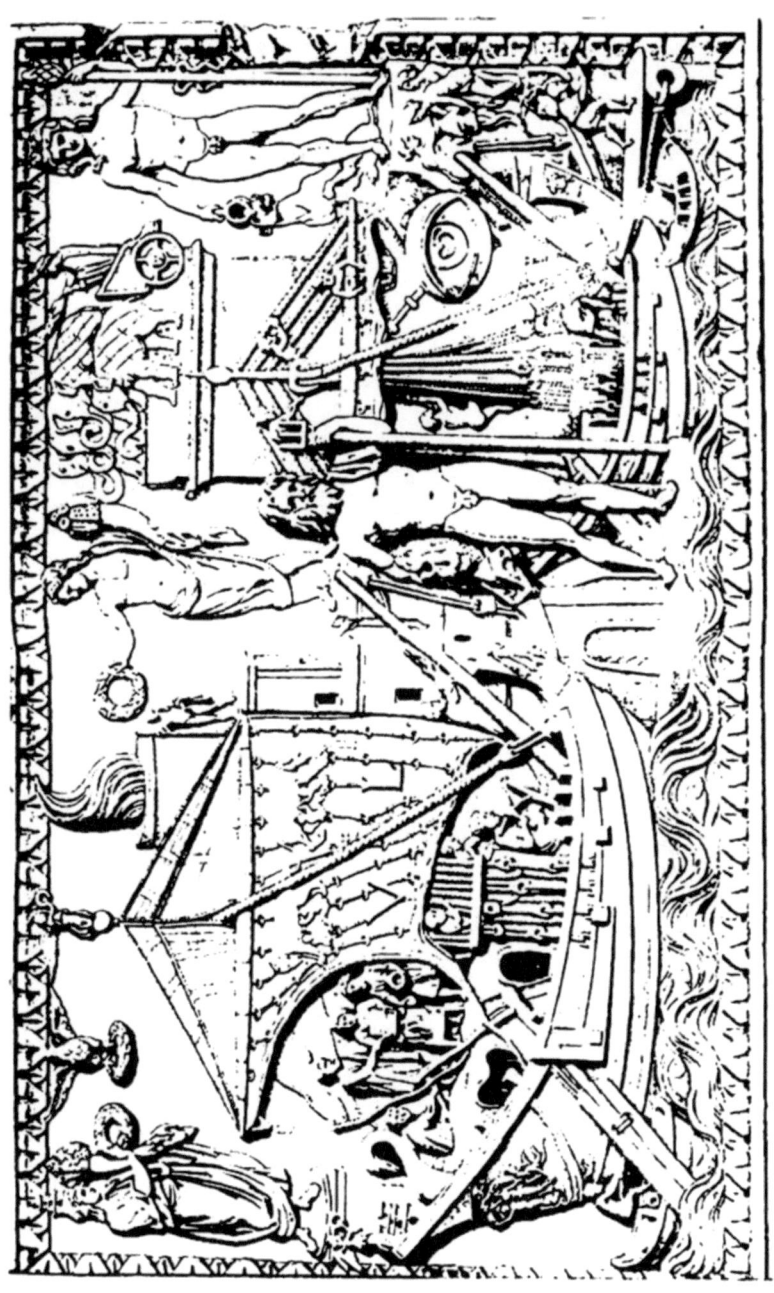

FIG. 21. ROMAN MERCHANT SHIP.

artemon mast that was the forerunner of the modern bowsprit. One can estimate the size of the mercantile ships of the Mediterranean of about the first and second centuries from Lucian, who refers to a merchantman engaged in the corn-carrying trade between Egypt and Italy. Her length was 180 feet, her breadth a little more than a quarter of her length, while her depth from upper deck to bottom of hold was 43½ feet. The registered tonnage of the largest trading ships was about 150.

We have in Fig. 21 a very instructive illustration of two Roman merchant ships of about the year 200 A.D. This has been copied from a relief found near the mouth of the Tiber. The advance in shipbuilding since the times of the Egyptians has continued. The great high stern is still there, the bow remaining lower than the poop. The steering oar is very well shown, together with the "rudder bands" that we have just spoken of. They will be found to be two in number, coming down from the ship's quarter, and passing through holes bored in the blade of the rudder. The tiller is of considerable length. The decoration under the stern with classical figures is very beautiful, while above is the familiar swan's neck which accentuates the general duck-like lines of the ship. Three bollards aft and four forward, are seen for mooring purposes. The shape of the stem is worth noting for this must have been fairly common in big ships, and we shall find something very similar in the vessels of Northern Europe up to the fourteenth century. The rigging shows to what knowledge they had attained by now. The dead-eyes for setting up the shrouds, the purchase for getting the powerful forestay down tight, together with a similar arrangement on the artemon mast, are deserving of careful notice. The mainsail will be seen to be hoisted by two halyards, foot-ropes apparently being provided for the men sent up to furl it. I have noticed that in most of the old illustrations depicting men going aloft, the sailors usually ascend

F

naked. This will be observed in the present illustration. The obvious conclusion is that they wished to be perfectly free and unfettered in their movements and to run no risk of their garments being caught in the rigging. The ships are moored to the quay by taking the stay of the artemon ashore. There is a different figurehead on the bows of each ship, while in the background, to the left of the middle of the picture, will be seen the warning beacon previously alluded to, the building below it with small windows being probably the leading lights for coming into the harbour. The sail has a triangular top-sail in two pieces without a yard of its own. The yard of the main-sail appears now to be made in one piece instead of two, but the point where, owing to the binding together of the two pieces, the yard was thickest, is still so in the centre. The sheets and braces will be recognised at once, but we must say a word regarding the brails that were now employed. If the reader will examine the sail shown set in this illustration, he will find

FIG. 22. ROMAN SHIP ENTERING HARBOUR.
From an earthenware lamp in the British Museum.

that the brails pass through rings on the fore-side of the canvas, then either through the top of the sail or just over it, between the yard and the edge of the sail itself, and so down to the stern. In the picture three of the brails are seen coming down so as to be within reach of the steersman. The action of brailing or reefing, then, must have been somewhat similar to the process of drawing up the domestic blinds that are familiar to us by the name of Venetian. The reader will no doubt have seen many drop-curtains in our theatres of to-day worked on the same principle as these brails worked the Roman sails.

The sails were not infrequently ornamented. The present illustration shows a sail bearing the devices of a Roman emperor. Topsails had come into use quite a hundred

FIG. 23. FISHING-BOAT IN HARBOUR.
From an earthenware lamp in the British Museum.

and fifty years before this ship, but they were far more popular on the Mediterranean than in the more boisterous waters of Northern Europe.

Fig. 22, taken from an earthenware lamp in the British Museum, shows another ship of this period entering harbour. The sail is furled to the yard, there is a crew of six on board, one of whom is at the helm, one is at the stern blowing a trumpet announcing their approach—an incident that one often sees depicted in the early seals of English

SAILING SHIPS

ships—three men are engaged in furling the sails, and the man in the bows is standing by to let go the anchor. At the extreme left of the picture will be seen the lighthouse. I am sorry it is not possible to give the reader a better illustration of this lamp, but it is of such nature as almost to defy satisfactory reproduction. Fig. 23, taken from another lamp in the same museum, represents a harbour with buildings on the quay in the background. A man is seen fishing from his boat in the foreground, with another man ashore about to cast a net into the water.

I am fortunate in being able to supplement our previous knowledge of ships of this period by some important information that has been brought to light through excavations and discoveries near Tunis in Northern Africa. These were completed by M. P. Gauckler only as recently as the year 1904, and I am indebted to his very interesting account* for much of the information to be derived from these.   In a building at Althiburus, near to Tunis, a mosaic was unearthed containing about thirty representations of several kinds of sailing and rowing boats. Below nearly every one the artist has thoughtfully put the name of each craft, usually in both Greek and Latin.   Not one of these is a war-vessel.   This is exceedingly fortunate, since hitherto we have possessed far less information of the trading vessels than of the biremes, triremes and Liburnian galleys.   But the ships in the Althiburus mosaic all belong entirely to the mercantile marine.   The discovery, in fact, has brought to light the most complete and precise catalogue we possess of ancient ships of Rome. M. Gauckler thinks that this list has been taken from some glossary or nautical handbook written about the middle of the first century before our era.   He fixes the date of the mosaics as about 200 A.D., and the evidence of

* "Un Catalogue Figuré de la Batellerie Gréco-Romaine — La Mosaique d'Althiburus," par P. Gauckler, in "Monuments et Mémoires." Tome douzième, Paris, 1905.

the ships themselves certainly confirms the view that they belong to some period not much before the time of the birth of our Lord.

The mosaic includes a number of craft that were not sailing ships, such as the *schedia* or raft, the *tesseraria*, a rowing boat called the *paro*, the *musculus* or *mydion*, and the *hippago*, a pontoon for transporting horses across a waterway. But whether sailing or rowing boats, they all bear unmistakable traces of the influ- ence of the Phœnician, Greek and Roman war-galleys. Almost every craft shows an effort, not altogether success- ful, to break away from the design that had dominated the Mediterranean so long, for we must not forget that it is an historical fact that the Romans, though they brought the war-galley as near perfection as possible, did this at the expense of the merchant ships, which they sadly neglected. It is only natural, of course, that a nation that is always at war has no time to expand its merchant shipping. The reverse was the case with the Egyptians, who, being more of a peace-loving nature, developed their cargo ships far more, for it was not until fairly late in Egyptian history that the warship was attended to ; we may even go so far as to assert that it was not until the time of the Middle Ages that the merchant ship both of the Mediterranean and the North of Europe, made any real progress. As long as civilisation was scanty and pirates were rampant on every sea, commerce was bound to remain at a standstill. In- deed, in the time of the early Greeks, it was thought no act of discourtesy to ask a seafaring stranger whether he was a pirate or merchant. So accustomed are we in these days to peace and plenty that we have need to remind ourselves constantly that there were no trade routes kept open, no policing of the seas, no international treaties nor diplomatic relations to prevent a peaceful merchant ship from disappearing altogether on the high seas, or staggering into port with the loss of her cargo and most of her crew.

SAILING SHIPS

The Egyptian stern still survives in these mosaics with modifications, but the greatest difficulty the naval architects appear to have had was with the bow. What to do with the ram-like entrance has obviously been a source of great worry. In the end, so that the merchant ship might not look too war-like, a curve has been added above the bulwarks at the bows to balance the curve at the waterline of the ram. The rowing arrangements exhibit a square hole in the gunwale for the oar to pass through.

Of the sailing boats and ships depicted in mosaic the *corbita* shows a freer design than the others. She is more or less crescent-shaped and not unlike the earlier caravels in hull. A ship of burthen, she has a mast, and the steering oar is seen at the starboard. Another illustration of this type of "corvette" is shown with a steering oar at each side, the sail furled to the yard, a couple of braces and the mast supported by six shrouds—three forward and three aft. The mast has a great rake forward, and there appears to be a narrow platform running round the hull as a side-walk, a relic, no doubt, of the flying deck that kept the marines separate from the rowers.

Another sailing ship called the *catascopiscus* obviously derived her name from the corresponding Greek word meaning to reconnoitre or scout; for she was famous as a light, fast-sailing ship. Her mast and sail are shown in the mosaic, as well as the halyards and the brailing lines.

The *actuaria* was a light, easily propelled ship, similar to the last. The mosaic (reproduced in Fig. 24) shows the sail furled to the yard and, what is significant, a rope-ladder, up which one of the sailors is ascending. Of the other two men one is sculling with two oars, while the captain is seen in the bows holding a mallet, which he knocks on the boat that the sculler may keep correct time and rhythm in a manner not very far separated from the exhortations of the "cox" of our University eights. This was the kind of ship which Cæsar employed during an expedition to Brittany, and will be referred to again in the next chapter.

Another sailing ship, called by the artist a *myoparo*, shows two halyards, and the sail divided curtain-like as we saw in the Phœnician ships. She also has the Egyptian

FIG. 24. NAVIS ACTUARIA.
From a mosaic at Althiburus, near Tunis.

stern and a modified galley bow. The *myoparo* was a light, swift vessel, chiefly used by pirates. The stem of the English word "peir" (meaning to *attempt* to rob) is thus found in the name of the ship. Plutarch makes use of the name of this species of ship. The *prosumia* contains just such a sail as we saw in Fig. 21, the brails being very clearly shown. A sailing ship called a *ponto* has a small artemon foremast and main. The former has shrouds to support it, but the yard and sail are not shown.

They would be kept in the hold somewhere, and only fitted when specially needed. This ship is of Gallic origin, and is mentioned by Cæsar, who refers to the "pontones quod est genus navium Gallicarum."* Finally, in these mosaics, we have the *cladivata*, a ship that resembles the vessel referred to by Mr. Torr in his "Ancient Ships" as having been found at Utica, and belonging to about the year 200 A.D. This *cladivata* has also two masts and sails of similar size, with the brailing arrangement of this period as already shown. There is some uncertainty concerning the derivation of the word, but it possibly owes its origin to being named after Claudius.

Such, then, was the development of the sailing ship in the waters of Southern Europe. We shall now, leaving behind the first ships that sailed the Mediterranean, proceed in our enquiry to the shores of Northern Europe, and consider what was the nature of their ships which had to voyage under conditions far less encouraging than those of the warm southern seas.

* "De Bello Civili," iii. 29.

CHAPTER IV.

THE EARLY SHIPS OF NORTHERN EUROPE.

THE evidence that we possess, in order accurately to judge, of the early ships that sailed the seas of the Baltic, German Ocean, Bay of Biscay, and English Channel, is both conclusive and diverse. We have in the writings of Cæsar and Tacitus, many details of ships that are of considerable interest. This literature is supplemented by the old Sagas * of Scandinavia, which, though highly informative, err on the side of exaggeration. Rock sculptures existing in the land of the Vikings, though somewhat the subject of controversy, are, in the writer's opinion, of real, valuable help in the study of sailing ships. There is also some evidence of later ships in the old coins of Northern Europe. But it is when we come to the important excavations that have revealed —nearly always accidentally—the ships of a bygone age, many hundreds of years old, that we are confronted with

* Sagas—or "says," narratives—are records of the leading events of the lives of great Norsemen and their families. Hundreds of these records exist, though many of them are purely mythical. They date from a period not earlier than the sixth century of our era, but the downward limit cannot be exactly fixed. Not unnaturally, in such national epics as centre round the kings of Sweden, Norway and Denmark, we find references to sailing ships both frequent and detailed.

the most undeniable and complete source of information that one could desire.

These excavations have revealed discoveries of two kinds, which we shall deal with as we proceed. In Great Britain, and in Germany, various examples of the pre-historic " dug-out " have been unearthed. The Museums of Edinburgh, York, Bremen, and Kiel, happily contain these interesting craft, preserved for the wonder of future generations. The second class is more valuable still, and far more picturesque, for thanks to the burial customs of the old sea-chiefs, there have been excavated from certain mounds in Norway, wonderful old Viking ships in a state of preservation that is remarkable when we consider how many centuries they have lain under the earth. Therefore, fortunate as we deemed ourselves in being able to have such sources of information as models and reproductions of the ships of Southern Europe, we are far more happy in our present section for we can go to the fountain head direct—the ships themselves.

To us members of the Anglo-Saxon race, the importance of the forces at work during the period we are about to consider cannot be lightly estimated. The influence of the Viking, or double-ended type of ship, dominated the whole of the coast-line from Norway to the land as far south as the northern shores of Spain, right from the period that followed the construction of mere dug-outs, until almost the close of the fifteenth century of our era. That is to say, as soon as ever the North European became sufficiently civilised to *build* rather than to hew his craft : as soon as he undertook the making of ships rather than of boats—he came under the power of that naval architecture, which we see illustrated in the ships of the Veneti and Scandinavians ; and, irrespective of geographical position, of language, of tribe or of nation, the civilised inhabitants living on that vast stretch of littoral, from the North Cape to the southern boundary of the Bay of

Biscay, continued in the same conventions of design and build for many hundreds of years. It is a striking proof of the accurate knowledge in ship-building and ship-designing possessed by these early Northerners when we remember that, even to this day, that influence, far from disappearing, shows a strong tendency to increase, at any rate, in the architecture of yachts and fishing boats. Thus, the Egyptians, who moulded for ever afterwards the lines of the ships of the Mediterranean, have in Northern Europe, their counterpart in the Norsemen. What the galley was to the south, the Viking-ship has been to us living in colder climes.

The obvious question occurs at this point as to what, if any, is the connection between the Mediterranean galley and the ship of the North Sea. That there is some similarity will be realised when we collect the following characteristics. And first, the very shape of both kinds of vessels—long, narrow, flat-bottomed; then the arrangement of the large squaresail with its braces and rigging; the mode of steering at the side; the pavisado that ran round the ship to protect the men from the enemy; the spur with which they rammed the enemy's ships; the girdle that went round the ship to prevent damage caused by ramming; the ornamentation of the head of the vessel; their very methods of naval warfare, and finally, their adoption later of fore-castles and stern-castles—what else do these similarities show but that there existed a common influence? With such evidence before us, it becomes somewhat difficult to find agreement with those who contend that between the two classes of ships there is no connection whatever, except such as chance might have brought about. I am not denying that there are important differences between the ships of the two seas, but I contend that such important resemblances to each other need an explanation more scientific than can be ascribed to chance.

But assuming that we are right in our surmise, by

what means were these early Norwegians affected by the southern design? Were they influenced by Roman civilisation? That they certainly were not. Then the southerners came to them?* Here is our contention. Though we have no actual proof, it seems justifiable to suppose that those great travellers and sea-folk, the Phœnicians, who, we have seen, were unsurpassed in their time for seamanship and shipbuilding; who have been said to have voyaged to the setting sun as far as America, and to have crossed the Bay of Biscay to Ireland and Cornwall, might have taken advantage of the prevailing westerly wind which blows across our land and have held on until they had touched the shores of Denmark or Norway. But why should they, do you ask? We have seen that the Phœnicians were not merely great sailormen, not merely adventurous, not merely eager explorers, but practical business-men, merchants, traders. If they had found ore in Cornwall, would they not have been inclined to seek other lands for what they could barter or wrest ere returning to their own homes? Even supposing the Phœnicians never crossed to South America, we know that they circumnavigated Africa. A land that bred seamen of that daring and ability would not be lacking in the kind of men to discover Norway.

And there is still another reason, it seems to me, why the Phœnicians might have felt tempted to go eastward after Cornwall. Ignorant as they were of the world's geography, might they not have thought that, just as by

* "This northern civilisation," says Du Chaillu, in his account of these people ("The Viking Age," vol. i. p. 4, London, 1889) "was peculiar to itself, having nothing in common with the Roman world, Rome knew nothing of these people till they began to frequent the coasts of her North Sea provinces, in the days of Tacitus, and after his time, the Mediterranean. . . . The manly civilisation the Northmen possessed was their own . . . it seems to have advanced north from about the shores of the Black Sea, and . . . many northern customs were like those of the ancient Greeks."

sailing round always to the starboard they had encircled Africa, so having performed roughly a semi-circle from the Mediterranean to the English Channel, if they kept their course over the wilderness of sea in front of them, they would ultimately find that Europe, like Africa, was an island, too, and that the nearer they approached the rising of the sun the sooner would they see their homes again ?

And if we are told to explain the differences between, on the one hand, the ships of the Phœnicians or their later descendants the Greeks and Romans, and on the other, those of the Vikings, it is but natural that, given a general design which has originated in the smoother waters of the Mediterranean, it must necessarily be somewhat modified for the nasty seas of the Baltic and German Ocean, where sudden changes of wind are but the harbingers of the rapid approach of bad weather. Cæsar, when he came north into Brittany, was struck, in comparing the ships of the Veneti with his own, by the superior seaworthiness of the former, and adds significantly that "considering the nature of the place and the violence of the storms, they were more suitable and better adapted." * There is to-day a far greater difference in England between the sailing ships of one port and another than there was between the old Viking vessels and those of the Phœnicians. If you cruise round from one coast of Great Britain to another, you will find in the Scotch fishing craft, the Yorkshire cobble, the Yarmouth fishing smack, the Lowestoft "drifter," the Thames "bawley," the Deal galley, the Itchen Ferry transom-sterned cutters, the Brixham "Mumble-Bees," the Falmouth Quay-punt, the Bristol Channel pilot, and the Manx lugger, a wonderful complexity of designs and rigs, but the reason is always that that particular design and rig have been found to be the most suitable adaptation for each particular coast.

* Cæsar, "De Bello Gallico," iii. chap. 13: "Pro loci natura, pro vi tempestatum, illis essent aptiora et accommodatoria."

SAILING SHIPS

So it was with the Vikings. They modified the Phœnician design to their local requirements, without, nevertheless, neglecting those features essential to a good ship. After they had been shipbuilders for some time they would rapidly learn for themselves the values of length and beam, of draught and sweet lines, of straight keel, with high stem to breast a wave, and high stern to repel a following sea. Double-ended as they were, there was a reason for this essential difference from the Phœnicians. Such seas as they had in the North would not suffer their ships to be beached always in fine weather. So in order that they could be brought to land with either end on, and in order, too, that in sea-fights they might easily manœuvre astern or ahead, the Viking ships were built with a bow both forward and aft.

But long before ever the Phœnician ships came to the shores of Northern Europe there were boats and sailing-ships. No doubt the pre-historic man in the north was driven to finding some means of transportation across the fjord by the same stern mother Necessity that first induced that primitive whom we saw learning his elementary seamanship on the Tigris or Euphrates. That ancient Northener of the Stone Age made a wonderfully historic discovery when he found that be could make an edge to his stone, and that thereby he was able to cut both flesh and wood. "For," says Mr. Eiríkr Magnússon in his interesting essay,* "on the edge, ever since its discovery, has depended and probably will depend to the end of time the whole artistic and artificial environment of human existence, in all its infinitely varied complexity. . . . By this discovery was broken down a wall that for untold ages had dammed up a stagnant, unprogressive past, and through the breach were let loose all the potentialities of

* "Notes on Shipbuilding and Nautical Terms of Old in the North," a paper read before the Viking Society for Northern Research by Eiríkr Magnússon. London, 1906.

the future civilisation of mankind. It was entirely due to the discovery of the edge that man was enabled, in the course of time, to invent the art of shipbuilding."

The monoxylon—the boat made from one piece of timber—as fashioned by the early sailorman of the Stone Age, is even still used in parts of Sweden and Norway. Indeed it still bears the name which is the equivalent of "oakie," showing that it was originally made out of the oaktrunk, which is the thickest and therefore the most suitable trunk to be found in the forests of the North Sea coast, a region, that in the time of the Stone Age was densely wooded with oak trees. Afterwards, this monoxylon or dug-out, in order that she may be made so strong as to carry as many as forty men, is strengthened with ribs, and the flat bottom has the modification of a keel added. The vessel that was found at Brigg in Lincolnshire in May 1886 (*see* Fig. 25) is of this kind. A similar kind of boat was found in the Valdermoor marsh in Schleswig-Holstein during the year 1878, and is now in the Kiel Museum. As there are other similar boats in existence, perhaps it may interest the reader if we deal with these discoveries a little more fully.

The Valdermoor boat has the following dimensions: length 41 feet, greatest width 4.33 feet, depth inside 19 inches, depth outside 20½ inches. The thickness of the wood is 1½ inches at the bottom and 1¼ at the top. The boat had eleven ribs, of which nine now exist. On the gunwale between the ribs, eleven holes were made for inserting oars. Both the stem and stern are sharp. The keel, 6½ feet in length, is worked out of the wood at both ends of the boat, leaving the middle flat. I am sorry not to be able to present an illustration of this before the reader, but the director of the Kiel Museum informs me that the boat is in such a position as to prevent it being photographed.

However, the Brigg boat is very similar to the Valdermoor and may serve the purposes of illustration equally well. This craft was found by workmen excavating for a new gasometer upon the banks of the river Ancholme, in North Lincolnshire. It had been resting apparently on the clay bottom of the sloping beach of an old lagoon. It was obviously made out of the trunk of a tree, and perfectly straight, its dimensions being: 48 feet 6 inches, long, about 6 feet wide, 2 feet 9 inches deep. The stern represents the butt end of a tree with diameter of 5 feet 3 inches. The cubic contents of the boat would be about 700 cubic feet. The prow is rounded off as if intended for a ram, and a cavity in the head of the prow appears to have been intended for a bowsprit, whereby the forestay could be made fast. In fact, a piece of crooked oak suitable for this purpose was found adjacent to the prow. Whilst the bottom of this dug-out is flat, the sides are perpendicular and there is a kind of overhanging counter at the stern.

The boat was formerly in the possession of Mr. V. Cary-Elwes, F.S.A.,* to whom I have to express my thanks for his courtesy in supplying me with some information regarding the boat here reproduced. The ship was offered by this gentleman to the British Museum, but was declined as being too big. It therefore remains in a small provincial town difficult of access and for the most part unknown. It would be impossible to remove the craft now, without risk of total destruction, but is it not a little humiliating that continental and provincial museums should see fit to harbour similar relics as this Brigg boat, while our great national store-house refuses a gift of such importance? I make no apology to the reader for giving in detail the result of this Brigg discovery, for it is one of the finest if not the most instructive of any craft of this kind that has come to light in Northern Europe. An interesting account has been written by the Rev. D. Cary-Elwes, son of the above,

* It was presented to the Hull Museum while this book was in the press, June 1909.

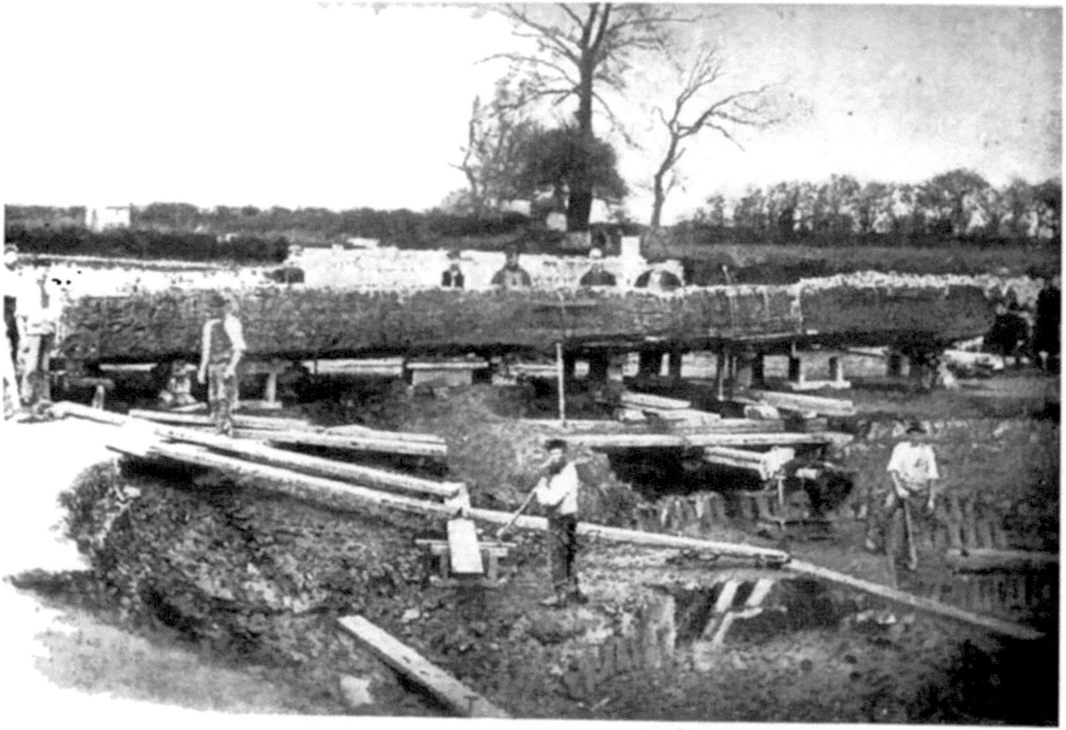

FIG. 25. THE VIKING BOAT DUG UP AT BRIGG, LINCOLNSHIRE.

and to this I am indebted for some of the following facts.*

The boat is hollowed out of one huge oak log, which, from the dimensions given above, would necessitate a tree 18 feet in circumference, and of such a height that the branches did not begin until 50 feet from the ground. Such a tree would be gigantic. The bows are almost a semi-circle when viewed from above, and are rounded off gradually to the bottom and sides, the latter being about two inches thick and the bottom four inches. The stern, however, is no less than sixteen inches. The transom has had to be fixed separately on to the trunk, and the difficulty was to perform such a piece of ship-building so as to make this part of the vessel as strong and watertight as the sides and bottom. The caulking of the joints has been done with moss, the transom fitting into a groove across the floor. In order that the sides of the ship might not give, in bad weather, Mr. Cary-Elwes thinks, a tight lashing was thrown across from one side to the other, coming round abaft of the stern, and so keeping both sides and transom tightly together. This transom was found a little distance away from the boat and is 4 feet wide at the top and 2 feet 5¾ inches deep, there being a projection some 2 feet aft, beyond the transom, so as to form an overhanging counter.

Along the whole length of the boat, close to the upper edge, holes, 2 inches in diameter, have been pierced at irregular intervals of about 2 feet. It is uncertain what these were intended for. Although there are no such evidences as a step for the mast, to indicate whether she was a sailing boat, it is not safe to condemn her as having merely been propelled by paddles. There are evidences of decks and seats, and the primitive man would, no doubt, after he had learned to harness the

* "A Prehistoric Boat," a lecture by Rev. D. Cary-Elwes. Northampton, 1903.

wind, maintain his mast in position perhaps by thongs to the seat or by means of the decking. It has even been thought that the fragment of rounded wood found with the boat and already alluded to as a probable bowsprit, was a mast. To me this latter supposition seems more likely than the theory of a bowsprit. It has also been surmised that the holes running along the boat were either for lacing to keep the ship's sides from coming asunder or for receptacles of pegs to hold washboards in bad weather. Personally, I think the latter is the more probable, for it was a very early custom. We have, in a former chapter, mentioned it as being a practice on the Mediterranean in classical times, and we shall see presently that the Vikings also used this method for keeping out the spray. It happens also to be the custom among modern savages.

Evidently during her career of activity this vessel had the misfortune to spring a leak, for she has been patched, and the work of the boatbuilder is most interesting to us of to-day. On the starboard bilge a rift of 12 feet long has been made. To repair this, wooden patches and moss have been used. The biggest patch is 5 feet 8 inches long and 6½ inches wide in the middle, tapering gradually to a point at either end, and is of oak. The patch was let into the rift from the outside until perfectly flush with the outer part of the boat. On the inner side of the patch, three cleats a foot long and four inches deep, with a hole in the centre of each, have been attached. Wooden pins were passed through these holes, so that pressing firmly against the solid wood on either side of the rift, they kept the repair in position. Besides this, holes three-eighths of an inch in diameter were made along the outer edges of the patch, corresponding holes being also made in the fabric of the boat by means of which the patch could be sewn to the ship with thongs. This custom, it seems to me, would have survived in the most natural manner from the time when the shipbuilder sewed the seams of his skin boat. Finally, all holes and crannies were caulked with moss. Mr. Cary-Elwes has carefully preserved a small portion of this lacing material, which appears to be of some animal substance, and probably twisted sinews. He has also taken some of this caulking moss from the boat and finds that it is of two kinds, both of which grow on sandy soils in woods, and are now largely used in the manufacture of moss-baskets and artificial flowers.

The important fact must not be lost sight of that while all the repairs have been made either by wood pegs or thongs, not a trace of metal was found in the fabric of the boat. This coincides with the argument that we have been proceeding on, viz., that such ships as these belong not to the age of metals but to that of stone. And, as if to convince those who scoff at the possibility of being able to fell trees—and oak trees especially—by means of stone implements, Mr. Cary-Elwes refers to the interesting fact that the Australian aborigines, a type of humanity as low and primitive as one could wish to find, had all their tools of agriculture, war and forestry, made of stone or wood, iron being unknown to them; yet indeed they knew how to fell the giants of the forest, such a tree as the Jarrah red gum, now used for paving London streets, being every bit as hard as our oak. " Within quite recent times," adds the same author, " the inhabitants of the South Sea Islands worked exclusively with stone implements. I came across a good collection of these old time weapons in New Zealand, and what is more to the point here, sundry canoes and boats hollowed by their means. My father, who was with me, and who is a member of the Society of Antiquaries, and not unlearned in these matters, pointed out to me not only the similarity that existed between these stone weapons and the pre-historic adzes and axes of the stone age, but also the interesting fact that the canoes hollowed out by fire or stone tools were as cleanly cut and as cleverly wrought as the old Brigg boat." The same writer, from the evidence of the geological strata where she was found, concludes that the age of the Brigg boat must be between 2600 and 3000 years, which would bring the date to between 1100 and 700 B.C.

In addition to the Brigg boat other dug-outs have been found in various parts of our country. In 1833 one was discovered near the river Arun in Sussex. Her length was 35 feet, breadth 4 feet, depth 2 feet. Her sides and bottom were between 4 and 5 inches thick. There are also other similarities to the Brigg boat. In 1863 a smaller, but similar boat, 8 feet 2 inches by 1 foot 9 inches, was also unearthed. She had washboards like those we have attributed to the Brigg boat. Another craft a foot smaller still was found near Dumfries in 1736, containing a paddle. In 1822 near the Rother in Kent an immense ship of this class measuring 63 feet long, and 5 feet broad was unearthed also. It is interesting to remark that it was caulked with moss in the manner already described. On the south bank of the Clyde another of these craft was found having an upright groove in the stern similar to that in which the sternboard of the Brigg boat was fixed. There is also a twenty-five footer in the Museum at York.

This Brigg Boat, and the Valdermoor one, probably belong to the class ascribed by Tacitus * in 70 A.D. to the Batavians and Frisians. Some have also thought that it was in such boats as these that the Romans crossed from Gaul to Britain. At any rate there can be no doubt that boats of this kind were to be found at this time still existing in Britain and along the shore washed by the English Channel and North Sea.

In addition to those dug-outs already enumerated, a similar craft was found in 1876 in Loch Arthur, about

* Tacitus, "Hist." v. 23.

six miles west of Dumfries. She is 42 feet long and like all the others is hollowed out of oak. Her width and other characteristics show her to resemble very closely the Brigg boat, and accentuate still more the existence of a prevailing type of craft in Northern Europe during pre-historic times. The prow, like that of the primitive Koryaks, is shaped after the head of an animal. Unfortunately not the whole of this relic is preserved, but at least one third of her, and that the bow end, is to be found in the Museum of the Antiquarian Society of Edinburgh. More than twenty canoes of this same class have also been found in the neighbourhood of Glasgow. Almost all were formed out of single tree-trunks of oak and afford evidence of having been hollowed out by blunt tools such as the people of the Stone or Bronze Age would possess. Two obviously later boats were dug up in 1853 and were found to be of more elaborate construction, planks having now been introduced. The prow resembled the beak of an ancient galley, the stern being formed of a triangular piece of oak. For fastening the planks to the ribs oak pins and metallic nails had been used. For caulking, wool dipped in tar had been employed. Boehmer in his exceedingly valuable and careful paper on " Prehistoric Naval Architecture of the North of Europe," * to which I am greatly indebted for some important facts, points out that in the bottom of one of these canoes a hole had been closed by means of a cork-plug, which Professor Geikie remarks could only have come from the latitudes of Spain, Southern France, or Italy. The inference is, of course, that notwithstanding their island home, even the very early inhabitants of Great Britain were in communication with distant parts of the Continent.

* "Annual Report of Regents of the Smithsonian Institution: Prehistoric Naval Architecture of the North of Europe," by George H. Boehmer. Washington, 1892. (See p. 527.)

SAILING SHIPS

There can be no doubt that, at any rate among the least progressive peoples of Northern Europe, this dug-out, monoxylon type of boat lasted till very late, for an account is given by Velleius Paterculus, who about the year 5 A.D. served under Tiberius as prefect of cavalry. He distinctly refers to the Germanic craft as dug-outs, "cavatum, ut illis mos est, ex materia." Pliny the elder speaks of the piratical ships of the Chauci, one of the most progressive of the coast tribes of Northern Europe, as having visited the rich provinces of Gallia. These ships were dug-outs and carried thirty men. This fact is interesting, as being the first time the Teutons had ventured on the open sea.

During the years 1885 to 1889, while excavations were being made at the port of Bremen at the mouth of the Weser, as many as seven of these dug-outs were found in the alluvial land at depths of from 6½ feet to 13 feet below the present level of the surface. They were made of oak-trunks, and had apparently been fashioned by axes. They were as usual flat-bottomed, without keels, but with prow cut obliquely and with holes for the insertion of oars. Of the seven four were entirely demolished, but of the remaining three the dimensions were respectively: 35 feet long by 2 feet 6 inches wide; 33 feet 4 inches long by 3 feet 6 inches; 26 feet 7 inches by 3 feet 3 inches. The height varied from 1 foot 5 inches up to 2 feet 2 inches. Several specimens of this type are preserved in the municipal museum of Bremen.

So much, then, for the earliest type of craft. We have seen that the dug-out in the course of time became strengthened with ribs. The next stage in the advancement of the pre-historic shipbuilder is to dispense with the strenuous work which necessitated the hollowing out of a whole tree trunk of hard oak. The affixing of ribs has given him an idea. So, utilising the hides of the wild animals which he has shot whilst hunting, he stretches these over the same framework that he had used for strengthening his oak-trunk. He is still in the Stone Age, so nails are not yet invented. The skins have to be sewn together to fit the framework, and the result is precisely that of the coracle even now used in Wales and off Connemara. If the reader should happen never to have seen one of these, a visit to the Victoria and Albert Museum will quickly clear up any misunderstanding. Though we have no actual specimens of ancient skin-ships existing—and indeed we should not expect such a relic—yet the interesting survival of the boat-building language of that primitive time is found both in the Norwegian and English language of to-day. Thus, when you have allowed a ship to lie high and dry in the summer sun so that the planking warps and daylight can be seen through, what is the expression you would use to express this? Would you not remark that she has opened her *seams?* Now "seam" is an Anglo-Saxon word connoting the joining together of two edges of some texture by means of a needle. But let us take a further instance. Do you not constantly hear shipbuilders and designers refer to the planking that covers a ship's ribs as her *skin?* Thus we have still in common use the very words which our sires employed in reference to the sewn hides of their primitive craft. Indeed, when one considers that all through history, even until now, shipbuilding has been an industry apart from ordinary occupations, and that both ships and seamen are, as we said in our introductory chapter, the most conservative of all peoples or created things, this survival is not so unnatural as might seem at first. We could continue to give other examples in the pertinacity of ancient seafaring expressions, but that would only be to digress from the immediate subject before us. We need only make reference to the interesting fact that Cæsar during his first Spanish campaign in the civil war, when he required some boats at the banks of the river Sicoris to get across,

ordered the soldiers to make boats of the build that they had learned in former years from the British use. Thus first the keel was obtained and ribs were fashioned of light stuff; the rest of the boat's body being then woven together of osiers and finally covered with hides.*
According to Pliny the Britanni also in the first century of our era put to sea in wicker vessels done round with a covering of ox hide. In such vessels they would take a six days' voyage to the Island of Mictis, whence the tin came.

We come now to the Bronze and Iron Ages. With the advent of metals we find a revolution scarcely inferior to that caused by the discovery of the edged stone. For whereas the latter could cut, yet its efforts were confined within narrow limitations. It was capable of felling a tree and of hollowing out its trunk with the expenditure of considerable labour and tediousness, yet that was its highest achievement in the department of shipbuilding. But now that the introduction of metals, of iron and bronze, is made, the primitive man finds that his sphere of energy is vastly widened. Instead of hollowing out the tree he cuts it up into planks. Instead of having to sew the outside together with thongs of hide, he has metallic nails as fastenings. To the same kind of ribs that framed his skin-boat, he can now nail down planks of oak and fir. He has a lighter and more easily propelled boat than the dug-out, and a stronger and more seaworthy ship than that made of stretched skins, although it is only fair to observe that the hide-boat was capable of far more than one would suppose. Mr. Jochelson in the account of the Jesup Expedition already referred to, relates his experience of being taken for a sail in one of the skin-boats of the

* Cæsar, "De Bello Civili," book i. chap. 54: "Imperat militibus Cæsar, ut naves faciant, cujus generis eum superioribus annis usus Britanniæ docuerat. Carinæ primum ac statumina ex levi materia fiebant: reliquum corpus navium viminibus contextum, coriis integebatur."

Koryak. He was delighted by the endurance which the skins (of seal) exhibited. Not the least remarkable feature was the fact that the skin was capable of sustaining enormous weights without bursting. But in Europe our ancestors must have been glad to be able to discard the hide for that of wood, since the wear and tear in beaching on rock, pebble, or snag, exposed them to instant uselessness.

Although ship-building proper comes with the Metallic Age, we must not assume that the change was made universally or at once. The transition would be made rapidly or but slowly in proportion as the tribe or nation were enthusiastically maritime or otherwise. In some parts of Europe the skin-boat or even the dug-out would be in use, while other shores were seeing built vessels of planks and ribs. The first historic account that we possess of these more modern vessels is to be found in Cæsar's account of the Naval Campaign against the Veneti in the year 54 B.C. From this narrative we learn that the ships of the Veneti were somewhat flatter than those of the Romans, so that they could more easily encounter the shallows and ebbing of the tide.* The prows, we are told, were raised very high, and the sterns likewise—" proræ

---

* Cæsar, " De Bello Gallico," III. xiii.: " Namque ipsorum naves ad hunc modum factæ armatæque erant: carinæ aliquanto planiores quam nostrarum navium, quo facilius vada ac decessum æstus excipere possent: proræ admodum erectæ atque item puppes ad magnitudinem fluctuum tempestatumque accommodatæ; naves totæ factæ ex robore ad quamvis vim et contumeliam perferendam: transtra pedalibus in altitudinem trabibus confixa clavis ferreis digiti pollicis crassitudine; ancoræ pro funibus ferreis catenis revinctæ; pelles pro velis alutæque tenuiter confectæ, [hæc] sive propter lini inopiam atque ejus usus inscientiam, sive eo, quod est magis verisimile, quod tantas tempestates Oceani tantosque impetus ventorum sustineri ac tanta onera navium regi velis non satis commode posse arbitrabantur."

Mr. St. George Stock in his edition (Cæsar, " De Bello Gallico," books i.-vii., edited by St. George Stock, Oxford, 1898) understands " transtra " not to mean the rowing benches but crossbeams or decks.

admodum erectæ atque item puppes "—so that they were suited for the force of the waves and storms which they had been constructed to sustain. We have, then, here a new design in naval architecture recorded—the Viking type of ship—although it had been in existence for a considerable time in the North. The high prows and sterns would immediately impress those who had come from the more peaceful waters of Italy. Further it is said that these ships were built of oak throughout and designed to be enormously strong. The crossbeams, made of logs a foot thick, were fastened by iron spikes as thick as a man's thumb. The anchors were made fast by iron chains instead of cables, while their sails were made of skin and dressed leather. These were used because they lacked canvas or the knowledge to apply it to such a use, or more probably because they thought canvas would be of too little strength to endure the tempests of the ocean and violent gales of wind, and that ships of such great burden could not be managed by them. Perhaps in the use of hides for sails, we have the parent of the practice of using tanned sails so common in our fishing fleet and barges. The relative character of the two kinds of ships Cæsar points out, as we mentioned earlier in the chapter, was that the Roman fleet excelled in speed alone and in oarsmanship. Otherwise the ships of the Veneti were, considering the nature of the place, and the violence of the storms more suitable and better adapted on their side. Nor could the Roman ships injure severely the ships of the Veneti by means of their beaks, so strong were they. And further, so high were these ships that the Romans found great difficulty in hurling weapons at them. Whenever a storm arose and the ships of the Veneti ran before the wind, they could weather it more readily and heave-to safely in the shallows, and when left by the tide feared nothing from rocks and shelves, for—" the risk of all such things," ends the account pathetically, " was much to be dreaded by our ships."

Those who are familiar with the terrible tides and treacherous coast of northern France * will readily understand how such able Viking-like ships as the Veneti possessed, appealed to the Romans with their fast but unsuitable craft. The difference would be that between the smart Thames skiff and the tubby though seaworthy dinghy of a North Sea fishing smack. For we know pretty accurately now, thanks to the Althiburus mosaics referred to in the previous chapter, just what Cæsar's craft were like. Hitherto we have known them as *naves actuariæ*—that is, light vessels of surpassing speed. But if the reader will refer back to Fig. 24 he will find that the *navis actuaria*, whilst propelled both with oars and sail, was nevertheless not much of a ship to be caught in off the rocks and narrow channels in a breeze of wind. Although these *actuariæ* were neither freight ships (*onerariæ*) nor war-vessels properly speaking, yet they still possessed rams and were used on this expedition for a war-like purpose. There cannot be much doubt that the

---

* The Veneti lived in the extreme north-west corner of France, and have left behind the name of the town Vannes, facing the Bay of Biscay, and opposite Belle Isle.

The Greeks and Romans having learned their seamanship on the practically tideless waters of the Mediterranean must have been appalled by the ebb and flow of the Northern Seas. Cæsar was ignorant of the moon's relation to tides until taught by bitter experience. He was taught only by the damage done to his ships in Britain. (" De Bello Gallico," iv. 29). The Veneti, however, understood all these things, for Cæsar remarks, "quod et naves habent Veneti plurimas, quibus in Britanniam navigare consuerunt, et scientia atque usu nauticarum rerum reliquos antecedunt." Further on he refers to the Bay of Biscay as the great, boisterous, open sea, " in magno impetu maris atque aperto." (" De Bello Gallico," book iii. chap. 8). It is to Pytheas (referred to previously) that Plutarch gives the credit of having detected the influence of the moon on tides.

The reader wishing to pursue the subject is referred to " Cæsar's Conquest of Gaul," by T. Rice Holmes. London, 1899.

SAILING SHIPS

Veneti had obtained their design and ideas of shipbuilding from the Norsemen who relentlessly swept down from their colder climes and plundered and pillaged from one end of the coast of Northern Europe to the other. As we shall see presently, this design was prevalent for many years before Cæsar came, and as we shall also see from the following chapter it had altered but little at the time when William the Conqueror left the French shores for England in the eleventh century.

In the year 15 A.D. we learn from Tacitus [*] that Germanicus had built near the mouth of the river Rhine a thousand ships with sharp bows so as to be able to resist better the waves. Some had flat bottoms to enable them to take the ground with impunity. Some had a steering apparatus at both bow and stern in order that thereby they could be rowed in either direction. Many were decked for the accommodation of throwing machines. They were equally useful as rowing and sailing ships, and just as in the mediæval times ships were built with towering decks for " majesty and terror of the enemy," so as early as this period these vessels were imposing as to their size whilst inspiring confidence to their own soldiery. Good serviceable ships as they were, yet after defeating the Cherusci at the mouth of the Ems they were shipwrecked in a storm although the wind blew from the south. It is only fair to add, however, that the ancients, especially the

---

[*] Tacitus' "Annals," ii. 23 and 6. "Mille naves sufficere visæ properatæque, aliæ breves, angusta puppi proraque et lato utero, quo facilius fluctus tolerarent, quædam planæ carinis ut sine noxa siderent : plures adpositis utrimque gubernaculis, converso ut repente remigio hinc vel illinc adpellerent : multæ pontibus stratæ, super quas tormenta veherentur . . . velis habiles, citæ remis augebantur alacritate militum in speciem ac terrorem " (ii. 6).

Mr. Henry Furneaux in his edition of the "Annals" (Oxford 1896), commenting on " pontibus," thinks these formed a partial deck across the midships which would have the appearance of a bridge when viewed from bow or stern.

Romans, were wont to build their vessels very quickly * and consequently they erred, no doubt, in constructing them too slightly. The Saxons who, after the death of Alexander the Great, came to the mouth of the Elbe and subjugated the Thuringians, and who are said to have possessed the art of tacking, already referred to, had such light vessels as belonged to the stone age. They were wonderfully light, made out of willows and covered with skins, but had a keel of knotty oak; yet these daring navigators, without compass or chart, and with but a feeble knowledge of the stars, managed to find their way to the Orkneys.

We pass now from the English Channel and the Rhine to consider that land which has given birth to a long line of robust, vigorous ships and men, who after the Phœnicians are the finest race of seamen that ever sailed a sea. A little clumsy like their ships the Scandinavians have always throughout history stood for manliness and strength. And if we were right when we submitted that a nation's character exhibits itself in a most marked degree in its ships, surely of no people could this remark be made with greater truth than concerning the inhabitants of that Northern peninsula who, in the early days of our own country, harassed our forefathers beyond all endurance, but left behind to us the heritage of a love of the sea.† There is in the Viking ship and its descendants not so much beauty as nobility, not prettiness but power. The first mention of these Northerners is by Tacitus‡ who

* Roman ships were sometimes built in 60 days, while there is a record of 220 having been built in 45 days.

† Du Chaillu points out the interesting fact that it was not until after the Danes and Norwegians had succeeded in planting themselves in this country that the inhabitants of our land exhibited that love of the sea and ships which has been our greatest national characteristic for so many centuries. Certainly when the Romans invaded Britain our fore-fathers had no fleet with which to oppose them.

‡ Tacitus, " De situ, moribus et populis Germaniæ libellus," chap. 44 : " Suionum hinc civitates, ipsæ in Oceano, præter viros armaque classibus

refers to them as the Suiones. (Tacitus died A.D. 108.)
As Cæsar was struck by the difference between the
Roman ships and those of the Veneti, so Tacitus remarks
that the ships of the Suiones differ from the Romans', too.
Although these were not sailing ships—*nec velis
ministrantur*—yet they were of the same design as those
which were fitted with mast and sail. Double-ended, they
could easily be beached and in battle could the more
rapidly manœuvre ahead or astern.

But we have much earlier information than the writings
of the Roman chronicler. We have history written in
stone, obvious, illustrative and imperishable. In many
parts of the Scandinavian coast, beginning as far north
as Trondhjem and extending right round to the isle of
Gothland, are to be found many rock sculptures depicting
the forms of both ships and men. A few have also been
found in Denmark as well as on the shores of Lake Ladoga
in Russia. These rock carvings are really history set
forth in picture language, primitive yet intelligible. In
spite of all the hundreds of years that have rolled by, and
the winds and rains that have dashed against them, they
are still quite decipherable. Professor Gustafson in his
book on Norwegian antiquities* gives several interesting
pictures of these rock-carvings, and I am able here to
reproduce one for the reader who will no doubt agree
that the evidence here afforded is exceptionally striking.
Fig. 26 shows the Viking-like ship beyond all doubt.
Frequently these carvings are represented in groups
and it has been thought that they record naval battles
fought in the vicinity, the several representations of ships
denoting fleets. The human figures perhaps are there

valent. Forma navium eo differt quod utrinque prora paratam semper
appulsui frontem agit: nec velis ministrantur, nec remos in ordinem
lateribus adjungunt: solutum, ut in quibusdam fluminum, et mutabile,
ut res poscit, hinc vel illinc remigium."

* "Norges Oldtid," by Gabriel Gustafson. Kristiania, 1906.

as an eternal memorial of their admirals who perished or distinguished themselves in the fight. There are two kinds of craft in these carvings, Magnússon * points out. First there is the ship with the very high stem, and stern, and there is the other kind of vessel which lacks

FIG. 26. ANCIENT SCANDINAVIAN ROCK-CARVING, SHOWING VIKING SHIP-FORMS.

just these features. The former appears to have a double keel which makes it look as if the ship were put on a sledge. There is at the bow-end a structure which is most probably a ram. As to the sledge-like formation below the body of the ship, I am inclined to think it may have been a removable keel to be attached to the ship when sailing and so give her flat-bottomed hull greater stability. In an old-fashioned part of the world, which is not so very far removed from Norway and which was in earlier times over-run by the Norsemen, in whose inhabitants to-day the flaxen hair and blue eyes and the Norwegian name are still to be found—in the counties of Norfolk and

* "Notes on Shipbuilding and Nautical Terms of Old in the North," by Eiríkr Magnússon. A paper read before the Viking Club for Northern Research. London, 1906.

Suffolk—the trading wherries have just such an arrangement as this. When they have a full cargo on board and come to a shallow part of the river, they unhook the whole length of keel which is attached to bow and stern by an iron band, and leave it on the bank until they return down stream. Until quite recently not much change has taken place in the craft of this neighbourhhood for ages, and it is quite possible that this double-ended wherry was as much swayed by Norwegian as by Dutch influence.

On some of these carvings a mast amidships is shown and their date belongs either to the Stone or the Bronze Age, though more probably the latter. Professor Montelius discourages the idea that the Phœnicians established themselves on the Baltic for the reason that the bronze culture found its way up to the North overland from the shores of the Mediterranean and especially the Adriatic. But in spite of this argument these sculptured forms show many points of resemblance to those of the Phœnicians' ships as the reader will not fail to notice. Many northern archæologists think that these sculptures have been wrought by the hands of foreigners, and Mr. Magnússon suggests that in that case they may have been the work of the Veneti. Be that as it may, and let it be disputed whether they belong to the year 1500 B.C. or as late as 50 B.C., whether they were carved by the Vikings or the enemies of the Vikings, there they are still to be seen, admittedly of great antiquity and corresponding to the description of the ships of the Suiones as given by Tacitus.

But long before this latter date the Suiones must have been afloat. They could not suddenly have become owners of a mighty fleet—*classibus valent*. The very prefix " Nor " which is so common in this region—in the words " Norge," " Nordheimsund," " Norse," to give but the first instances that come to one's mind—signifies ship. It is the same stem that is found in the Greek *ναυς* and

112

Fig. 113. The Gokstad Viking Ship

Photo. O. Væring, Christiania.

„ 113

Photo. O. Væring, Christiania.

p. 118.

Fig. 29. The Gokstad Viking Ship.

the Latin *navis*. In the Irish language *noe* also means ship and is found in the oldest tractates of the ancient laws of Ireland. We have already mentioned the important fact that Pytheas of Marseilles led an expedition in the fourth century B.C. by sea to Norway in the interests of the commercial community of Marseilles. This rather goes to show that the Gauls and Scandinavians had met on trading terms before and that one or both of the parties had journeyed to each other's shore previously.

We know that the Norsemen sailed in early times frequently along the Eastern shores of the Baltic. We know that they voyaged to Denmark, Jutland, Germany and Russia, for they have left behind them unmistakable relics. For just as we are indebted to the funeral customs of the Egyptians for so much important knowledge of their ships, so to the burial rites of these hardy Northerners we owe a great debt of thanks for information as to their vessels. There were three kinds of burials adopted by the Norsemen. First, and this is the one we wish to draw immediate attention to, there was the custom of cremating the deceased Viking. His ashes, together with his personal property, were buried on land in a boat-shaped grave. The outlines of long, narrow, pointed shapes formed by a single line of stones in the countries just mentioned indicate the ship-shape resting places of these men who were so faithful to their vessels, who revered them so highly for having carried them during their lives safely across the turbulent sea, that even in death they desired not to be separated from them. Thus on land the very design of the stones was after the lines of that which is the noblest and most beautiful of all the creations of man.*

* Du Chaillu (" The Viking Age," *vide supra*) attributes these ship-form graves to the Iron Age, and remarks that similar monuments have been found in England and Scotland. "One of the most interesting," he adds, " is that where the rowers' seats are marked, and even a stone placed in the position of the mast" (p. 309, vol. i.). This is reproduced in Fig. 27.

But there were two other modes of burial, each in its own way magnificently impressive and in keeping with the vigorous character of the Viking spirit. Of these two the first consisted in placing the body of the deceased in his own ship, then, setting the whole thing ablaze, the ship

FIG. 27. VIKING SHIP-FORM GRAVE.

and its owner were carried out to sea a red, glaring mass, flaming up against the dark background of the horizon. This kind of obsequies, magnificently as it appeals to our imagination with its suggestion of colour, of grandeur and solemnity, has been inimical to the pursuit of historical knowledge. But even in spite of this, remains of unburned ships have been found among both the outer and inner shores of Trondhjem Fjord.*

But it is the third kind of burial that tells us as much about the Viking ship as the Brigg discovery taught us about the primitive dug-out. For instead of sending them out to sea there was also the custom of dragging the huge ship ashore, and placing the distinguished seaman's body in the bow, a sepulchral chamber (clearly shown in Fig. 28) of wood was erected above. Together with his horse, his dogs, his weapons and other belongings he was left to sleep in peace. Finally over the whole boat a huge mound was raised towering to a great height, and the proceedings were completed. Now, within recent years some of these mounds have been excavated with

* For further details as to the Viking mode of burial, the reader is referred to vol. i. chap. xix. of Du Chaillu's " The Viking Age."

results of remarkable historic value. Ever since the beginning of the nineteenth century the Norwegians have taken a real interest in their national antiquities, and these ancient craft have been treated with the care and reverence to which they have every right. But besides Norway these ships have been found elsewhere. Even in England relics of a Viking ship 48 feet long, 9 feet 9 inches wide, and 4 feet high were found near Snape in Suffolk during the year 1862. Viking remains have also been discovered in the Orkneys. In 1875 an enormous specimen was found at Botley, a charming little place up the river Hamble which flows out into Southampton Water opposite Calshot. This was probably a Danish ship and a relic of one of her nation's incursions against our shores. She has been thought to belong to the year A.D. 871 when the Danes invaded Wessex. At any rate she was in length 130 feet while her upright timbers measured 14 feet 10 inches. The caulking was found to be of ferns and moss and indeed the impression of the leaves of the former was still visibly outlined on the wood. The timber was oak as far as could be discerned, and bore evidences of having been burned. Nowadays there is not enough water at Botley to float such a ship, but at high tide, and allowing for the silting up of the river it would have been as snug a place as ever could be found along the south coast, after the Vikings were wearied with fighting and the buffeting of the waves.

Of the other Viking ships discovered we shall give to each for convenience the name of the district where she was found. The Nydam ship was discovered in October, 1863, in the Nydam Moss to the north-east of Flensburg in the Duchy of Schleswig. Nydam is in a dale and was once part of a bay of Als Sound, and in former times was navigable. Systematic diggings were undertaken at the expense of the Danish Government and afterwards the ship was placed in the hands of an expert restorer. She is as usual built of oak, her lines being very similar to the Scotch fishing boats that flourished on our coasts up to the middle of the nineteenth century, and resembling the boat well known as a whaler. The rudder was placed on the starboard about 10 feet from the stern and was about $9\frac{1}{2}$ feet in length. She is sharp at both ends with high stem and stern posts ; 77 feet long, as much as 10 feet 10 inches across her midships, she was clinker-built of eleven oak planks. The keel is an inch deep and eight inches thick, being broad at the middle but diminishing gradually toward the sternpost. The planks were fastened with large iron nails and caulked, as was the custom, with some woollen stuff and pitch. She had twenty-eight oars, was flat-bottomed, and her date has been estimated as about the middle of the third century of our era. I admit she is not entitled to be called a sailing ship, but as she will be found to belong so closely to the sailing class we cannot afford to neglect her. With her was also found another similar ship but of fir and armed with a ram low down at each end. Remains of another boat were also discovered with her as well as bronze brooches, silver clasps, wooden boxes, bone combs, many shield boards or *pavisses* (also seen in the Gogstad ship, Fig. 28), 106 iron swords, spear shafts and heads, 36 wooden bows, iron bits still in the mouths of the skeleton horse-heads, pots, bowls, knives, axes, clubs, and thirty-four Roman coins, belonging to dates between 69 and 217 A.D.* These composed the personal property, already alluded to, that was always buried with the Viking. Professor Stephens (see note) was of the opinion that one or more of these three boats had been scuttled and sunk in order to avoid capture by the enemy, and goes on to refer to the fact that in the twelfth century the Wends and Slavs employed the same means when pursued. Their tactics

* See "The Old Northern Runic Monuments of Scandinavia and England," vol. i., by George Stephens, F.S.A., London, 1866.

included dragging the ship ashore, scuttling her and then decamping and seeking shelter.

The Tune ship was found in Norway, near the town of Frederikstad in the year 1865. She is of especial interest to us as being the first specimen of a sailing craft that we have from the North. She was found under the funeral mound that had been raised over her, and measured 45½ feet long; her width is supposed to have been 14½ feet, for not the whole of the hull was rescued. Her height from keel to bulwark has been estimated as about four feet. Clinker-built of oak, there were found just abaft the mast the unburnt bones of a man and his horse. From internal evidence this ship has been thought to belong to the Iron Age, and is obviously a Viking ship.

About the year 1873 the Brosen ship was found near Danzig. She was 57 feet long, 16 feet wide, 5 feet high and pointed at both ends. Her planking was 1½ inches thick of oak and clinker-built. The caulking consisted of the hair of elk, bear, or some other wild animal, with an application of tar. The bottom was flat. In 1890 the Gloppen ship was found during excavations of a mound on the fjord of that name near to Bergen. I understand that the remains are preserved in the Bergen museum.

But far surpassing any of these we have already mentioned is the great Gogstad ship discovered in the year 1880 near to Sandefjord. The mound in which she lay was 18 feet above sea-level, and the prow was placed looking seaward, as if ready for a voyage again. The condition in which this fine old ship was found is nothing short of marvellous, and is attributable to the fact that the blue clay in which she was embedded had preserved her from the air. The upper part has unfortunately been damaged, owing (thinks Du Chaillu) to the clay being mixed with sand, and so allowing the air to penetrate

She is clinker-built, entirely of oak, and caulked with cow's hair spun into a sort of cord. Her planking is of oak, $1\frac{3}{4}$ inches thick, and her length over all is 79 feet 4 inches, beam $16\frac{1}{2}$ feet, and depth 6 feet amidships, but $8\frac{1}{2}$ feet at the extremities. She weighs about twenty tons, displacing about 959 cubic feet. Her gunwale above water is amidships 2 feet 11 inches, while at bow and stern it rises to $6\frac{1}{2}$ feet. Her draught is only 3 feet 7 inches. In many respects she resembles the Tune ship, but this is indeed a sailing vessel. There is a step for the mast, and thirty-two oars were carried—sixteen on either side—the oar-holes being provided with shutters so as to keep out the sea. Through the courtesy of the British Consul at Christiania I am enabled here to show two excellent photographs of the ship as she now lies in the keeping of the Royal Frederiks University, Christiania. Professor Gabriel Gustafson has been instrumental in preserving the ship from further decay, and the reader who desires a complete description of the Gogstad ship is referred to the latter's publications concerning her. It is quite evident from her construction that her builders possessed the greatest experience and that her designer, whoever he may have been, thoroughly "understood the art, which was subsequently lost, to be revived in modern times, of shaping the underwater portion of the hull so as to reduce the resistance to the passage of the vessel through the water." * It is the opinion of experts in naval architecture that for model and workmanship this vessel is a masterpiece, nor for beauty of lines and symmetrical proportions could she be surpassed to-day by any man connected with the art of designing or building ships.

As rebutting the statement of those who would limit the possibilities of these early ships to short voyages, it may not be out of place to mention that at the end of the

* "Ancient and Modern Ships," part i., "Wooden Sailing Ships," p. 60, by Sir George C. V. Holmes, K.C.V.O., C.B., London, 1900.

nineteenth century an exact replica of this Gogstad ship was built, and sailed across the Atlantic on her own bottom. She proved to be a capital sea-boat and was for some time a source of great attraction at the Chicago exhibition. From the various articles of antiquarian interest that were found in the Gogstad ship, as well as from the style of carving with which the vessel was decorated, she has been given the date of somewhere between the years 700 and 1000 A.D. According to the Sagas such a ship as this would carry two or more boats propelled by from two to twelve oars. It is therefore interesting to remember that fragments of three were found within this mother ship.

Fig. 28 shows the *bakbordi* or port side looking forward from the stern. The dark triangular erection towards the bows is the sepulchral chamber in which the old sea-chief was laid. The unfortunate break in the ship's side below was evidently the work of thieves bent on stealing some of the articles of value while the ship was under the mound. The wooden shields, or pavisado to protect the oarsmen from the enemy, are much in evidence, and the beautiful lines of her stern cannot fail to be admired. She has a somewhat flat floor amidships for greater stability, but the general sweep of her lines is exquisite. Fig. 29 is even more interesting still as showing the *stjornbordi* or starboard side looking forward. The height of the stern, and the planking, are here clearly discerned: but especially claiming our attention is the rudder. Here it is now a fixture, having developed like the Mediterranean ships from a loose oar at the side. It remained as we see it here until the beginning of the fourteenth century. In this Gogstad ship the rudder is fixed to a projection of solid wood, on which it is pivoted. Into the neck of the rudder a tiller was fitted, which we shall see quite clearly in the illustration of the seal of Winchelsea in the following chapter. Even nowadays, while in the modern

Scandinavian ships the rudder is at the end and not at the side of the ship, the steering helm comes round at the side so as to avoid the high sternpost. Figs. 30 and 31, which have been sketched from modern Norwegian and Russian ships, will show not merely how wonderfully has this Viking type prevailed up till to-day, but how the tiller also has altered only very slightly. From the stern of the Gogstad ship will be noticed the rope for pulling up the rudder clear of the water-line (as in St. Paul's ship) so as to avoid damage when beaching. The steering side was of course always the starboard, whence this word originates. On this side the reader will notice the oar-holes mentioned above. The class to which this Gogstad ship belongs is that of the *skuta*, which was extensively used in Norway. Such craft as these, though they were not the biggest of the Viking ships, were nevertheless of great speed. The actual word *skuta* indicates "to shoot," in the sense of passing speedily. No doubt the familiar Dutch craft *schuyt* is, at least in name, derived from this.

FIG. 30. NORWEGIAN SHIP.

Being an open ship it was customary to stretch a tent, called a *tjald*, over the vessel under which the crew could sleep at night or shelter in bad weather. This was extended by means of cords and wooden stretchers. A pair of these latter have been found in the Gogstad ship with carved figure-heads. Very similar to the ships depicted in the

120

Bayeux tapestry, as we shall presently see, the Gogstad ship may be regarded as a typical Viking ship, such as we are accustomed to read of in the literature of the Sagas.

Since this last ship was unearthed there has also been found another Viking ship, which we shall refer to by the name of Oseberg. This was discovered on the western side of the Christiania Fjord, in the district of Vestfold, in the year 1903. Its resting place was, as usual, deep down in a mound. Happily the work of excavation was

FIG. 31. RUSSIAN SHIP.

put into scientific hands, and the University of Christiania sent Professor Gabriel Gustafson to Oseberg to superintend the digging, which proceeded with great care, and about Christmas, 1904, the whole ship was fully disclosed. The various pieces were subsequently put on board a lighter and brought to Christiania, where for the present at any rate they are stored in the military arsenal of Akershus, each piece having previously been numbered so as to facilitate reconstruction. She is of similar dimensions to the Gogstad ship though a little shorter, but unfortunately she has not been so well preserved. She has in fact suffered severely by the earth pressing up from beneath while her own weight, together with that of the mound above her, have damaged her frames considerably. In ornamentation she is indeed superior to the Gogstad ship and some detailed carving at the ends of the ship runs

121

along the gunwale. However the wonderful collection of personal property found in her has not yet been surpassed. Although she also had suffered at the hands of thieves, there were discovered in her :—a loom with a tapestry full of small pictures resembling those on the Bayeux tapestry, implements of various kinds, a carriage but no weapons, which latter had probably been stolen unless we suppose that his wife and not the sea-chief himself had lain buried here.

With regard to the internal arrangements and fittings of the Viking ships, the rowing benches were placed at either side of the ship with a gangway running down the centre. In calm weather the ship was of course propelled with her oars. In the centre of the gangway, fitted to the keelson, was placed the step—*stalbr*—for the mast, room being left so that the mast could conveniently be raised and lowered. Like those of their ancestors in the Mediter- ranean, the masts of these ships were lowered by means of a tackle on the forestay before going into battle, and also when compelled to resort to oars on meeting with a head wind. Stays supported the mast from the top to the high stem-post, as well as shrouds on each side. The halyards passed through a hole below where the shrouds met. Wooden parrals called *rakki* were used to hold the yard to the mast, and these are clearly seen in old manuscripts of English ships of mediæval times. Braces came down from the extremities of the yards, leading away aft.

The sail was square and was not practicable for tacking, consequently it frequently meant waiting for a fair wind or resorting to oars. We learn from the Sagas that Harald Sigurdson wishing to visit Constantinople, on his return from Jerusalem, waited with his fleet a whole month and a half for a side wind to enable him to display his magnificent sails all glorious with rich velvet. The sail was much wider at the foot than on the yard, and

122

exceeded the breadth of the ship. Fig. 30, as we have already remarked, represents a modern and practically an ancient Scandinavian ship—so little have these craft altered in the march of time. It will be noticed that she has no boom. However, the Russian ship in Fig. 31 is correctly shown with one. That, in fact, is the characterising difference between the ships of these two peoples. That a tacking-boom or *beiti-ass* was in use we know from the Ynglinga Saga. It is said to have reached so far beyond the gunwale that it could knock a man overboard from a boat when sailing too close past.[*] This boom was probably used when wishing to sail fairly close to the wind. Apparently when the *beiti-ass* was not in use the braces were called sheets.

The sail itself was made of home-spun until with civilisation came the cultivation of flax. It was strengthened with a hem of rope, and was frequently striped. Sometimes it was embroidered or decked with pall. It is perfectly clear that the Vikings did know of the art of tacking for we find the word in the Norse which means this—*beita.* The portions of the sail were sewed together with thread, rings being attached to the leach in such a place that the sheets could be conveniently made fast when the vessel had need to shorten sail. Small ropes or reefing points were also affixed to the sail. We shall see this quite easily when we come to consider similar ships in the next chapter. Mention has just been made of Sigurdson's sails of velvet. Very highly did the Vikings respect their wings. Gorgeous sails were worked by their women folk, with cunning designs and beautiful embroidery, even historic incidents being included. White sails were sometimes striped with red and with blue, whilst others of double velvet were made gay with exquisitely woven patterns in red, purple and gold. As is the case in regard to many other details this custom of

[*] Magnússon's "Notes on Shipbuilding," &c., *ut supra*, p. 50.

decorating the sail was passed on to the English, and it is a matter for regret that our seas do not still witness these picturesque spots of warm colour flitting over the cold green waves.

Very poetic, too, are the phrases in which we find, from the Sagas, the Norsemen referred to their sail. Thus such happy expressions as " The Cloak of the Wind," " The Tapestry of the Masthead," " The Sheet spun by Women," " The Cloth of the Wind," " The Beard of the Yard," " The Fine Shirt of the Tree," are found. With a ship-load of thirty or fifty lusty Norsemen singing and swing-ing to their oars, with a sail above bellowing out its purple and gold over their flaxen heads, with their red and white striped hull, and their standards and gay weather-vanes waving at her extremities—what a feast of colour, what a sight for mortals she must have made as she came sliding down the billows towards the unprotected yellow shore !

There were three distinct classes of ships possessed by these Northerners. Firstly, the war-ships, including the Dragon type, so called from the figure-head at her stem ; the *Snekkja*, named after the Long Serpent or Snake ship ; the *Skuta* or swift, "shooting" ship, to which the Gogstad and the Nydam craft belong, the *Buza* resembling the *Skuta* ; and finally the longship, or, to give her the native word, *langskip*. But far and away the largest of this class was the Dragon, whilst the most celebrated for beauty of design was the not inaptly named " Long Serpent." Indeed, right until the twelfth century this vessel dominated the design of most other ships built around the North Sea and English Channel.

Secondly there were the ships of burthen, modifications of the warships : and finally the small boats, also fitted with mast and sail, which were carried on board the bigger craft.

In almost every case there was but a single row of oarsmen on each side, protected by the overlapping wooden shields from both arrows and waves, whilst the name given to the rope surrounding the ship so as to guard against the shock of ramming was the *viggyrdil.* Whilst the dragon's head was on the stem-post and the tail of the dragon ornamented the stern, the tiller, and, as we know from the Gogstad ship, the handles of the oars were also decorated. We have a relic of this custom in the beautifully carved dogs' heads so often found on yachts and other craft before iron helms came so much into practice. With regard to the nomenclatures of these old vessels we find such figurative terms as " Deer of the Surf," " Snake of the Sea," " Lion of the Waves," applied to them : but it is not without interest to remark that not until about the time of the introduction of Christianity is frequent mention made of the naming of a ship at launching. They carried with them, on board somewhere, rollers wherewith to beach and launch their ships. These are referred to in the early accounts of the Viking burials and launchings.

In building a vessel there were three chief classes of shipwrights employed. There was the head-smith, the stem-smith, who was responsible for the construction of her framework, and finally the strake-smith. Besides these came also the joiners, nail-makers, blacksmiths and other workmen.

When making a passage every oarsman kept his weapons underneath his seat in a chest, and when the fight began, the ships—following the practice of the early Mediterranean galleys—of the aggressor and the enemy were locked together so that the warfare resembled a land battle. This custom naturally was handed on to the English, and there are not wanting in old manuscripts illustrations showing this method of warfare. The prow had its raised deck and the stern likewise. In between, but considerably lower, was the maindeck. At the poop, in his historical position, stood the commander. Here, too, immediately below him was the ship's arsenal for whenever fresh arms had to be served out. Each ship had five compartments, two being in the stern as just described —the commander's room called the lofting, and the fore-room used for the next in rank as well as for the arms. We have also mentioned the central space of the ship where the mast and rowers were placed. And forward beyond that were quartered the important men who were responsible for defending the stem and who also bore the standard, this bow section being divided into two sections. One can readily understand how essential it was that only picked men should be in this part, for when once the bow end had been stormed, it would be with difficulty that the enemy, coming aboard, could be repelled from the rest of the ship.

As to the navigating methods of the Vikings, although they understood the cardinal points of north, south, east, and west long before the loadstone was invented, yet their voyages mostly consisted of coasting from shore to shore like the ancient Greeks. But as to how they were able to make such long voyages as to Iceland, and thence across to what are now the New England states of America without compass or sextant, I offer no explanation, beyond attributing success to that wonderful additional sense and intuition which seamen possess and which is, we find all round our coasts, developed in a high degree in fishermen unlettered and untutored. Of course they had the rising and setting of the sun to enable them to distinguish east from west, and the stars, too, would be for their assistance, but with such slender aids to navigation and in spite of being blown off their course as such shallow ships must frequently have been, they very rarely got wrong in their bearings. But perhaps we ought to admit that usually the Vikings were wise enough not to fight against nature wantonly ; for they confined their sailing seasons, following the example again of the Mediterraneans, to spring and summer. Except when they were in some country too far distant, the Vikings always returned home about the autumnal equinox and "brought their ships to the roller."

Because the Vikings coasted as a rule instead of making a passage across the Ocean, they were frequently able to go ashore at nights to sleep. But whether they slept ashore or afloat each man turned-in in a leather sleeping-bag. Under that awning and on board such able ships the possibilities of comfort were perhaps not so limited as one might imagine at first. The cooking could only be done on land, so this was an additional reason for hugging the shore. In fact a municipal law of Bergen in the year 1276 assumed this, for it enacts that the mate shall, whenever the ship lies at anchor in harbour, cause the crew to be put on shore and brought back on board once a day: but the cook is to be allowed ashore three times—once to take in water and twice to take in food. Bronze cooking vessels belonging to the ships have also been found.

Thus we conclude our investigation of these eternally fascinating sailing ships of the land of pines and fjords, of glacier and keen biting air. We leave them with reluctance, but our regret is tempered with the knowledge that henceforth wherever we discuss the sailing ships of our English nation, we shall know that either obvious or concealed there is the Viking influence lurking in her design, her manner of construction or her sail and rigging.

CHAPTER V.

THE DEVELOPMENT OF THE SAILING SHIP FROM THE EIGHTH CENTURY TO THE YEAR 1485.

It is the custom of some writers concerning mediæval ships to deplore the existing information as being too scanty to afford us any adequate idea as to vessels that sailed the seas during the first half of the middle age. For myself I think that such a statement cannot be maintained.

The evidence on which we are able to construct afresh in our minds the ships of this period, is scarcely as slender as has been supposed, though not unnaturally we must make allowances for obvious inaccuracies, for exaggerations, and for ignorance. But, even when we have done this we shall find the sources of information far from shallow. I have used as the basis for this chapter, the evidence of mediæval seals, both English and Continental : England, Scotland, France, Spain and Flanders all affording interesting details of ships by this means. I have gone carefully through old coins, and though representations of ships thereon depicted have necessarily had to suffer through the limitations imposed on the artist by the size and shape of the coin, yet this evidence used collaterally

FIG. 32. HAROLD'S SHIPS.
From the Bayeux Tapestry.

FIG. 33. WILLIAM THE CONQUEROR'S SHIPS.   p. 129.

From the Bayeux Tapestry.

with the rest, goes a long way towards completing the picture we are endeavouring to paint.

During the eleventh century, certain merchants from Bari on the Adriatic made an expedition to Lycia and brought back the remains of St. Nicholas, Archbishop of Myra, who had lived and suffered persecution in the fourth century under Diocletian. Thence grew up a wide-spread cult of this saint. Not only did he become patron saint of Russia, but of all sailormen throughout Christendom. In ancient pictures we sometimes see a ship caught in a terrible storm with sails and gear carried away, Boreas or his colleague, raising his head above the waters, blowing with inflated cheeks at the helpless ship, while above the picture, St. Nicholas appearing in the clouds, comes to the aid of the skipper seen praying on the poop for deliverance from the horrible seas. In England this cult was not wanting either. There are between three and four hundred churches in our land dedicated in St. Nicholas' honour, and the reader as he journeys along the coast, will frequently find that in an old seaport the parish church bears this dedication. We need not go too far into this matter, but the famous parish church of that very ancient seaport of Great Yarmouth (whose seamen used to have goodly quarrels with the men of the Cinque Ports, and who, long prior to the coming of William the Conqueror, were busy with the herring fishery), and also of Brighton, are notable instances of this devotion to the sailor's saint. The font of the Brighton church and of Winchester Cathedral—although the design in each case is conventionalised—cannot fail to assist us. The date of the former belongs to somewhere between the years 1050 and 1075: as to the latter, Dean Furneaux informs me that the date is about 1180.

Mediæval manuscripts both English and foreign have happily preserved to us not merely actual facts, but exquisitely coloured illustrations of ships. We see the vessels in every conceivable way—in course of construction, ashore, afloat, with sails spread, with sails stowed. We see them on rivers and seas, embarking and disembarking. We see them in peace and in war, bound for the Crusades, or ramming each other, grappling, hurling darts and arrows from their elevated forecastles and sterncastles, or casting destruction down on to one another's decks from the fighting top above.

We have, too, some slight evidence in contemporary stained glass, which by reason of the demands of an exceptionally conventionalised art must be regarded with caution and only to confirm other evidence. We have the clear and valuable evidence of certain mosaics in St. Mark's Venice, which help us more than a little with regard to the fourteenth century, and, few though they be as we remarked in Chapter I., there are some artists whose pictures of ships in mediæval times can be relied upon, after making certain allowances already indicated. In this class we may include especially Carpaccio, Giorgione and Memlinc. The more artistic the mode of expressing these ships becomes, however, so much the more prone to inaccuracy does the evidence incline, and to this category belong the tapestries, models in precious metals, paintings on china and earthenware and tiles. In most cases the distortion of truth has been in respect of length, breadth, and height.

When we remember how thoroughly the Vikings harassed the shores of France and England sailing up the Seine and the rivers and creeks of our own land, committing piracy on the sea and pillage ashore, and finally settling down and conquering the territory, it is not to be wondered that their sway in naval architecture and construction should have been universal in northern Europe. We have in the previous chapter already dealt with the primitive craft of early Britain, and it is generally supposed that the ships which were sent from this country to assist the Veneti against Cæsar had by this time become wooden and not skin-ships. With the Roman invasion of Britain would come the introduction of Roman craft, and there can be little doubt that the Deal "galley" of to-day, which is the characteristic ship of that part of England which was so frequently the landing-place for visitors from Gaul, is a relic, much modified, from the Roman times. After the withdrawal of the Roman influence from these shores, the Saxons and Angles coming in their double-ended Viking craft quickly banished almost all the customs that the Britons had learned under the Romans. And having effected this complete transformation the Saxons settled down and practically forsook the sea and shipbuilding.

But now from the year 787 until the coming of William the Conqueror our forefathers were constantly being invaded by the Northmen in the kind of ships that we discussed in the last chapter. But before the end of the ninth century Alfred succeeded to the throne after the country had been ravaged and despoiled by these raiders along the north-east coast as far west as Southampton Water. Acting on that blessed maxim which alone preserves our country to-day, that he who would be secure on land must first be supreme on sea, he set himself the task of improving on the Viking ships. This he carried out by making his longships—so the Saxon Chronicles inform us—twice as long as the Danish, and swifter, steadier and with more freeboard than any war vessels that had hitherto been seen in England. Nor did he neglect such important details as the seasoning of the timber. But to show how utterly lacking his subjects were in all knowledge of seamanship, his oarsmen—some of his ships carrying as many as sixty—were all hired pirates from the seafaring district of Friesland. Still, for all that, he succeeded in his object and defeated the cruel foe.

SAILING SHIPS

Hakluyt quotes from one Octher, who voyaging to " the Northeast parts beyond Norway reported by himselfe unto Alfred the famous king of England, about the yere 890 " that he " tooke his voyage directly North along the coast, having upon his steereboard alwayes the desert land and upon the leereboard the maine Ocean : and continued his course for the space of 3 dayes. In which space he was come as far towards the North, as commonly the whale hunters use to travell." . . . "The principall purpose of his traveile this way, was to encrease the knowledge and discoverie of these coasts and countreyes, for the more commoditie of fishing of horse-whales, which have in their teeth bones of great price and excellencie : whereof he brought some at his returne unto the king. Their skinnes are also very good to make cables for shippes, and so used." We see, therefore, that if the Saxons had sunk in maritime pursuits this Octher from " Helgoland " was one of a class in the northernmost parts of Europe that was wont to sail far across the seas. From the same traveller we learn that it was evidently at this time the custom for a ship on a passage and not making port before to " lay still by the night."

Edgar, too, who reigned from 959 to 975, took a keen interest in his navy. In fact, I would much rather call him the first of our yachtsmen than bestow the title on Charles II. as is customary. For "this peaceable king Edgar," says Hakluyt, "(as by ancient Recordes may appeare) his Sommer progresses and yerely chiefe pastimes were, the sailing round about this whole Isle of Albion, garded with his grand navie of 4000 saile at the least, parted into 4 equall parts of petie Navies, eche one being of 1000 ships, for so it is anciently recorded." From the same source we learn that the number was 4800, although it has been also estimated at 3600. One thousand two hundred were kept on the east coast ("in plaga Angliæ Orientali "), and similar numbers to the west, the south and the north respectively, for the defence of his kingdom. Under Edgar's rule every three "hundreds" (probably only of those along the coast-line), were compelled to furnish a ship. Nor must we suppose that the mercantile marine was entirely at a standstill, for there is frequent mention of the English fleets after the time of Athelstan, and whilst the men of Kent were busily engaged in the herring fishery, trade was regularly being carried on with France and Flanders. Under the reign of Edward the Confessor the merchant navy grew very greatly.

The Anglo-Saxon ships of the eleventh century were less of the Gogstad or *skuta* type, than of that bigger class to which the "Long Serpent" or *snekja* belongs. We do know from a certain Scandinavian Edda what the Viking ships of about the year 1000 were like in dimensions. We learn that the "Long Serpent" was 117 feet long, and carried as many as 600 men aboard. She was decked after the manner described in the last chapter, and had the five cabins already mentioned. As in the Mediterranean the ships of burthen developed from the ships of war, so in the Anglo-Saxon times the merchantman differed from the battleship only in being more beamy, and consequently not quite so fast as the longships.

As to the Scandinavians, they did not confine their activities to fighting. Their fleets voyaged as far away as the Levant in the south and Iceland in the north, and further still to Greenland. It is from the colony of Iceland that they are said to have sailed across to the New England States in North America. As to their sails at this period, there is a Scandinavian coin of the ninth century of our era * which shows that the usual lines of a Viking ship were continued, with high poop and bow. The mast is shown supported by three backstays and one forestay, whilst pavisses of shields hang round as in the

* Reproduced on p. 126, fig. 536, of Prof. Gustafson's "Norges Oldtid."

Gogstad ship. The sail is particularly interesting, as it much resembles that of the Mediterranean boats found on the Althiburus mosaics, the surface giving the appearance of net-work. This is no doubt the joining of the stripes of coloured material plus the rows of reef points. In addition to the different classes of ships enunciated in the previous chapter, there were also during Anglo-Saxon times vessels called "ceols." These came from Saxony, and it is not without interest to remark that the same word "keel" is still given to those somewhat beamy ships, carrying one huge Viking-like square sail, that to-day are seen navigating the canal that connects South Yorkshire with the same river Humber up which the Saxons sailed.

We come now to the year 1066, when William setting forth from St. Valery-sur-Somme on the evening of September 27, with a fair wind, disembarked before mid-day on the following morning, Before starting there was trouble with the reluctant crews, and even when lying at anchor off St. Valery several ships foundered. Happily details of William's ships are preserved to us by the Bayeux tapestry, which is supposed to have been worked by his consort, Queen Matilda. From certain variations between this interesting, painstaking work and contemporary records we know that it is not absolutely correct. Nor, indeed, should we have expected otherwise from the work of imaginative ladies unlearned in maritime matters. But having made due allowance for that, the Bayeux tapestry taken in conjunction with the other evidence is most valuable. The photographs which are here reproduced have been taken from the copy of this tapestry in the South Kensington Museum.

In Fig. 32 we see the striped ships of Harold. To the left of the picture the ship is being "quanted" off from the shore in the manner we saw adopted by the Greeks. Two men are wading out to her; while on board one of the crew, having just got the anchor up, is keeping a look-

134

out. Three others are ready to row as soon as in deep water, while another sailor is stepping the mast. The ship next to her has a backstay and forestay as well as shrouds. Behind her she tows a small rowing boat for going ashore. Some excitement appears to be going on aboard her judging by the man forward of the mast who is shouting to the helmsman—possibly informing him that they are getting into shoal-water, for the man in the bows is seen to be sounding with a pole. Notice that a part of the crew has collected aft, the sheets having been eased. In the next ship it is clearly shown that these sailors have come to the stern in order to put their weight on to the shrouds so that the mast may be lowered away gently. The sail and mast will be seen to be partially lowered, a look-out man being still up the latter, and the man forward is about to drop the anchor overboard. The ships, as we have already seen was the Viking custom, are striped as to their hulls. The present writer has seen a modern Scandinavian boat of this type though smaller with stripes of black and yellow. The pavisses are seen in both ships, being apparently coloured alternately. The sail, too, is striped in accordance with the prevailing custom. The shield-like forms hanging down over the stern outside may probably be the North European equivalent of the aphlaston as a protection against ramming. The decoration of a dragon's head on stem and stern will be easily seen.

In Fig. 33 we see another ship of this kind, with rudder still affixed to the starboard, and tiller. We see also that William's men, having been commanded to build ships specially for the purpose of sailing across the Channel, are felling trees. They are seen to be stripping off the bark and planing the wood, whilst other shipwrights are engaged in putting the craft together. Very interesting is the mode of launching shown here. A line attached to the bows is taken through a ring on a stake, and five

135

men haul away on that. Excepting that nowadays the ship would also be put upon a cradle and a capstan or tackle would be used, the same method is used for hauling ashore. Finally, in the same picture also we see the weapons and armour and wine being carried down to the ships (see Fig. 34). It is an historical fact that this wine played no small part in urging the unwilling men to embark on this expedition.

Touching the size of the Norman ships, they did not exceed thirty tons burthen, and as we have seen from the above illustration they were put together on the beach. We have seen, too, that the mast was lowered *forward*, not aft, and with the sail and yard fixed to the mast. This practice is confirmed by an illustration shown in an old manuscript, in which the sailors have gone aft for the purpose of either raising or lowering the mast. Hanging on to the stays they are even standing right out on the top of the stern-post. The yard is clearly seen from these illustrations to have been kept fixed to the mast and not lowered separately, so that to furl the sail when the mast was not taken down the sailors climbed the rigging and tied the sail to the yard. In the Brighton —or as this old fishing village was then called, Brighthelmston—font this is shown quite clearly, as also is a figure holding a tiller, which is correctly shown to be on the starboard side. The high bows and stern are typical of the Viking type, while the construction appears to be clinker. As we shall see from seals and other illustrations while we go down through time this may be regarded as the characteristic ship of Northern Europe until the end of the fifteenth century, although the tendency was gradually to get away from the "longship" idea and to develop into a crescent form. In the Winchester font which is about a hundred years later than the Brighton one, this newer shape is most noticeable. Both fonts refer to a scene in the life of St. Nicholas.

At the masthead of the ships of this period, the chief ship of the fleet carried a vane or flag. The Bayeux tapestry also shows the *Mora*, William's flag-ship. The truck is surmounted by a cross, and there appears to be a lantern immediately below of somewhat similar appearance to that on the Bœotian ship in Fig. 11. We do not know to what exact knowledge of seamanship the crews of William the Conqueror had attained,* but they would, at least some of them, have crossed many times between the two countries before in connection with trade, and they would have been able to acquire by experience and observation, the necessary knowledge of the strong channel tides which, although the coastline between Pevensey to the eastward has altered since the eleventh century, probably were not much different from what they are to-day. They would have an excellent mark in Beachy Head whereby to make a good land-fall, and a sandy beach further to the eastward on which to disembark in the bay, nicely sheltered from westerly winds. William, having once landed in this country and vanquished Harold, did not neglect the care of the navy. By 1071, or roughly the date when the font was being placed in Brighton church just a few miles to the westward, there was a fleet in being. Trade, too, between France and England would now be even less fettered than before, and this would naturally make for an increase in the merchant shipping. Neverthe-

---

* Evidently the early Europeans did not merely make rash voyages, trusting entirely to good luck to reach their port. It is quite clear that they had given serious study to seamanship by the early part of the fifth century, for when Lupus and German, two Gallic prelates, crossed the Channel to Britain in the year 429 A.D., they encountered very bad weather, and Constantius adds that St. German poured oil on the waves. The latter's earlier days having been spent in Gaul, in Rome and as duke over a wide district, he had evidently picked up this item of seamanship from the mariners of the southern shores. (See Canon Bright's "Chapters of Early English Church History," Oxford, 1897, p. 19 and notes.)

less the crews of William's fleet would be more Norman than English. Nor was shipbuilding neglected in other parts of Great Britain, for Hakluyt gives a chronicle of the Kings of Man, in which we find that Godredus Crovan, who gathered together a fleet of ships and sailed to the Isle of Man, vanquished its people, and subdued Dublin, and "so tamed the Scots that none of them durst build a ship or a boate with above three yron nailes in it."

Under Henry I. the maritime industry prospered much, and the king collected a squadron of great size. Up to this time it had been the custom that any cargo cast ashore from a wreck became *ipso facto* the property of the king. But Henry caused a law to be put into force that should any one escape from a wreck alive, the ship should not be treated as lost, and her contents should not have ceased to belong to her owner. In this reign too, we learn of *La Blanche Nef*, a fifty-oared vessel that had as many as three hundred souls on board when she foundered on the rocks off the race of Catteville in the year 1120.

Portsmouth, even as early as this period, was springing into importance as a naval port, and under Henry II.'s reign, London and Bristol, which in after years were to come into such prominence and to witness so many fine expeditions setting forth to explore all parts of the unknown world, now became the two chief ports of England. Ships were gradually getting bigger and bigger, until we read of one in the year 1170 carrying as many as 400 people. Henry II. contributed his share in encouraging the progress of shipping by good naval legislature, for it was he who enacted that no one should buy or sell any ship that was to be carried away from England.

In the next reign we reach an important stage in the history of sailing ships. Richard I. had set his mind on undertaking a Crusade to the Holy Land, and this expedition had lasting effects on the design of the ships that subsequently were built. Instead of coasting to Ireland or France or the Orkneys, or even to Norway, England now sends her first expedition across the Bay of Biscay to the South, the beginning of that wonderful series of great voyages of the English nation which in Elizabethan times made our country so famous through her enterprising mariners. I have already referred in our first chapter to the influence that was effected by the opportunity afforded to English sailor-folk of seeing the ships of the Mediterranean. The ships of this Sea had developed on two separate lines. There was first the galley type, which had remained wonderfully similar to the galley of Greek and Roman times. She was essentially a rowed vessel, having sails as auxiliaries. In after times all sorts of adaptations resulted from this, which we shall see as we proceed through the Elizabethan period. The root of the word "galley" is found in the various craft designated "galleass," "galliot," and "galleon," but it was the first of these three that represented the rowed ship in her largest dimensions. The other two were sailing ships, although preserving some similarity in name.

The second class of Mediterranean craft consisted of a rounder, broader type of vessel—the descendant of the classic merchant vessel as distinct from the "long ship." This in fact has been the general division in the history of sailing ships through all times. Under this heading will come the various classes of Mediterranean sailing *ships* —not galleys—designated respectively "caracks," "great ships," "busses" or "buccas," "caravels," "barks," and "dromons." If we keep these two classes distinct in our minds—"galleys" and "ships"—we shall not get far wrong during the ensuing centuries. Sailors in all ages have always had an unfortunate habit of mixing the various classifications of vessels, and we shall see as we proceed to what inconvenience this has attained.

In the records of the Crusades we find mention made of the larger and second class of the Mediterranean ships of sail. Near to Beirut the English espied in the distance a great ship with three tapering masts, strongly built, painted green and yellow, with 1500 men aboard. On being hailed she pretended at first to belong to Richard's colleague in the Crusade, the King of France, whose flag indeed she was flying, but she was soon discovered to be a Saracen ship, and after some difficulty was rammed and sunk by the English Viking-shaped and smaller vessels. In Hakluyt's account of this ship she is described as a "carack." She was probably not very much different from the caravel shown in Fig. 43. The three tapering masts which astounded the Englishmen in their one-masted Viking ships and the tall sides of the carack which gave Richard's men so much difficulty in assault from their comparatively small vessels of low freeboard, would not fail to bring forth changes in English shipbuilding as soon as internal and external peace was assured and sufficient technical skill had been acquired. This big ship or carack class—call it what you will—marks a determined stand in naval architecture to build real ships as distinct from big boats. From her evolved the vessels that sailed across the Atlantic with Columbus, that carried Elizabethan explorers to all points of the compass, that fought the Armada and the Dutch, and became adapted in time to such wooden walls as the *Victory* and others, and which are not radically dissimilar from the modern full-rigged ships, though made of iron instead of wood, with steel rigging and a much larger spread of canvas.

Although the carack class was not rare in the Mediterranean in the twelfth century, it was some time in making itself felt in English naval architecture. We must needs wait for another three centuries. But what seem to have had an almost immediate effect were the castles on the Mediterranean galleys at bow and stern. These may have come into use in England during the remaining years of Richard's or during John's reign. I have seen no illustration of either of these reigns which shows these castellated constructions; but in the reign of Henry III. in the seal of Sandwich this structure is shown in the bows, at the stern and at the top of the mast. And we can be quite sure that unless it were a prevailing type it would not have figured in the port's official seal. Fashions moved but slowly in those days, so that it is not unreasonable to suppose that these castellated structures had been in use for some years prior to the date of the seal—the year 1238. At the same time the seal of the City of Paris, which represents the first seal of its "Merchants of the Water," belonging to the year 1210, shows the Viking shape pure and simple—without any germ of the castle—as were the ships of this type which accompanied the rest of Richard's fleet to the South. The high stem- and stern-post, the clinker-build, the three stays forward to support the mast, and three aft, seen in the seal, show how determinedly the Viking type had overrun the north coast of France. But there is nothing surprising in the French not having adopted the fighting castles by this date.

Richard having despatched his navy by the "Spanish seas" to meet him at Marseilles, himself travelled overland, and having waited eight days in vain at Marseilles, "for his Navie which came not he there hired 20 Gallies, and ten great barkes to ship over his men, and so came to Naples" and eventually to Messina in Sicily, where to his great joy he found his fleet had arrived. After the departure of the French King from Messina, Richard followed "with 150 great ships and 53 great gallies well manned and appointed." They were caught in a strong southerly gale, but only two of his fleet appear to have foundered. Later on, in the account included in Hakluyt, we find that the whole fleet that was gathered at the port of Lymszem consisted of "254 tall shippes, and above threescore galliots."

SAILING SHIPS

Fig. 35 represents a Mediterranean warship of the thirteenth century and well shows how far ahead the Southerners still were of the North Europeans. Notice

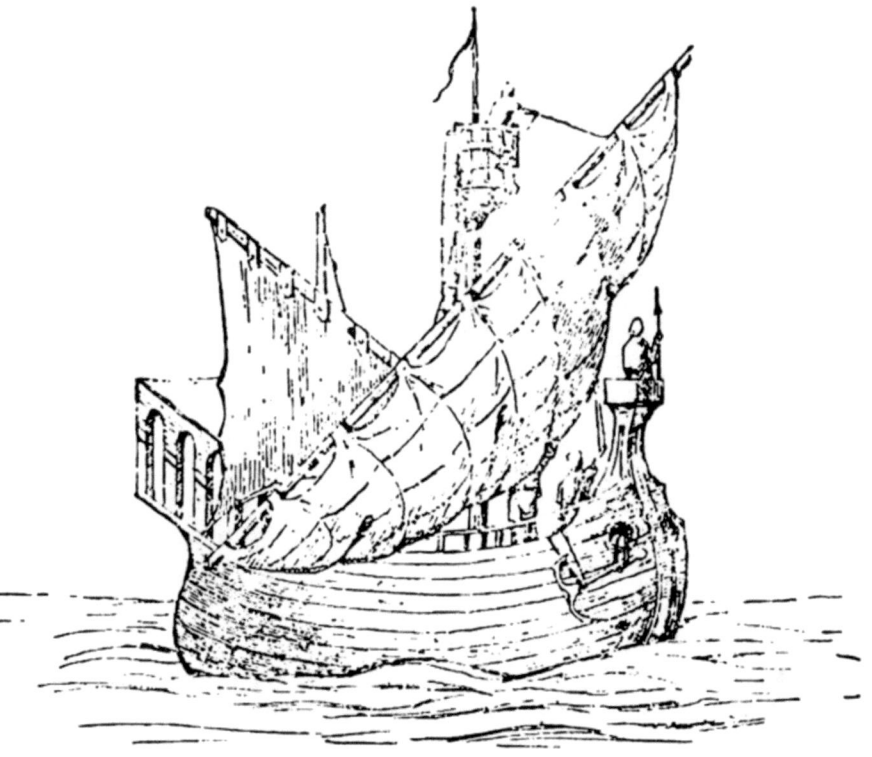

FIG. 35. MEDITERRANEAN WARSHIP OF THE THIRTEENTH CENTURY.

especially the sterncastle and forecastle. The former is open at the sides and differs not very much from the sterncastle in the clay model shown in Fig. 17. In the forecastle of the thirteenth-century ship before us will be seen a warrior standing ready to hurl down spears at the galleys over which his ship towered so high. The large cage-like fighting-top is used as well for steadying the unwieldy yard of the main sail as for purely warlike
142

purposes. The rope ladders are also seen, and the rig consists of a large squaresail on the main with a lateen on the mizzen. The latter, having been for many hundreds of years seen up and down the Mediterranean, would but naturally find its way into the rig when a second mast was added. It would be very acceptable as being far handier than the big squaresail and capable of being easily stowed in a breeze. When her commander was endeavouring to sail a tubby old craft like this as close to the wind as she could get, the help of the lateen mizzen by sending her head up into the wind would counteract the tendency to fall off from the breeze. I attach considerable importance to this illustration as it is the earliest picture I know of giving us anything of a satisfactory idea of the kind of ships, other than the galley class, that sailed the Mediterranean during about the time of Richard's crusade. Perhaps this is one of those " great ships" already alluded to. At any rate she belongs to the sailing-ship days. The method of stowing her anchor is clearly shown. Very interesting, too, is the manner of bending the sails to the yard. No lacing of any kind seems to be employed, but strips of the sail appear to pass round the yard and then meet the cloth again on the other side.

This is a Venetian ship, and when we consider that at this time Venice was the foremost maritime power in the world, it is not surprising that her vessels subsequently influenced Spain and thence Northern Europe to a wonderful extent, as soon as the latter nations had begun to discard the Viking type which had so long been the model of their shipbuild. This illustration is from the work of one of Giotto's pupils.

As to the other ships which Richard had with him besides the Viking type, there were the Mediterranean galleys, somewhat similar to those shown in Figs. 57 and 58. A "dromon" or "dromond" is also mentioned, but this word was used very loosely, as for instance the

143

word "barge" and other examples already given in our own times. Sometimes "dromon" referred to a vessel of large tonnage, but the reader will see in Fig. 36 a much smaller ship bearing the same appellation. This mosaic is

FIG. 36. A FOURTEENTH-CENTURY DROMON.

taken from the ceiling in St. Mark's, Venice, and belongs to the year 1359. The incident depicted is that of bringing St. Mark to Alexandria from Egiddo. The rig is lateen and the rake of the mast is about the same as seen in the modern dhow-rigged yacht shown in Fig. 101. In the dromon St. Mark is at the stern sheltered from the following sea by a bulwark that would seem to have been super-added to the hull. Notice, too, that by this time a rudder has been fixed to the ship at the extreme stern, and that it appears to be worked by means of a rope leading in through
144

a hole in the gunwale. Of the crew of two one is holding on to the vang, which comes down from the peak of the sail, a relic, no doubt, of the brace of the squaresail, while the man forward has just hoisted up the sail. Nowadays, that part of the mast seen to project beyond the sail would be cut off in a dhow-rigged vessel, the yard coming flush with the truck of the mast.

There was also in the fleet of Mediterranean craft which joined Richard, a ship of the class called a *buss, bucca,* or *buzzo.* This was a Venetian type of merchant ship, bluff-bowed and highly useful as a transport. Levi * derives the name, not from the Italian word meaning "stomach," although she has a hold capable of stowing away much cargo, but from *buco* meaning a hole or small, dark room, into which the cargo was thrown. The various kinds of galleys are spoken of under the names of gallion, galliot, galleass—though in course of time a different and distinctive meaning has been assigned to each of these words—and the *visser* was a shallow transport perhaps not differing much from the *hippago* of the Althiburus mosaic. A "barge" was probably more like one of those tar-covered "coasters" that one sees loading in every port—in hull, that is, but with a square-sail and of course no triangular head sails.† Of the Viking class Richard had with him some of the *esneccas* or "Long Serpent" type as well as some "Cogs." The latter class was also of Scandinavian origin and probably somewhat bigger than the skuta type. Hakluyt includes a letter sent from our King Henry III. to Haquinus, King of Norway, granting permission to Norwegian merchants to come and go freely into English ports. "Wee will and command all bailifes of Portes," reads the mandate, " at which the Cog of Norway (wherein certaine of the king of Norwaie his souldiers, and certain Merchants of Saxonie

* " Navi Venete da codici Marini e dipinti," by Cesare Augusto Levi, Venice, 1892.
† See the ship in the seal of Dam, Fig. 40.

are coming for England) shall touch, that when the fore-
said Cog shall chance to arrive at any of their Havens,
they doe permit the said Cog safely to remain in their said
Havens, &c." Perhaps she was a new type of Viking ship
and, like the " Long Serpent," gave her name to the class
of ships built after her model.

On a MS. in the possession of Corpus Christi College,
Cambridge, we see a couple of galleys ramming each
other with the spur some distance above the waterline.
The largest of Richard's galleys in the Mediterranean had
thirty oars, and the Viking type of steering paddle was still
used, since the rudder affixed to the farthest end of the
stern had not yet been introduced into ships of North
Europe. Masts and sails were carried as usual. The
larger ships of Richard's fleet that we have mentioned also
carried engines for projecting darts as well as terrible
explosives. The banner under which they fought at this
time was that of St. George. As to the equipment of this
first great English fleet the chief vessels had each three
spare steering paddles, thirteen anchors, thirty oars, two
sails, three sets of all kinds of ropes, and duplicates of all
gear except the mast and boat. There are not wanting
plenty of references to the *esnecca* or "Serpent" class.
Thus there is a record of payment "to the men of the
esnecca" (Pipe Roll, 5 Henry II., p. 45. Pipe Roll Socy.);
" paid out to me of the snecca for the Queen's passage
and that of Henry FitzGerald with the treasure and of
Nicholas de Sigillo £30 : 10 " (Pipe Roll, 6 Henry III.,
p. 47); " to the sailors of the snecca twenty shillings by
the king's writ " (Pipe Roll, 8 Henry II., p. 35). The
ship that was reserved for carrying royalty across from
England to France was always at this period called the
" esnecca."

The resulting effects on England of this crusade were
not confined to her naval architecture. Although it was not
the first time that a North European or even an Englishman
146

had sailed in the Mediterranean, it was the first instance of a naval expedition on a large scale setting forth from these shores to the Levant. It gave our sailors in a smaller way just that experience which the recent world-cruise of the fleet of the United States from the Atlantic to the Pacific and back again has obtained for American sailormen. It made deep-sea sailors of the men who had only been coasters, and showed them in what directions their ships could be improved upon. But its effect on the trade of England was to expand it, to create new sources of imports and fresh outlets for her exports. England owes a great debt to Richard I., besides, for his attention to maritime legislature. Hakluyt gives a list of the laws the king ordained for his navy during this expedition, as, for instance, that any one who killed another on board ship should be tied to the dead man and thrown overboard: and that if he killed him on land he should in like manner be tied "with the partie slaine, and be buried with him in the earth." It was from the Levant that Richard brought a roll of laws regulating maritime affairs, and which, being held in high honour on the Southern sea, he ordered to be observed in English waters. Very drastic were these laws of Oleron, framed for the benefit of the merchant service. Thus if a pilot from ignorance or otherwise lost the ship entrusted to his navigation and the merchants thereby sustained damage, the pilot was to make full satisfaction if he had means, and if he lacked these he was to forfeit his head. It is interesting to note the care that was taken to prevent ships fouling each other's anchors, for it was enacted that all anchors were to be indicated by buoys. But no modern sailor will read without a smile the regulation that if a vessel were wind or weather-bound, the master, when a change in the conditions had occurred, was to consult his crew, saying to them, "Gentlemen, what think you of this wind?" and to be guided as to whether he should put to sea by the opinion of the majority. It is

147

not difficult to imagine what the verdict of such a consultation would be to-day on a big barque, for instance, after the men have returned from their carouse ashore, if the law were still in force. The "gentlemen's" opinion of the wind would be something unprintable.

During the reign of John, ships reached a size as big as eighty tons. Hakluyt contains a reference to the time when Louis invaded England to aid Archbishop Langton. "Hubert of Borough (then captaine of Dover) following the opinion of Themistocles in the exposition of the oracle of the woodden walls, by the aide of the [Cinque] Port townes, armed fortie tall ships, and meeting with eightie saile of French men upon the high seas, gave them a most couragious encounter, in which he tooke some, sunke others, and discomfitted the rest." Under John the English navy was considerably improved, and this was the first of our sovereigns to retain seamen with permanent pay. Instead of being alternately pirates, fishermen and fighting men of the state, the sailor became endowed with a higher status. The privileges first granted to the Cinque Ports by Edward the Confessor, William the Conqueror and their successors, did much to assist the progress of the sailing ship; but in addition to the ships supplied to him by these south coast ports, John had also ships of his own. This reign is notable, too, as the first instance of our country claiming to be "The Sovereign of the Seas."

Nor under Henry III. was this progression in maritime matters arrested. Every year the size of ships was becoming greater. Thanks to the Mediterranean influence they were getting away from the Viking type to a more protected and seaworthy kind. Decks and cabins and more than one mast were introduced, and in 1228 a vessel that was sent to Gascony with the king's effects had expended on her a certain sum of money "for making a chamber in the said ship to place the king's things in." In 1242 there is a direction for the cabins of the king and

148

queen to be wainscotted. The seal of Sandwich, one of the Cinque Ports, of the date of 1238, shows the customary Viking hull, as usual, clinker-built. But some notable additions have been made. Both in the bows and stern a raised structure has been added to enable the men to hurl the same destruction from a height that they had seen the Mediterraneans operate during the Crusade. The space underneath the stern-castle was used as a kind of roofed deck-house or cabin, but open at the sides, and we see one of the barons of Sandwich sitting in a dignified manner under this shelter, while a couple of the crew are aloft on the yard, evidently about to unfurl the sail. At the top of the mast has been placed a fighting-top. A very thick forestay, two backstays, and four shrouds are shown, but possibly the two halyards did duty also as backstays. A small rowing boat is seen carried on board, as well as two more crew.

Fig. 37 has been sketched from the seal of Winchelsea in the British Museum. For detail of information it is pre-eminent : the date is the end of the thirteenth century. The reader, after making allowances for the limitations of space and shape imposed on the artist, will at once remark the similarity of the lines, especially at bow and stern, between this and the Gogstad ship. The stem- and stern-post are depicted very high. Forward is seen the forecastle taking its Gothic curves from the architecture on shore. Above, floats a flag. Below the stern-castle sits the baron or commander protected by the roof and arches, whilst over him two trumpeters are pealing forth. We have seen this trumpeting at the stern also depicted in the ancient Mediterranean ship coming into harbour (Fig. 22), and the practice was evidently still a common one in the middle ages when entering or leaving port so as to give due warning to approaching vessels. Hakluyt contains a reference to Richard when he had wearied of waiting at Marseilles and had sailed to Messina. "After

149

that he had heard that his ships were arrived at Messana in Sicilie, he made the more speed and so the 23. of September entred Messana with such a noyse of Trumpets

FIG. 37. SEAL OF WINCHELSEA (END OF THE THIRTEENTH CENTURY).

and Shalmes, with such a rout and shew, that it was to the great wonderment and terror both of the Frenchmen, and of all other that did heare and behold the sight."

The rigging, the sail furled to the yard, and the two braces are so clearly shown as to need no comment. But two other points are of considerable interest to us. Firstly, notice that the rudder, on the starboard side, is almost identical with that of the Gogstad ship. From the hull projects a bracket to support the rudder, while above, the tiller or *clavus* fits in at right angles and comes inboard to the helmsman. Secondly, notice that the two men forward are getting up the anchor and that the cable

FIG. 38. SEAL OF HASTINGS (THIRTEENTH CENTURY).

leads aft to a winch—probably a great wooden drum like that found on the Dutch schuyts of to-day—for the two men in the stern are clearly shown working away with their handspikes, which would fit into the windlass drum in the manner the reader will notice any day he likes to take a stroll and look at the Dutch craft lying off Billingsgate. In a few moments the ship will be under way, for one of the crew has been sent aloft to unfurl the sail. The fighting-top is not shown on this seal, but that

151

is possibly accounted for by the fact that the artist was cramped for space. Winchelsea, or as Hakluyt speaks of it, "Frigmare Ventus"—and not inaptly so-called, as those who have been caught in the nasty chilly squalls off this ancient shore will agree—was one of the original five Cinque Ports before the others were added, and in the time of Edward I. had to provide ten ships, though during the reign of the third Edward this was increased to twenty-one with five hundred and ninety-six mariners.

Fig. 38 has been drawn from the seal of Hastings in the British Museum. The date is the thirteenth century, and although no forecastle is shown, the erection in the stern scarcely requires any further comment. The high stem and stern are seen again, and what is of considerable interest, the three rows of reef-points. This seal depicts an incident in one of the many engagements that took place about this time along the coast between Beachy Head and the North Foreland. Both ships, it will be noticed, are sailing, and one has rammed his enemy and cut his ship down to the water. An unfortunate warrior is seen swimming in the foreground of the picture. On the banners at bow and stern of the victorious ship are shown the arms of the Cinque Ports. All three warriors are seen clad in mail.

The seal of Dover, another of the Cinque Ports, of the date of 1284, bears out the general characteristics we have been discussing. The castles at bow, stern and top of mast: the trumpeters—this time at the bows: the two men getting in the cable: the one man going aloft to unfurl the sail—these details are all depicted. Both Dover and Sandwich seals contain a bowsprit after the manner of that seen in the Roman merchant ship moored alongside the quay in Fig. 21. It is therefore probable that a small square sail was used occasionally at this time for tilting the ship's head off the wind.

The model by Mr. Frank H. Mason, R.B.A., repro-

152

duced in Fig. 39, was in the Franco-British Exhibition and is now in the South Kensington Museum. It may perhaps assist the reader to obtain a more living picture of the ships of the thirteenth and fourteenth centuries. The castles will be at once recognised. Frequently the sail was decorated as shown. The detachable " bonnet," still used by the sailors of Scandinavia and Norfolk, can just be seen below the decoration. The steering oar, or rudder, is attached to the starboard side, but the reader can just see the handle coming up. The massive wooden fenders were both to strengthen the ship and for a protection when going alongside an enemy. Since so frequently the same ship that was used for fishing or trading was also employed as a battleship or even pirate, the unwieldy, top-heavy castles were made so as to allow of them being removed in times of peace. The ship before us probably represents one of the larger, esnecca type, and the snake's head coming inboard from the stern-post is very noticeable.

From the mast-head of the commander-in-chief's ship by day flew a banner, and by night a lantern hung in order to direct the sailing of the fleet. The officers of the Cinque Ports were ordered to cut adrift the banner of a hostile commander in an engagement, so that the whole of the enemy's fleet might be thrown into confusion. Before the close of Henry II.'s reign another crusade was undertaken, but the ships of the Southern sea seem to have reached to larger dimensions by now. There is a record of a ship built in Venice for France in the year 1268. She was 110 feet long, 40 feet broad, and 11½ feet deep in the hold. She had also 6½ feet of head-room on her main deck. Her crew totalled 110 officers and men, and she was of about four or five hundred tons burthen.* The English ships had another opportunity of testing their sea-going qualities in the Mediterranean, for

* "Social England," edited by H. D. Traill, D.C.L., and J. S. Mann, M.A., London, 1901. See article by W. Laird Clowes, vol. i. p. 589.

during a storm in the year 1270 the English squadron was the only part of the allied fleet that escaped without loss.

During Henry II.'s reign the magnet seems to have been first commonly used in navigation. From an old MS. in Corpus Christi College Cambridge we see the derivation of that anchor which is also freely used by balloons nowadays and which seamen find extremely useful when dragging for a lost anchor or cable—the grapnel with its several flukes projecting from a common centre. The MS. mentioned illustrates a sea-fight, and sailors are seen keeping the enemy's galley close alongside by means of one of these anchors or grappling irons. The other anchors, as will have already been noticed by the reader in the illustration of the warship by Giotto's pupil in Fig. 35, were stockless.

Edward I.'s charter, granted to the Cinque Ports, ordained that each time the king passed over the sea the Cinque Ports should " rigge up fiftie and seven ships " every one of which was to be manned with twenty armed soldiers. These were to be maintained at the ports' own cost for fifteen days together. In this charter we come across the expression, so familiar to us now, " before the mast." Thus it adds : " And that they be free of all their owne wines for which they do travaile of our right prise, that is to say, of one tunne before the mast, and of another behind the maste."

About the time of Edward I. two-masted ships became more general. One of the first acts of his reign was to revive the wool trade between England and Flanders: this necessarily made for the extension and progression of shipping. Fig. 40 represents the seal of the town of Dam in West Flanders. The actual date of the seal in the British Museum, from which this has been drawn, is 1309, or two years after the death of Edward I. This represents one of the larger or barge class of ships. The most striking feature is her apparent modernity, for if we were to remove the fore- and stern-castles and rig her as a ketch by adding a mizzenmast and triangular head sails we should have before us one of those black traders which even the

FIG. 40. SEAL OF DAM (WEST FLANDERS) (A.D. 1309).

most casual observer must have looked at many times during his summer holidays by the sea. She marks a very decided departure now from the Viking type, but we must remember that she represents only one species of ship. The prevailing type elsewhere in Northern Europe continued to be a modification of the Norwegian. The ship before us would be rigged with the usual single squaresail. Perhaps also she used a smaller square head-sail occasionally, as the bowsprit is present, but the most important feature of all is the change that has come in the

155

steering arrangement. Hitherto we have always seen the rudder at the side; but now we get to that stage where the rudder is placed at the extreme stern of the ship, where it has remained ever since. Such a ship as this in the North Sea would be no doubt the counterpart of the Mediterranean *buzzo* of the same century. I believe this ship of Dam (spelt also Damme) to be the earliest illustration of any North European vessel showing the rudder thus placed, although the seal of Poole dated 1325 has her rudder also in this position. The Viking ships of Norway did not adopt this steering method until the beginning of the fourteenth century also. In England there is an additional example in a man-of-war built for Edward III. at Lynn, Norfolk, in 1336. She was named *La Félipe.* It is worth remembering that it was off Damme that the English fleet in the reign of John inflicted a severe defeat upon the French.

The ship shown in the Poole seal marks another development in the fore- and stern-castles, which by now appear to be not so much superstructures as part of the hull itself. We shall see as we continue through the ensuing centuries how this " castle " idea increases. Another point of interest exhibited in the Poole design is a large anchor hanging from the bows. This now has a stock in the usual place as distinct from that in the illustration by Giotto's pupil. This Dorset craft has some resemblance to the previous Viking type, but instead of being after the pattern of the " longships " she shows the tendency towards crescent-shape. As evidence that the pure Viking influence was still extant in Europe let us take the seal of San Sebastian, Spain, which is to be seen in the British Museum. The date is 1335, and it is remarkable that this type should have spread so far south as the other side of the Bay of Biscay. She has the high stem and stern with a stern-castle, but not a forecastle. She has one mast with a streamer, the sail being furled by two men along the yard

156

as usual.   The mariner steers with a rudder to starboard, and the braces as well as the bowsprit are shown.

In the reign of Edward III. the current gold coin called a noble showed a ship-design still more crescent-shaped than the Poole seal.   By now the sterncastle has come right down on deck, the rudder hung on pintles is seen at the extreme stern, and the back stays lead not into the hull but to the top of the sterncastle.   The actual length on the water-line is much smaller now and the overhang greater.   The date of the noble is 1360.   An imitation of this coin, and bearing a similar ship, was struck by David II. of Scotland in 1357.*   In the seal of Boston belonging to the year 1375 the sterncastle is seen to have come down to the deck, the sheer of the ship coming up, so to speak, to meet it.   The forecastle has also come lower, but projects away ahead of the vessel. There are three masts and three fighting-tops, and the shrouds come outside of the hull.   Edward III. admirably continued the example of the kings of England and helped forward the steady improvement of the navy, while the glorious victory in the Battle of Sluys, in which the French fleet was utterly routed, gave the English seamen their opportunity of showing their superiority.

From the " Black Book of the Admiralty " of the reign of Edward III. we see that the admiral's ship carried two lanterns at her masthead when sailing at night in order that the masters of other ships of the fleet could see the course being taken by the flagship.   The king's ship was to be distinguished by three lanterns arranged triangular-wise.   As to the armament of this period, they consisted of bows and arrows, archers from the fighting-tops and castles at bow and stern being able by means of their

* See " Handbook to the Coins of Great Britain and Ireland in the British Museum," London, 1899.

The Edward III. coin will be found to be reproduced on all the publications of the Navy Records Society.

superior height to do considerable damage. Cannon were introduced in 1338, and before the close of the fourteenth century guns and gunpowder were becoming common, but the influence which cannon had on the design of ships we shall notice presently.

Nor did the enterprising spirit imbued through the Crusades perish. As early as 1344 an Englishman, of the name of Macham, sailed as far south as to discover the Island of Madeira, but unfortunately his lady-love had fallen a victim to sea-sickness during the voyage, and after going ashore with some of his company, the ship either dragged her anchor or parted her cable and " with a good winde made saile away, and the woman died for thought." However, after building a chapel over her grave, Macham, according to the account of Antonio Galvano given in Hakluyt, " ordeined a boat made of one tree (for there be trees of a great compasse about) and went to sea in it, with those men that he had, and were left behinde with him, and came upon the coast of Afrike, without sail or oare." It was the information given by Macham and his men that induced the French to voyage thither and also to discover the Canary Isles.

In 1360 Nicholas of Lynn, " a Franciscan Frier, and an excellent Mathematician of Oxford," a good astronomer and experienced in the use of the astrolabe, " went in companie with others to the most Northern Islands of the world, and there, leaving his company together, hee travailed alone, and purposely described all the Northerne Islands with the indrawing seas." We get some idea of the speed of the ships of olden days by the statement made that from Lynn (Norfolk) to Iceland is not more than a fortnight's voyage with an ordinary wind. Reckoning the distance between the two as roughly a thousand miles this would give the day's run at about seventy miles. It was from this same Lynn that sixteen ships and 382 mariners were contributed to the enormous fleet of English ships

158

which Edward III. had in 1347, when he besieged Calais. Some idea of the development that had gone on since Arthur's time may be obtained when we recollect that the English ships at Calais numbered 700 and the mariners over 14,000, without including the assistance of Ireland, Spain, and other helpers.

We pass over the reign of Richard II. as being anything but prosperous for the progress of the sailing ship. His successor, Henry IV., however, entered into commercial treaties with Prussia and the Hanseatic League, much to the advantage of shipping. Piracy had become so rampant on the North Sea as to cause merchants to abstain from sending their goods across from the one country to another. This Henry did his best to stop. He endeavoured to remove all hindrances to the herring fishery, and all English merchants were to have full liberty to arrive with their goods and ships at any port in Prussia. The list of claims for satisfaction and recompense set forth in the agreement between Henry IV. and the Hanseatic Towns throws a light on the ships of the time. Thus we find reference to "a ship of Newcastle upon Tine called *Godezere* . . . being of the burthen of two hundred tunnes . . . which ship together with the furniture thereof amounteth unto the value of foure hundred pounds." Mention is also made of the *Shipper Berline of Prussia*, belonging to the port of Hull; of a ship called the *Cogge*, belonging to William Terry of Hull, carrying a cargo of both broad and narrow cloth. Another ship from the same port was called the *Trinitie*; another bore the name of the *Hawkin Derlin of Dantzik*. Among other acts of piracy, that perpetrated near Plymouth on "a certaine barge called the *Michael of Yarmouth*," is mentioned. Another vessel, braving superstition, bears the name *Friday*, another which was robbed of her "artillerie, furniture, and salt fishes," and herself captured and taken to Norway, was named the *Margaret*. A similar misfortune had happened

159

to the *Nicholas* and also to the *Isabel*. Other unfortunate vessels included the *Helena*; a certain ship classed as a "crayer," and named the *Peter;* and two fishing vessels called respectively the *Doggership* and the *Peter of Wiveton.* Another fishing ship also called the *Dogger* was robbed of her fish and "furniture," while she was at anchor and her crew were fishing near by. Another "crayer" is mentioned called the *Buss of Zeland,* and still a further one called the *Busship.* One ship was of 300 tons burthen—this being measured by tuns of wine—and carried a crew of forty-five.

Other ships of the following reign were the *Jesus* (1000 tons), the *Holigost* (760 tons), the *Trinity Royal* (540 tons), and the *Christopher Spayne* (600 tons). In the navy were also seven caracks, barges (see Fig. 40), as well as the "ships" that had taken the place of the Viking galley. The largest caracks were between six and five hundred tons burthen, the barges a hundred tons, whilst a class of vessel called "ballingers,"* ranged between one hundred and twenty, and eighty tons. It was during Henry V.'s reign also that, the Battle of Agincourt having been fought, the king set forth two years later from Southampton for a fresh invasion of France, having caused to be built for this purpose ships the like of which was to be found nowhere, "naves quales non erant in mundo," as the old chronicler quoted by Hakluyt expresses it.

"The Libel of English policie, exhorting all England to keepe the sea," contains in the following rhyme some references to the vessels we are considering :

> And if I should conclude all by the King
> Henrie the fift, what was his purposing,
> Whan at Hampton he made the great dromons,
> Which passed other great ships of all the commons:
> The Trinitie, the Grace de Dieu, the Holy Ghost,
> And other moe, which as nowe bee lost. . . . .

* Ballingers were long, low vessels for oars and sails, introduced in the fourteenth century by Biscayan builders.

FIG. 34. LADING ARMS AND WINE.
From the Bayeux Tapestry.

FIG. 51. ELIZABETHAN MAN-OF-WAR.   p. 169

FIG. 39. THIRTEENTH CENTURY ENGLISH SHIP. *p.* 161.

or again :

> And when Harflew had her siege about,
> There came caracks horrible great and stoute. . . .

The reign of Henry VI., at least as regards ship-building, was about as unsatisfactory as had been that of Richard II., owing to the scarcity of money consequent on the war with France. Further, the unhappy Wars of the Roses kept men's minds too tightly gripped to allow of them thinking much about commerce or the ships that were to carry it. But towards the close of Edward IV.'s reign, after peace had been made between England and France, matters began quickly to improve, and in the time of Richard III. England was sending her ships and merchandise to Venice, to Genoa and other Mediterranean ports.

But let us now go back to trace a little more fully the designs of the ships according to the illustrations that have survived through history. Firstly with regard to Southern Europe. The Mediterranean had still maintained her lead in the designing and building of able, roomy vessels. Happily we are helped by the work which one or two Italian painters have left behind them. There is a most interesting picture by Gentile da Fabriano, representing a ship of the early fifteenth century. The original which is in the Vatican is called " The Miracle of St. Nicholas." * She is a fine, strong ship, with a square stern and rudder fixed to the middle of the latter. She has two masts as well as a bowsprit, and the hull is somewhat crescent-shaped The artist has depicted her scudding before a terrific storm, which has split the mainsail along the foot where the bonnet seems to be laced. Evidently the ship has been caught in one of those sudden squalls not unknown to the Mediterranean, for otherwise the skipper ought not to have

* See "Gentile da Fabriano," p. 134, by Arduino Colasanti, Bergamo 1909.

carried on so long without unlacing the bonnet. At the stern he is seen praying to St. Nicholas who appears in the clouds coming to his assistance, while amidships a sailor is seen jettisoning some of the cargo. The forecastle resembles that of contemporary English ships with a projecting bowsprit. The mizzen-mast and sail are clearly shown, the latter being furled to its yard as the ship is running before the wind. Pulleys are now prominently indicated, whilst a couple of braces are attached both to the main and mizzen-yard, while the mainsheet leads right aft to the starboard quarter and comes in through a hole in the gunwale pretty much in the same way adopted in a square-rigged ship to-day. Two rope ladders are shown, one at either side, hanging down over the stern, evidently in order to facilitate getting into the ship's boat (seen towing astern) if the ship herself shall founder. A fighting-top is depicted at her masthead. The picture is altogether most fascinating and instructive.

Carpaccio, the great Venetian artist, whose period is covered by the dates 1450–1522, has left behind more pictures containing ships than any artist of his time. There is in one of his paintings a striking example of a contemporary Mediterranean warship. She is shown as having a main-mast with square sail and very small topsail. Aft she has both a mizzen-mast and bonaventure-mizzen, each carrying a lateen sail. She is fitted also with a small foresail, spritsail, and carries eight oars on each side.* Like Memlinc and other artists, Carpaccio utilises the celebrated story of "The Pilgrimage of St. Ursula," for some of his best work. It is, indeed, owing to this story, necessitating the introduction of ships into the picture, that we possess much of our knowledge concerning mediæval craft. For instance, in "The Arrival of the Ambassadors," in "The Return of the Ambassadors," in "The Arrival at Cologne," and "St. Ursula taking farewell of her parents," we have

* See Fig. 37 in "Navi Venete."

presented many valuable details bearing on our subject of sailing ships. We see a small open boat in the first of these pictures. She has a tiller and one large single lateen sail, coming almost down to the water. In the background we see the big ship in which the ambassadors have travelled. She has a high poop, one mast and square mainsail. In the second picture we see a Mediterranean galley with her enormous sail. She still retains her name " trireme," and it is remarkable how generally she continues to resemble her Roman ancestor. In the last of the four pictures mentioned above, we see a large ship resembling somewhat the caravel type.*

The most famous of all the works of that delightful Flemish painter Memlinc is the reliquary of St. Ursula. Those who saw the wonderful collection of " Primitives " brought together in Bruges in the year 1902 will recollect the eight exquisite miniatures on the reliquary. Happily no less than four of these contain representations of the ships in which St. Ursula and her accompanying maidens journeyed. The date assigned by Mr. Weale † to these paintings is not later than 1489. In Fig. 41 one of these panels is reproduced. We cannot regard these Memlinc pictures of ships as absolutely truthful: some allowance must be made for the artistic temperament. There is, for instance, no indication of any braces shown in the illustration. But Bruges is not far from the sea, and during the fifteenth century it was the great centre of commercial activity of the prosperous Hanse towns, and Memlinc would have plenty of opportunity to study the details of contemporary craft. It may fairly be assumed that in spite of a small inaccuracy here and there the general drawing of the ships is nautically correct. From other pictures and MSS. and stained glass windows of this time

* See "The Life and Works of Vittorio Carpaccio," by Pompeo Molmenti and Gustav Ludwig, London, 1907.

† "Hans Memlinc," p. 46, by W. H. James Weale, London, 1901.

we know that this is so. Looking at the picture before us
we see at once how the Viking lines have been modified.
The forecastle and sterncastles are seen in their latest
form: that is to say, they have long since passed the time
when they were mere additional structures to the hull of the
ship. They have, in fact, now been absorbed into the
general design of the whole vessel. There is still one mast
supported by backstays, shrouds, and forestays, and there
is one large mainsail which furls still to the yard. The
lines of the ship are tubby, but we can easily see the pro-
genitors of the Dutch craft which went on developing
until the sixteenth and seventeenth centuries and there
halted for ever after. Notice, too, that the rudder is in
its proper place. Such a ship as this resembles in many
points the one in " The Miracle of St. Nicholas " referred
to above. The length of the Viking ship has given way
to breadth. Roundness has taken the place of straight-
ness: free board has added to her seaworthiness. We
shall find this evidence before us confirmed by a certain
mediæval Italian illustration * in which a Mediterranean
ship is being tossed mercilessly about by the Wind, who,
with inflated cheeks raises his head above the water and
blows vigorously into the sails. Men are seen tumbling
into the sea, the mainmast has gone by the board, and
general confusion reigns. A somewhat similar kind of
ship is also seen in a reproduction from a stained glass
window of this period. †

In a beautiful French manuscript of the fifteenth
century similar ships to those in Memlinc's work are shown
with considerable ability.‡ Perhaps these French vessels

* Reproduced in " Navi Venete," Fig. 96.
† See " Musée Rétrospectif de la Classe 33," &c.
‡ This MS. has been carefully reproduced in "Monuments et Mémoires,"
par Georges Perrot and Robert de la Steyrie. Tome onzième. See article
on " Un Manuscrit de la Bibliothèque de Philippe le bon à Saint-Pétersbourg," Paris, 1904.

FIG. 41. PANEL OF THE SHRINE OF ST. URSULA, AFTER MEMLINC (1489).

show the Viking influence somewhat more certainly, especially in their bows. We are shown in one illustration a scene of the river Seine at Rouen. A ship with a stern-castle, now modified rather to a square platform, is seen by the shore. She appears to be carvel- and not clinker-built; this is a notable fact. She has shrouds at the sides, a forestay, and also an additional stay coming forward from the mast to a spot midway between amidships and the bow. This may have been in the original ship to act as a further support to the sail or it may only be the product of the artist's imagination. If the former it would be analogous to the lee-runner but placed forward, and must have chafed the sail a good deal. The latter is furled to the yard in the usual way. We see in the same MS. ships starting forth bound for the Crusades. They are fine, bold vessels, broad of beam, with plenty of freeboard, clumsy but probably good sea-boats. These French craft appear to have a certain amount of overhang at the bows and some of them carry a large fighting-top, partly supported by means of a stay coming up from both bow and stern.

Such seals as the following throw light on the ships of England in the fifteenth century. That, for instance, of Richard Clitherowe, Admiral of the West of England, 1406, shows a decorated sail and flies an ensign at her stern. The reason for this flag being always placed aft lies in the fact that the raised poop was the place of honour reserved for the commander. Similar ships are seen in such seals as those of Thomas Beaufort, Duke of Exeter, Admiral of England, Aquitaine and Ireland (1416–1426): John Duke of Bedford, Regent of France, Lord High Admiral of England, Ireland and Aquitaine (1435): John Holland, second Earl of Huntingdon, Admiral of England, Ireland and Aquitaine (1435–1442). This last seal shows the Admiral's lantern hanging over the poop. Similar ships may be seen in the seal of Richard Plantagenet, third Duke of Gloucester, Admiral for Dorset and Somerset (1461–1462); in the seal of Rutherglen (co. Lanark), 1493; in that of the English merchants of Holland—a fifteenth century seal found at Harrow and now

FIG. 42. SEAL OF LA ROCHELLE (A.D. 1437).

in the British Museum—and in various others of this period. Their general characteristics include a crescent-shaped hull with forecastle and sterncastle, fighting-top, sail decorated with the arms of France and England, &c., forestay, two backstays, and a rudder at stern. The seal of Rye, belonging to the fifteenth century, shows three rows of reef-points, an ensign with the cross of St. George as well as streamers on the mast. Fig. 42 represents the seal of La Rochelle of the date 1437. It is interesting as showing that while in England, in Damme, in Paris (see the seal of the city of Paris of the year 1415) and else-

167

where, the crescent-shaped ship with castles was in vogue, this town kept strenuously to the original Viking type. The bonnet with three rows of reefs is clearly indicated, and similarly the sheets and stays.

We referred just now to the introduction of cannon as affecting the design of ships. At first they were placed on the upper deck and fired over the bulwarks, a modified pavisado of cloths or wood being hung round to conceal both guns and gunners. Next it was but an easy transition to make a hole through the bulwarks and insert the cannon. Hence we have the origin of the word "gun-wale" for the top "wale" or plank. Subsequently this introduction of cannon necessitated a much higher free-board, and in course of time tier above tier of guns, as in former times there had been tier above tier of rowers, came into being. Owing to the weight of the guns so far aloft an increase of beam became essential, but afterwards the exact opposite occurred. Lest the beams should be strained, considerable tumble-home or fall-inboard was made, so that the width of the upper deck became only about half of the greatest beam.* We shall see, too, how in later years this "tumble-home" was greatly exaggerated. As to the effect of the new armament on a ship's rig, we shall be able to discuss this when we come to the bomb-ketch in Fig. 62.

We have seen how the ships of England have developed into the crescent-shape by now. That, indeed, continued for some time, until the fashion came for bigger and more powerful ships under the Tudor *régime.* Practically with the end of the fifteenth century we bid farewell to the Viking influence as clearly expressed, although it were perhaps more correct to say that that design was not so much discarded in later years as absorbed : enlarged upon and modified rather than altogether supplanted. The first

* See "Ancient and Modern Ships," p. 74, by Sir G. C. V. Holmes, London, 1900.

important addition to the Viking design was that of the fighting castles. From thence it was not a great step to add decks, guns instead of bows and arrows, two masts instead of one, and an increase of beam and subsequently of depth.

CHAPTER VI.

THE DEVELOPMENT OF THE SAILING SHIP FROM THE TIME OF HENRY VII. TO THE DEATH OF QUEEN ELIZABETH (1485–1603).

E enter now upon a period that will always be memorable for the impetus given to maritime matters, and the consequent improvement that took place in sailing ships of all kinds. In the history of the latter there are two centuries that have witnessed the greatest developments in the production of that most beautiful of all things that man ever set himself to fashion out of wood or iron. The first of these eras was the sixteenth century, and the other was the nineteenth. But before we begin to consider the sixteenth, let us briefly sum up all that had been effected by the end of the fifteenth.

We have seen how the early type that prevailed so long in England was that of the Vikings, whilst in the Mediterranean the galley and carack were collateral kinds of craft. Whilst it is true that after the Crusades England did eventually begin to build real ships, yet long before this time out of the ports of Venice, Genoa and Barcelona were sailing big carrving ships of three decks and of several hundred tons burthen. Of enormous free-board, the carack and caravel were more able to encounter bad weather and to remain in commission both winter and summer. Able, too, to carry considerable quantities of merchandise and large numbers of passengers with a fair chance of making port in safety, they were from the first destined to become the ideal ship for the trader in prefer-ence to the galley. In war-time the galley was more handy because she could be manœuvred quickly with oars. But the carack and caravel, when guns were intro-duced, instantly exercised an undisputed superiority in another respect, for they could carry larger and more numerous cannon, and had the commanding advantage of height, though they were in comparison with the galleys decidedly cumbrous. Slow in stays, top-heavy and decidedly uncomfortable, pitching into every sea, they were far from the ideal. Thus the galley (or its cousin the galleass) remained in existence for fighting, as distinct from merchant service, side by side until after the Armada. An effort was made to re-introduce the galley in the English Navy under Charles II., but though the galley flourished in the Mediterranean until the eighteenth century, it was doomed in England gradually but surely from the beginning of the fourteenth century.

The Viking-like ships of England had gradually under-gone important changes. Alfred had tried the experiment of building them of greater displacement, and this increase in size had gone on steadily after the time of William the Conqueror. Moreover, as we have seen, the development of the forecastle and sterncastle had prepared the English sailors for the logical outcome of these—the ship with two or three decks. At first a mere light scaffolding, castel-lated at the top and capable of being affixed to a merchant-ship on the declaration of war, these castles had in the march of time assumed a more permanent character. Instead of being mere supports lashed together, the framework became more solid, and the design of the ship was adapted to suit these structures—the sweep of the hull, as we have seen, coming up to meet the platform, which steadily became lower and lower and projected less forward until both fore- and stern-castle were essential portions of the vessel.

But besides the knowledge that our forefathers had gained through studying the ships in the Mediterranean at the time of the Crusades and after, owing to the large carrying trade, some of the big ships from the three Mediterranean ports just mentioned were in the habit of coming into English waters with their merchandise of gold, silks and spices. Their stay here would not be too short for our shipwrights to study their build and architecture. Here was a new kind of ship that but few had ever seen. Their cargo capacity and high freeboard, and the fact that they held a crew numerous enough to fight pirates on even terms would instantly appeal to those who had eyes to see. As soon as ever peace at home gave a sufficient encouragement, shipbuilding was bound to go ahead on these larger lines. Henry V., too, had actually in his navy some Genoese ships of this type, and by the middle of the fifteenth century merchant ships of 100 tons were not rare, and some of even 300 tons were in existence, and trading to the Mediterranean, the Baltic and Iceland. The galley was fast disappearing, and instead of the one-masted ship, by the end of the fifteenth century a big vessel of 800 tons with four masts and a bowsprit began to be built.

The evolution of the number of masts was on this wise. When the single mast was multiplied two things happened. In the Mediterranean the additional mast forward of the main-mast had become the *mât de misaine* (Italian *mezzana*=foresail), or foremast. In Northern Europe the mast was added aft, but nevertheless called mizzen—still another instance of the confusion that has existed in nautical nomenclature. We know from the

172

illustrations on old manuscripts of this period that vessels possessed as many as three and four masts, and this is further confirmed by the inventories still extant of Henry VII.'s ships. The same evidence proves the introduction by now of topmasts as fixed though separate spars. There is even one instance of a topgallant mast. Instead, therefore, of the old rig consisting of one large sail on the one mast there is—reckoning from forward to the stern—a spritsail on the bowsprit, a squaresail on the fore and main masts with one small topsail on each of these two masts, and a lateen or triangular-shaped sail on a yard, but with no boom of course, hoisted up the mizzen-mast. The spritsail was a squaresail on a yard lowered from the end of the bowsprit. If the reader will look at the illustration in Fig. 46 he will see a badly drawn, but none the less interesting, illustration of a carack of the beginning of the sixteenth century. The ship in the foreground is the *Cordelière.* Though much of the bow end is not shown, there is sufficient to indicate how the fore- and stern-castles have come down to be part of the hull, and how the latter has been increased in length. The three masts will also be seen, though the bowsprit is not shown. The castellated structures have become large, roomy cabins. Guns will be seen on both the lower and main decks. It was about the end of the fifteenth century, also, that portholes were introduced, and the tiers in forecastle and poop reached as many as three. The guns in the ships of Henry VII. were serpentines, breach-loading, using lead, stone or iron ball. From the tops, picked men still hurled javelins or shot arrows from their bows on to the enemy's decks below.

When Henry VII. ascended the English throne, the first real effort in the direction of an adequate national navy was made. It was a critical moment. The country's finances had been drained by the long-drawn out Wars of the Roses, so that her navy had been utterly and grievously neglected. Notwithstanding that under Henry V. it had

increased to unprecedented strength—including as it did
as many as thirty-eight vessels ranging from 400 to 600
tons—yet on the death of this fifth Henry the thirty odd
ships that remained were, disgraceful to relate, sold out of
the service, and by 1430 the English Navy comprised only
two or three dismantled hulks.* It is true that Henry V.
had been at great pains to build ships, and Southampton
Water and Hamble, the pretty little village on the river
of the same name, were in those days as interested in his
ships of war as to-day they are in the industry which
yachting brings to both of these places. It is true, also,
that Edward IV. had at various times during his reign
bought some ships, including the *Grace à Dieu* and *Mary
of the Tower*, and the *Martin Garsia*, and that his successor, Richard III., had added to these three by the
purchase of the *Governor*. These four indeed came into
the possession of Henry VII. on his accession, but though
the administration in his reign represented an effort
rather than a complete reorganisation, yet it marked an
important advance. He prepared the way for his successor
Henry VIII., and showed his keen interest in the navy
and maritime matters generally. But his especial good
deed consisted in the building of two warships which were
a considerable advance on any the country had previously
possessed. Of these the *Regent*, of 600 tons, was inspired
by French naval architecture. She was built on the
Rother about 1490 and carried 225 serpentines. These
guns were not of much avail in penetrating the enemy's
sides, but they would be efficacious in destroying his sails
and rigging and in sending a sweeping fire over his decks.
She had a foremast, foretopmast, mainmast, maintopmast
and main topgallant mast, main mizzen and bonaventure

* "Naval Accounts and Inventories of the Reign of Henry VII.," edited
by M. Oppenheim, Navy Records Society, 1896. I wish to acknowledge
my indebtedness to this valuable volume for much information in connection with Henry VII.'s ships.

mizzen.* Both mizzen-masts, having lateen sails, were without topmasts. From the bowsprit, as already described, there was a spritsail. This, as we saw in Chapter III., had its origin in the Roman ships. I think there can be little doubt but that the spritsail was the lineal descendant of the artemon. It was scarcely very wonderful that it survived so long, seeing that the galleys had remained but little altered since classical times. We must not forget that the rig of the squaresail ship originated in the Mediterranean, so that the spritsail would come most naturally to the aid of the ship for her head canvas. Similarly the lateen, being everywhere seen on the Mediterranean and Nile—on feluccas and dhows alike—would be found at hand for the after canvas. The preference for a lateen sail for the mizzen was based on the reason that such a sail will hold a better wind—will sail at least a point closer to the breeze. Its position in the stern was to facilitate the steering. The *Regent's* topmasts and topgallant mast were separate spars fixed to the lower mast but could not be lowered or raised. The topgallant mast had a sail but no yard. It was not till many years after that the topgallant sails had yards. Mr. Masefield states that the topgallant sail began like a modern moonraker, *i.e.* a triangular piece of canvas, setting from truck to the yard-arm of the topsail yard immediately below.†

The *Sovereign* was of a similar type, though smaller. She had two decks in the forecastle, two in the summer-castle, and in the topgallant poop. What the summer-castle exactly was cannot be discovered, but Mr. Oppenheim suggests the very probable theory that it was the poop royal. At any rate it commanded an all-round fire

---

* In the Middle Ages it was the custom to refer to the masts of a ship possessing four in the manner as above. The after-most was the bonaventure.

† "On the Spanish Main," by John Masefield, London, 1906. See chap. xvi., on "Ships and Rigs."

and carried many guns. We shall see as we proceed how strong the tendency was in the sixteenth century to raise the poop to enormous heights. The *Sovereign* had no main topgallant mast as the *Regent* possessed. All the armament of both ships was carried in the waist, in the decks of the summercastle and poop, but there was no real gun-deck. With all this top-hamper, there is no wonder that the *Santa Maria*, Columbus' ship, pitched so terribly. But in spite of the guns, a considerable part of the fighting was entrusted to the archers. Mr. Oppenheim mentions that the *Sovereign* had on board 200 bows and 800 sheaves of arrows, and but small quantities of gunpowder and lead.

When the *Regent* and *Sovereign* were launched at the end of the fifteenth century the sensation which they caused can scarcely have been inferior to that in our own times made by the launch of the *Dreadnought* and *Bellerophon*. The country had never produced such ships before in size and equipment. But just as it would have been impossible for our builders or designers to have suddenly brought a *Dreadnought* into being, so in the case of the *Sovereign* and the *Regent* what was seen was the result of gradual progress. The fifteenth century shipwrights and architects had step by step been feeling their way to higher achievements, and had the Wars of the Roses never occurred there can be little doubt but that these big ships would have been launched in an earlier reign.

The standards flown by the ships of this period were of white linen cloth, with red crosses of " say " (*i.e.*, woollen cloth). The streamers with which they were wont to decorate their vessels in a somewhat profuse manner were also of linen cloth or " say." The *Regent* had no gilding or carving, except a gilt crown. Nor was any great expense made on the score of paint, for we find a record of the painting of the *Regent* and another ship called the

FIG. 43. A CARAVEL OF THE END OF THE FIFTEENTH CENTURY.

p. 172

FIG. 44. A FIFTEENTH-CENTURY CARAVEL.

p. 177.

Mary Fortune. The whole job was done by contract for the sum of £2 19s. 10d. The davits, both of this period and for many years after, were used not for hoisting the ship's boats aboard—which was done by means of tackles with poles and sheaves of brass—but for getting up the anchors. There were both fixed davits and movable ones that could be used in different parts of the ship. Most of the timber came from the New Forest and Bere Forest, not far from Portsmouth. Iron was bought by the ton and worked up at the royal forge into nails and spikes, &c.

In 1497 two smaller men-of-war, named respectively the *Sweepstake* and the *Mary Fortune*, were built. But these were much smaller than the other two, and carried three lower masts, a main topmast, as well as a spritsail on the bowsprit. The *Grace à Dieu*, which Henry had inherited on his accession to the throne, was renamed the *Harry Grace à Dieu*. She is said to have cost £14,000, to have had four pole masts, each with a circular top, a bowsprit, a built-up poop and forecastle, as well as two complete and two partial tiers of guns mounted in ports.[*] The late Sir W. Laird Clowes inclined to the belief that the drawing of the *Harry Grace à Dieu* in the Pepysian Library, Cambridge, represents not the ship of the same name built in the reign of Henry VIII., but that of which we are now speaking. By the beginning of Henry VIII.'s reign she had either disappeared or was known under a new name.

It was for a long time the custom of English monarchs in times of peace to let out on hire the royal ships to merchants. Nor did Henry VII. break away from this practice. Apart altogether from the importance which big ships possessed from a naval point of view, it was a profitable speculation to build large vessels. Merchants were glad to hire them, since it saved the necessity of

---

[*] See article by W. Laird Clowes in vol. ii. of Traill and Mann's "Social England," London, 1901.

having to build for themselves or of keeping them in commission when their voyages were ended. The larger the tonnage of the ship the more popular were they to the hirers, for the reason that they not only held more cargo and were less likely to succumb to pirates, but that they could voyage to virgin fields where trade could be established. Henry, in addition to the ships he had inherited and built, also hired some himself, both from his subjects and the Spanish. He even went so far as to purchase some vessels from the latter, but Spain eventually legislated to prevent Spanish-owned ships from being sold to foreign Powers.

We find references in the naval accounts of this reign to caulking with "ocum"; also to the "crane line," which led from the sprit mast to the forestay, and steadied the former. Among the details preserved to us concerning the *Grace à Dieu* we find that she had three bonnets for the mainsail, the lacing that secured the bonnet to the foot of the sail (after the manner adopted by the Vikings) being called "latchetes." There is a considerable similarity between the nautical terms of this period and of our own time. Corks were used for buoying anchors; "deadmen's eyes" (deadeyes, as we now call them, through which the lanyards of the shrouds are passed), "painters" (Mr. Oppenheim derives this familiar word from the old French *pantiere*, meaning a noose); hawse, used in its old sense, to mean the bows of a vessel—hence our modern expression "athwart hawse," meaning across the bows— these, as well as others, were in daily use among sailormen. We find mention of the fact that the *Grace à Dieu* had "a shefe (*i.e.*, a sheave or pulley-wheel) of brasse in the bootes halse." There were not always bulwarks or rails to ships of this age, and sometimes before going into action a cable was coiled round about the deck breast high in the waist, bedding and mattresses being also requisitioned as protection against the enemy's fire.

178

As to other details of equipment, we have mention of these ships possessing running glasses, *i.e.* sand glasses for the use of the log which time has not even now wholly abolished in spite of the patent log on sailing ships. Outriggers, or as they were called, "outliggers," "bitakles," (*i.e.*, binnacles), "merlyng irens," (*i.e.*, marlin spikes) were also in use. By 1514 at any rate, the usual length of a sounding line appears to be forty fathoms. There were winches apparently on the *Sovereign*, for we find mention of the "wheles for to wynde up the Mayne Sayle." In order that the large square sails should set as flat as possible, bowlines played an important part during this century and after. In the case of very large sails, the weight on the tack was relieved to some extent by adding luff hooks and chains. As will be remarked in the illustration of the *Cordelière*, in Fig. 46, *pavesses*, or wooden shields bearing the devices or coats of arms, were placed along the ship's waist, and sometimes too, on the forecastle and poop. The reader will recognise them as being survivals from the times when the Viking sea-chiefs hung their shields along the bulwarks. At a later stage we shall see these shields giving way to the waist cloth as a protection for this part of the ship.

It was under Henry VII. that the bounty system for encouraging ship-builders was introduced. It was during his reign, too, that Portsmouth Dockyard was founded, and that at this port the first dry dock was built in England, and the *Sovereign* was the first ship known to have gone into it. We find among the Naval Accounts of Henry VII., a record that on the tenth of October in the first year of his reign, the *Grace à Dieu* was docked at Hamble, or, as it was then known, Hamill. But Mr. Oppenheim points out that this docking here meant merely getting the ship high and dry on to the mud and then surrounding her with a fence of brushwood. The popularity which, during the fifteenth century, Hamble had shared with Southampton, was decreasing as soon as ships of the size of the *Regent* and *Sovereign* were built. Perhaps it was owing to the lack of water in this river that the Portsmouth dry dock was made.

All the time the unhappy Wars of the Roses had been wasting England's energy and finances, the people in the south-west corner of Europe were prospering exceedingly. Whilst England was at a standstill as regards development, Spain and Portugal were going rapidly ahead in maritime matters. They had acquired an immense amount of nautical knowledge from the Venetians and Genoese, and until the time came for England to wake up and set her house in order, Portugal was taking the lead in voyages of exploration. When Columbus set forth in 1492 on the voyage that led to the discovery of the West Indies, his fleet comprised his flagship, the *Santa Maria*, and two other caravels named respectively the *Nina* and the *Pinta*. We find that the *Santa Maria* proved to be " a dull sailer and unfit for discovery."[*] This statement is entirely borne out by Captain D. V. Concas.[†] For from historical data, a replica of the *Santa Maria* was built at Carraca by Spanish workmen in 1893, for the Chicago Exhibition. She was sailed across the Atlantic on her own bottom the same year with a Spanish crew. The course taken was exactly that followed by Columbus on his first voyage. The time occupied was thirty-six days, and the maximum speed obtained was about $6\frac{1}{2}$ knots. Captain Concas, who was in charge of her, reported that she pitched horribly. The illustration in Fig. 43 represents a caravel of this period, and will give the reader a general idea of the ships of this time. This

---

[*] See "Christopher Columbus and the New World of his Discovery," by Filson Young, London, 1906. The reader is especially advised to study an admirable article in vol. ii. of this work on "The Navigation of Columbus's First Voyage," by the Earl of Dunraven.

[†] See "Ancient and Modern Ships," by Sir G. C. V. Holmes.

is from a photograph of a model made by Mr. Frank H. Mason, R.B.A., and exhibited in the Franco-British Exhibition of 1908. It has since been presented by Lloyd's to the South Kensington Museum. The colouring of the underbody is quite correct, for we find mention of the "white bellies" of the Spanish ships of the sixteenth century being seen coming over the billows. The yard on the bowsprit for the spritsail should not be shown as a fixture for another hundred years later. The yards of the lower courses will be observed, and two topsails with fighting-tops and the lateen yard will be noticed aft. The rest of the rigging, including the stays and braces, are so clear as to need little comment further, except that the forestay should be provided with crane-lines as in Fig. 45. The *cresset* or lantern is shown in its correct place over the stern. A cresset was, strictly speaking, a hollow vessel for holding a light, and carried upon a pole. The light was produced from a wreathed rope smeared with pitch or rosin. The development now reached by the forecastle, and the tendency to exaggerate the height of the poop which became in Spanish galleons even higher still, are worthy of the reader's attention. Fig. 44 is from a photograph of the caravel model in the Royal United Service Museum, Whitehall. This is by no means an accurate model and is only put forward as an interesting representation of the manner of mounting the guns in these days, and showing how tubby in proportion to their length such ships sometimes were. It shows fairly accurately the proportion also to which the sides of the hull just above the water-line projected as compared with the narrow beam on deck. Whereas we saw in the illustration of the *bucco* in Fig. 35 a fighting-top of slender basket-work, we have now a much more solid structure. No topsails are shown here, but Columbus's ship carried a main-topsail. Mr. Mason's model shows a fore-topsail which was certainly carried on ships of this time, though not on the *Santa Maria*. The

181

Whitehall model should not carry the heavy figurehead, and a bowsprit should of course be shown. The topmasts are also too long. Falconer's "Marine Dictionary" derives the caravel from the Spanish word *caravela* as "a light, round, old-fashioned ship with a square poop, formerly used in Spain and Portugal."* Levi derives the word as from either *carabos*, meaning a kind of lobster, or from *cara-bella*, meaning a beautiful shape, in reference, of course, to the lines of her hull.†

In Fig. 45 will be found a reproduction of what is probably the only accurate model of the *Santa Maria* in existence. This has been constructed by Captain C. E. Terry, who has made it his hobby for some years to gather together every item of information in connection with Columbus's ship. For this purpose he has searched all through Southern Europe in order to collect every detail, and through his courtesy I am enabled for the first time to show this interesting little ship, which the reader may regard as approaching as nearly to accuracy as possible at this late date. The sails with the Papal and Maltese crosses, the flag of Ferdinand and Isabella flying above, the crucifix over the stern, the crane lines, the braces, sheets and other gear may be taken as reliable. The bonnet and drabbler will be found on the mainsail. On deck the brick-made cooking-galley, and the capstan, though not decipherable from the photograph, have been correctly placed. A careful examination of the lead or the gear will explain the rigging more quickly than by detailing every rope individually.

Not all the Spanish ships were rigged with square-sails. Indeed, the lateen sail in the Mediterranean gave way reluctantly to the rectangular shape, as is only natural in the seas so dominated by the felucca rig. Columbus's ship, which was reconstructed according to every known source of information, had of course a lateen

* London, 1830.   † "Navi Venete."

182

Fig. 45. Columbus's Flagship, the "Santa Maria."

FIG. 46. THE FRENCH SHIP "CORDELIÈRE" IN THE FOREGROUND, WITH
THE ENGLISH "REGENT" IN THE BACKGROUND, ON FIRE OFF BREST.

mizzen. She was three-masted, having a square mainsail with topsail of much smaller size, but "goaring" out considerably from a small yard. On the foremast was a square course but no topsail, while from the bowsprit was carried a square spritsail. In Mr. Filson Young's work already referred to, the interesting fact is mentioned that after Columbus and his three ships had set forth they had to put into Grand Canary for a new rudder to be made for the *Pinta*, and that while they were waiting for this to be done the rig of the *Nina* was changed from lateen to squaresail like that of the *Santa Maria*, so that the *Nina* might be able to keep up with the others. For a ship that was about to cross the wide ocean of the Atlantic no sailorman nowadays would dispute this wise proceeding on the part of Columbus. As to the relative size of these ships the *Santa Maria* was of about one hundred tons burthen, 90 feet long and 20 feet beam. Other accounts make her slightly larger, and she carried a crew numbering fifty-two. The *Nina* was a much smaller ship of about forty tons.

Inasmuch as we are studying not so much the history of voyages as of the ships that actually carried the voyagers there is not here the scope to enter into a discussion of the reasons that prompted Columbus to go West. But it may not be out of place to point to the fact that it was no mere haphazard undertaking. We mentioned in an earlier chapter that the Vikings who colonised Iceland in a previous century also sailed further on from there to the American Continent. Now Columbus had visited Iceland and may in all probability have heard of the tradition that there was land to the far west across the seas. As Lord Dunraven mentions, Columbus knew that the world was more or less round, and that consequently the more he sailed West the nearer he would come to the well-known regions of the East. We must remember, too, that for some time the Portuguese and Spaniards had been applying themselves to the study of charts and the science of navigation. Columbus, himself, was a mapmaker, and a man with a scientific mind. But besides all this there was the story of the "unknown pilot," whose ship having been blown from Spain or Portugal across the Atlantic had reached new land. Taking these considerations in conjunction with an age almost bursting with energy, that was thirsting for knowledge only to be obtained through adventure and perseverance, it was inevitable that the New World should be discovered.

As to the navigational instruments Columbus had with him a compass divided into 360° and 32 points as to-day, although the points were named somewhat differently. Nor was he prevented through lack of knowledge from taking observations of the sun. He had a cross-staff, a quadrant and a sea astrolabe. The voyage five years later of John Cabot, an Italian, to the mainland of America with a Bristol ship and Bristol sailors ; of Vasco de Gama doubling the Cape of Good Hope *en route* to India, and of other enterprising and courageous navigators could only have the effect of influencing the subsequent building of ships of greater tonnage and seaworthiness.

One of the largest ships of this time was the French *Cordelière* in Fig. 46. Although it is not quite safe to rely too much on the reported tonnage of these mediæval vessels, hers has been assessed at 700 while the *Regent* and the *Sovereign* have been estimated at 1000 each. Another famous contemporary French ship was the *Grand Louise* of 790 tons. The latter was a four-master. She had pavesses around her like those on the *Cordelière*. Cannon were carried on her deck. Her mainsail was decorated with a shield device, whilst the main-mizzen and the bonaventure mizzen carried lateen-sails. In the illustration just mentioned the *Cordelière* is in the foreground, the ship behind being the *Regent*. While the latter was attacking the French ship off Brest at the beginning of Henry VIII.'s reign both vessels caught fire and became a total loss. Our illustration, which is taken from a MS. in the Bibliothèque Nationale, shows this mournful incident depicted.

Not entirely had the galley disappeared yet. In a warrant dated January 29, 1510,* we find mention of caracks, galleys, row-barges, hulks, barks (great barks and "lesse barks"), ships and crayers. The latter were victualling ships. Thus when the *Sovereign* sailed from Portsmouth she had with her the *Trinity of Wight* (80 tons), the *James of London* (80 tons) and the *Katherine Pomegranate* as her victuallers. We find in this warrant also mentioned "twyne, merling (marlin), ropes, cables, cabletts (these were used for the mainstay), boyes (buoys), lynes, tacks, lists, toppe-armers, stremers, standards, compasses, ronnyng glasses (sand-glasses for the log), lanterns, shevers of bras, poleys, shrowdes" and other "taclyng." The same warrant directs the building of the *Mary Rose* of 400 tons and the *Peter Pomegranate* of 300 tons. The former foundered at Spithead in the year 1545.

It was in 1514 that the famous *Henri Grace à Dieu*, commonly known as the "Great Harry," was built. The custom having recently grown up of passing on the name of an obsolete ship to her successor, and of reserving special names for the largest class and still further of embodying in it the name also of the ruling sovereign, it was but natural that this great "Harry" should be so named. Of the available illustrations of this ship that shown here in Fig. 47 and reproduced from Holbein's painting in Hampton Court Palace, is perhaps the most reliable. The incident depicted is the embarkation of Henry VIII. from Dover, on May 31, 1520, to meet Francis I. at the Field of the Cloth of Gold. Besides this picture there exists another which hung for many years in Canterbury Cathedral, and is supposed to represent this vessel. It was afterwards

* See "Letters and Papers relating to the War with France, 1512–1513," by Alfred Spont, Navy Records Society, 1897.

presented by the Dean to Sir John Norris, Admiral of the Fleet, who died in 1749. In 1750 an engraving was made by Allen, and a copy is to be found in the Print Room of the British Museum. The original of Allen's engraving has been ascribed to Holbein, but it seems pretty certain that this print depicts, not the " Great Harry " of the reign of Henry VIII., but a ship of later date. Nor, as we have mentioned above, does it seem probable that the *Henri Grace à Dieu* in the Pepysian Library represents this vessel.

The *Henri Grace à Dieu* of the time of Henry VIII. had four masts with two decks and topgallant sails on fore, main and main-mizzen masts. On the bonaventure mizzen she carried a topsail above the lateen but no topgallant. The fore and main masts had topsails as well. Happily her inventory is still extant and will be found in Mr. Oppenheim's volume on the administration of the Navy of the reign of Henry VIII.* Her tonnage was 1500, and she represents still another advance in the construction of big ships. Her launching one day in the middle of June had been a memorable ceremony, in the presence of the Court, the ambassadors of both the Emperor and the Pope, as well as a distinguished crowd of bishops and nobles. Her armament, according to her existing inventory of 1514, included 184 pieces of ordnance, of which 126 were brass and iron serpentines.

Two more of Henry VIII.'s ships will be seen in Figs. 48 and 49. Both have been photographed from the coloured drawings of " The Rolle declaryng the Nombre of the Kynges Maiestys owne Galliasses " by Anthony Anthony in the Pepysian Library of Magdalene College, Cambridge. The date of the roll is 1546, one part being now in the British Museum and the other half

* " A History of the Administration of the Royal Navy and of Merchant Shipping in Relation to the Navy," vol. i., 1509–1660, by M. Oppenheim, London, 1896.

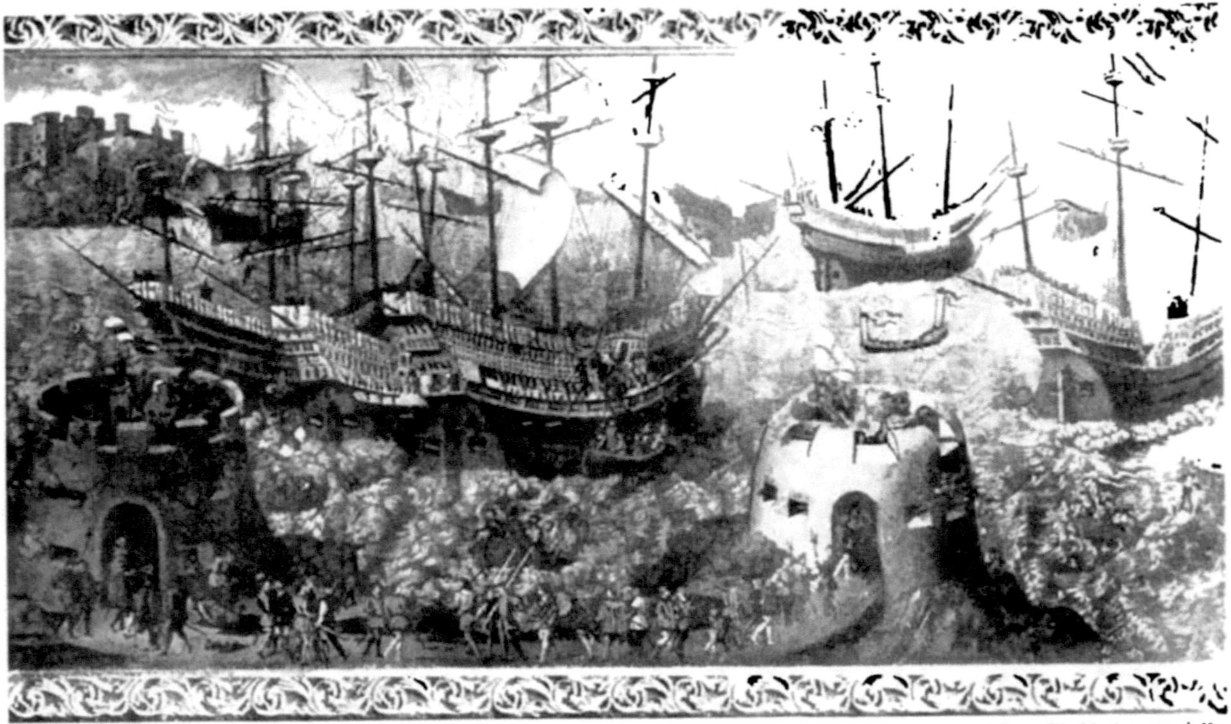

Fig. 47. The Embarkation of Henry VIII from Dover in 1520, showing the "Henri Grâce à Dieu."

p. 186.

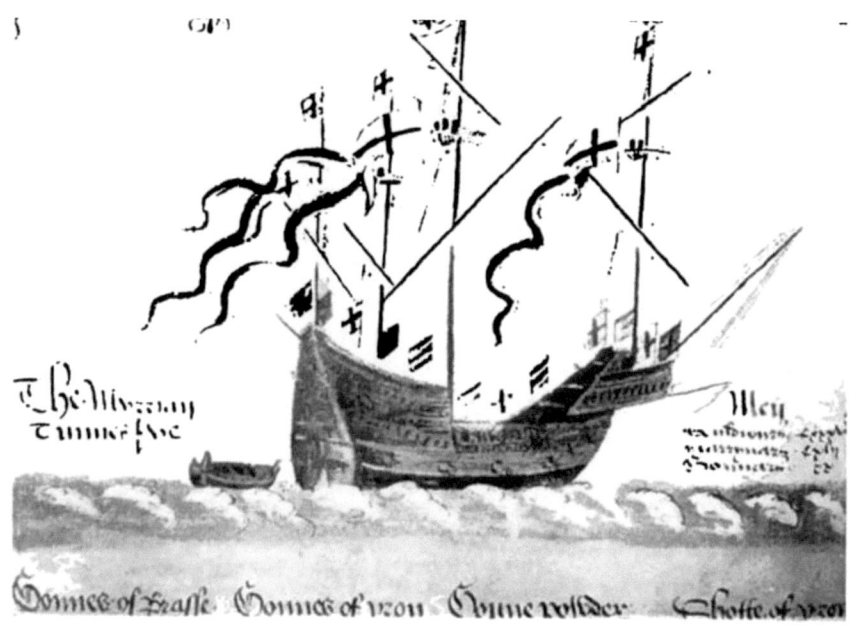

The Mary
Tinner fyre

Mey
...

Gonnes of Brasse   Gonnes of yron   Chyne roffder   Chotte of yron

c Otrus
...njel

Mey.
...

in the Pepysian Library, as stated. Originally, both rolls belonged to Samuel Pepys. Quaint as these representations are, they are contemporary records and of some real interest to us. The *Murrian*, in Fig. 48, was brought into the Royal Navy in 1545 and sold out in 1551. Her tonnage was 500, and she had 300 men, 10 brass guns and 53 iron guns. The reader will notice the manner of stowing the spritsail which is correctly shown. Along the waist of the vessel the pavesses can just be discerned. The netting spread over the ship's deck was as a protection against the enemy's missiles dropped from the fighting-tops. Astern the ship's biggest boat is seen towing, as was the custom when at sea, except in bad weather, " much as one may see a brig or a topsail schooner to-day with a dinghy dragging astern."* The boat's coxswain stayed in her as she towed, keeping her clean, fending her off, and looking out for any of the crew who happened to tumble overboard. The *Struse of Dawske* (*i.e.* Danzig) in Fig. 49, had been purchased in 1544, and was sold out of the service the same year as the *Murrian*. She was very similar to the other ship but slightly smaller. Her tonnage was 450, she carried 250 men, 39 iron guns, but none of brass.

Another ship in this roll called the *Jesus of Lubeck*, being of 700 tons, having been purchased by Henry VIII. from the merchants of Lubeck in 1544, shows steel sickle-shaped bill-hooks affixed to the yard arms, so that in battle she could sail alongside the enemy and tear his rigging to pieces, but it was inevitable that the aggressor would injure himself scarcely less than his foe, and these hooks had disappeared before the end of the century, though their origin was of great antiquity. (See also Fig. 56.)

From a delightful volume † of this reign entitled the

* " On the Spanish Main," by John Masefield, chap. xvi., on " Ships and Rigs."

† Reprinted in " The Naval Miscellany," edited by Professor Sir J. K. Laughton, M.A., R.N., vol. i., Navy Records Society, 1902.

SAILING SHIPS

" Book of War by Sea and by Land," by Jehan Bytharne, Gunner in Ordinary to the King, and bearing date 1543, we are able to verify the truth of the vain display of flags seen in the illustrations of the *Murrian* and *Struse.* There is so much interesting matter contained in this work respecting contemporary ships that I make no apology to the reader for dealing with its contents at some length. Although the earliest code of signals belonged to about 1340 and was given out for the guidance of the fleets at Sluys, yet we have now much more elaborate directions.

Bytharne tells us just what we want to know about the decoration of the ships of his time. The external ornamentation from the mainwale to the top of the castles ought to be painted, he says, with the colours and devices of the admiral. Likewise the forecastle and after-castle were to be decorated as splendidly as possible. All the shields—as we saw in the *Cordelière*—round the upper part of the castles were to be emblazoned with the admiral's arms and devices also. Above the forecastle on a staff inclining forwards was to be a (pennon) of the admiral's colours and devices, as also at the two corners of the castle. Amidships there should be two square banners, emblazoned with the admiral's arms, and on the after-castle high above the rudder he was to have a large square banner larger than any of the others. From the maintop a broad swallow-tailed standard was to be flown, of such a length as to reach to the water, and emblazoned with the admiral's arms and devices also.

For celebrating a triumph the ship was to be covered in and curtained with rich cloth and draped. " You may also paint your sails with such devices and colours as you choose, or with the representation of a saint if you prefer it." Then follow the signals to be employed for summoning the captains of the ships to come aboard the flagship. If a strange ship were espied, this was to be signalled by putting a square banner in a weft in the
188

shrouds half-way up on that side on which the strange ship was seen. At sunset all the ships of the fleet were to pass ahead of the admiral's ship and to shout three times, one after the other, and if they had trumpets they were to be sounded. At the third shout the master of the admiral's ship was to return the salute "causing all those of your ship to shout and the trumpets and drums to sound." And each ship as she made the salute was to ask for the watchword for the night and what course to steer. These having been given, the ships were all to drop astern again, and not pass ahead of the flagship during the night on pain of severe punishment.

Nor to any one gifted with imagination and a love of the beautiful can the following picture make an ineffectual appeal. For, after the above instructions had been carried out, the admiral was to cause to be sung the evening hymn to our Lady before her image, after which all lights were to be put out except those in the cabins of the gentlemen, who may have lamps trimmed with water covered with oil, but neither candles nor any other kind of light, owing to the risk of fire. The grandeur of these old ships with their plentiful freeboard towering high above water, pitching backwards and forwards to the swell of the sea, their highly coloured hulls lit up by the last rays of a glowing sunset, and the strong rough voices of the crew singing their solemn plain-chant as the freshening breeze wafted it to leeward—such an incident would have impressed itself on our minds scarcely less forcibly than the massive *Mauretania* to-day racing over the Atlantic eastward with the sun sinking astern, her masthead, port and starboard lights showing, while the rich notes of a grand piano come floating out from the luxurious drawing-room.

The admiral was further to appoint persons who should see that all the crew not kept up on duty were to retire—soldiers and officers alike. At the stern of the

ship a cresset with flaming combustibles was to burn so
that every one might recognise the admiral's ship and
follow, no other vessel being allowed to carry such a fire.
But if the fleet contained a vice-admiral, he was allowed
to carry just such a light, but the admiral must then
carry two instead of one. The ship was also to carry a
large lantern in which were three or four great lamps with
great lights to make a powerful illumination. The use of
this lantern in place of the cresset was when the wind was
blowing hard or from astern, and it became necessary to
put out the cresset lest the ship should catch fire. At
break of day the "two nimble ships" which sailed some
distance ahead of the fleet were to come back and salute
the admiral as at nightfall. They were then to take their
orders for the day, go on ahead again and keep just in
sight. At sunrise a fanfare was to be sounded on the
trumpets, the other ships to salute as at sunset, the
admiral's ship keeping under easy sail until they had done
so. Then "at such hour of the morning as shall please
you your chaplain" is to say a dry Mass.*

For his interest in the Navy, England owes a debt to
Henry VIII. Under him it became a separate, organised
force instead of being a mere auxiliary of the army.
About eighty vessels and thirteen row-barges of twenty
tons were added during his reign to the ships inherited
from his predecessor. Many were purchased from the
Venetians and the Hanseatic League, who were the great
merchant seamen of this time. Some also were prizes
taken from the enemy, but about forty odd were actually
built during this reign, among which may be mentioned
the *Tiger*, which was flush-decked without any superstructures and heavily armed; and the *Ann Gallant*.
Whereas clinker-built vessels had been almost universal
from the times of the Vikings, carvel-built ships were now

---

* This was the Missa Sicca (Messe Sèche), the "Messe Navale," or
"Missa Nautica," in which no consecration took place.

being used, as being both stronger and faster. Coloured cloths were put round the fighting-tops, and the hulls, besides being carved and gilded, were painted various colours. Sometimes the Tudor colours of green and white were seen, but ash and timber shafts became common under Elizabeth. In the ships of the seventeenth and eighteenth centuries the yellow colour above the waterline of our ships was more pronounced. The crews of Henry VIII.'s ships wore the Tudor colours of white and green also, cloth being used for the sailors and satin or damask for the officers.*

Under Edward VI. the power of the Hanseatic League began gradually to wane, and consequently the superiority which in respect of ships it had possessed over those of our nation became less marked. Perhaps no maritime incident of this reign is more interesting than the preparation, the setting out, and the partial accomplishment of the voyage from our shores to discover a passage by way of Archangel to China. Those who know their Hakluyt will agree that few yarns written nowadays by either professional or amateur sailormen are so absorbingly interesting as this record: those who have still to read this record will enjoy it thoroughly. It is not possible here to give even a summary of this lengthy voyage, in which Sir Hugh Willoughby and his crew perished of cold and starvation, though Richard Chancellor reached as far as Archangel. But there are some details given in the account that are pertinent to our inquiry of the sailing ship. Among the instructions given to the voyagers were that the fleet should keep together as far as possible. A log was to be kept by day and night, "with the points and observation of the lands, tides, elements, altitude of the sunne, course of the moon and starres." The fleet com-

* See "Companion to English History (Middle Ages)," edited by F. P. Barnard, M.A., F.S.A., Oxford, 1902; article on "Shipping," by M. Oppenheim.

prised the *Bona Esperanza*, flagship, of 120 tons, "having with her a pinnesse and a boate," the *Edward Bonaventure*, 160 tons, and the *Bona Confidentia*, 90 tons, the last two ships having the same number of boats as the first. Their progress down the Thames was not rapid, for it took them from the tenth of May till the twenty-second to get from Ratcliffe to Hole Haven. They could not sail nearer to the wind than seven points, for the statement is made that "the wind veared to the West, so that we could lie but North and by West.* Approaching a strange harbour, they would first send forth the ship's "pinnesse" before entering. They were not long in discovering that "the land lay not as the Globe made mention." The "Confidence being troubled with bilge water, we thought it good to seeke harbour for her redresse."

The cost of purchasing these three ships was £6000 according to another account also included in Hakluyt, and written by one, Clement Adams, who praises very highly the "very strong and well seasoned plankes for the building," as well as the skill of the shipwrights who "calke them, pitch them, and among the rest they make one most stanch and firme, by an excellent and ingenious invention." This invention is that "they cover a piece of the keele of the shippe with thin sheetes of leade, for they had heard that in certaine parts of the Ocean a kinde of wormes is bredde, which many times pearceth and eateth through the strongest oake that is." The reader will recollect that this "invention" was known to the inhabitants of the Mediterranean for many hundreds of years before this.† The same writer states that when they departed from Ratcliffe "upon the ebbe " "with the turning

* Manwayring, who fought in the English Fleet against the Armada, states that a "cross-sail" (square-rigged) ship in a sea cannot sail nearer than six points, unless there be tide or current setting her to windward.

† See chap. iii. p. 78. This revival in Edward VI.'s time of lead sheathing was copied from the contemporary custom among Spanish ships.

FIG. 50. THE "ARK ROYAL," ELIZABETH'S FLAGSHIP. BUILT IN 1587.

p. 192.

FIG. 52. THE SPANISH ARMADA COMING UP CHANNEL.

p. 192.

of the water" the "greater shippes" were "towed downe with boates, and oares, and the mariners being apparelled in watchet or skie coloured cloth, rowed amaine." The Court being at Greenwich they fired a salute while "one stoode in the poope of the ship, and by his gesture bids farewell to his friendes . . . another walkes upon the hatches, another climbes the shrowds, another stands upon the maine yard, and another in the top of the shippe." When they arrived at Harwich, to Chancellor's dismay, part of the victuals were found to be "corrupt and putrified" "and the hoggesheads of wine also leaked, and were not stanch."

During the reign of Mary the fishing and coasting traffic flourished, but it is when we enter upon the reign of Elizabeth that we find the greatest encouragement given. It was she who repealed all existing restrictions in connection with navigation laws, so that merchants were allowed to use whatever ships they possessed, whether foreign or English-built. More sensible and far-sighted than some of our modern legislators, she was wise enough to restrict the coasting trade to British ships. In this reign, too, telescopes were invented, Mercator's chart of the world completed, the art of navigation developed, hydrography taken up seriously, the harbours of England and estuaries well surveyed, pilotage and buoyage systematised and placed under the care of the corporation of Trinity House. The variation of the compass had been already observed by Columbus and Cabot, but under Elizabeth the matter was given serious study.

The carrying trade, which for so long a time between England and the Mediterranean had been the monopoly of ships belonging to Venice or Genoa or Spain, now belongs exclusively to English vessels. Our shipwrights, too, were building craft of finer lines and longer on the keel. Hawkins, perhaps the ablest shipbuilder of the reign and a practical seaman who had roved over the seas as pirate and slave-hunter too, was foremost in designing ships on what were then new principles. He it was who recognised that the enormously high poops and forecastles of the prevailing type were as unnecessary as they were unwieldy. These were cut down considerably, and the reader will notice the changes effected if he will compare the illustration of the *Ark Royal* in Fig. 50 with that of a Spanish galleon in Fig. 55. Practical test was made of the new type as soon as the Armada came sailing up the English Channel in July of 1588, with the usual south-west wind blowing. Howard's ships sailed closehauled out of Plymouth, succeeded in getting to windward of the Spanish craft, and keeping out of range of their guns, his own ordnance being of much longer range, poured a terrific fire into the enormous freeboard of the enemy, who found themselves at once both outsailed and out-cannoned.

By adding also to the draught of water the Elizabethans were making their ships more weatherly and less likely to roll in a seaway. Among other advantages arising from this would be better marksmanship than could ever be obtained on a galleon pitching her head into every sea and making good gunnery almost impossible except in calms. An interesting comparison is possible when we mention that the new English ships possessed a length three and a half times their beam; nevertheless, the galley had been about seven times the breadth. Besides the green and white colours, Elizabethan ships were also painted outside black and white, red, or the timber-colour previously mentioned. Figureheads, consisting of a dragon or a lion, were in vogue, and carved figures of men and beasts decorated also the interior. Cabins were painted and upholstered in green and white, whilst at the stern the royal arms were displayed in gold and colours. Sir Walter Raleigh in his " Judicious and Select Essayes and Observations," printed in London in 1650, refers to the recent invention of topmasts, which could be lowered or raised instead of being kept permanently fixed as hitherto had been the custom. He describes these as being "a wonderfull great ease to great ships, both at sea and harbour." * He also mentions as recent innovations chain pumps, studding sails, top-gallant sails and the weighing of the anchor by means of the capstan, and the introduction of the bonnet on the lower courses. But as to these last two items he is quite incorrect. The bonnet had existed at least from the Viking times, and we saw it on some of the seals. But below the bonnet was now laced on another called a drabbler. Instead of reefing as nowadays by taking in the foot of the sail, the drabbler would be unlaced, for one or two reefs, and the bonnet removed for a close reef. The yard would then be lowered away some distance from the mast. The same authority refers to the practice which had come into fashion of using long cables by which " we resist the malice of the greatest winds that can blow."

He tells us also how the *Marie Rose* of Henry VIII.'s time was lost when getting under way. She heeled over, and the water rushing in through her ports, which were only sixteen inches above the water, she sank. Raleigh goes on to say that they were now making such improvements in their ships as would prevent such a catastrophe occurring again ; but we know that more than one instance of this kind of calamity happened in later times owing to the same cause, notably the case of the *Royal George.* Royal ships, he tells us, were being strengthened by pillars fastened from keelson to the beams of the second deck and so keeping them from giving way in bad weather. He rejoices over the improvement of the lines in the new ships mentioned above " whereby they never fall into the sea after the head and shake the whole body, nor sinck a sterne, nor stoope upon a wind." He gives the following

* P. 16.

essentials for the building of a good ship: That she be strong, swift, stout-sided, able to carry her guns in all weathers, be seaworthy and stay well when boarding and turning on a wind. He advises that in order to make her sail well the ship should be given a long run forward and not sink into the water, but lie clear above it. He suggests, too, that her lowest tier of guns be four feet above water, and in order to be a good sea-boat she have a good draught of water and not be overcharged with towering poops, "which commonly the king's ships are." This "overcharging" compelled the ships in bad weather to "lie at trye" (*i.e.*, heave-to, hence the derivation of the word try-sail), under main-course and mizzen. In protesting against this excessive overcharging of poops and decks he adds, "two decks and a half is sufficient to yield shelter and lodging for men and mariners and no more charging at all higher, but only one low cabbin for the master."

Large ships had two decks, an upper one and a gun-deck underneath. Towards the end of the sixteenth century, a third deck, called a false orlop was laid in the hold to carry cabins and stores. The ship was divided transversely on both upper and lower decks by means of bulkheads where the forecastle and poop ended. Gravel ballast was used to such an extent that but little room was left for stores. A large portion of the space left in the hold of the ship in the waist was taken up by the cooking galley which was a solid structure of bricks and mortar. Raleigh * complains of the heat "that comes from the cook roome" as well of the risk of fire which it afforded, and of the unsavoury smells which emanated from this part of the ship. He therefore recommends that the "cook roomes" be placed in the forecastle instead, as was the custom already adopted by many of the merchant ships.

When Elizabeth came to the throne, the *Henri Grace à Dieu* had been accidentally burnt five years before.

* "Judicious and Select Essayes," p. 33.

Apart from the *Jesus of Lubeck* (700 tons), the *Triumph* was the largest English ship afloat. Built in 1561, her tonnage was over a thousand, and her crew numbered 500. Until the launching of the *Prince Royal* in 1610, she was the finest English ship afloat. But though there were improvements going on in regard to the building of the ships, the lot of the sailor was not entirely a happy one. Musty rations, want of clothes, and the harmful effects of the bilge water collecting in the bottom of the ship and emitting an unwholesome stench, caused scurvy and dysentery; and the sailors of both the English ships and the Spanish Armada suffered terribly from these. But on the other hand, we find that as early as the year 1601, Lancaster, during his first voyage for the East India Company, kept the crew of his flagship in comparatively good health by serving out lime-juice.*

The illustration in Fig. 50 is of the *Ark Royal*, from a contemporary print in the Print Room of the British Museum. Built for Sir Walter Raleigh in 1587, she was sold while on the stocks to Queen Elizabeth for £5000. Her name was to have been the *Ark Ralegh*, but on being purchased it was changed as above. Her name was, after the end of this reign, changed to the *Anne Royal*, and in 1625, while returning from Cadiz, she began to leak like the proverbial lobster-pot and only reached home with difficulty. In 1636, while lying in the Thames, she bilged on her own anchor and sank. It was this *Ark Royal* that was Elizabeth's flagship of the fleet that defeated the Armada, and for this reason, if for no other, she is deserving of a more complete consideration than we have room to devote to other ships of this period. Sir William Monson,† who was already a captain

---

* See article on " Public Health," by Charles Creighton, on p. 763, vol. i., of Traill and Mann's " Social England."

† " Naval Tracts of Sir William Monson," edited by M. Oppenheim, Navy Records Society. See vol. ii. p. 285.

by 1587, gives her tonnage as 800, and the number of her crew as 400. Happily the complete inventory of the *Ark Royal* is still in existence, and the reader is referred to the " State Papers Relating to the Defeat of the Spanish Armada, anno 1588." * It was compiled in September 1588 after the *Ark Royal* had come in for a survey, having been out in the Channel in the memorable victory. All the tackle and spars and sails, every item of the inventory down to the kettles for the cooking-room is mentioned. From this list we find that the spritsail, besides its yard, had clew lines, braces, sheets, halyards, and " a false tye." Sir Henry Manwayring, who also fought in the fleet against the Armada, in his " Seamen's Dictionary " defines ties as four-strand ropes, hawser-laid, being the ropes by which the yards hang. But the spritsail yard having no ties, was made fast by a pair of slings to the bowsprit. Among the items of the rigging of the foremast are included the " fore pennants," and both the falls and pennants of the " swifters." Referring to Manwayring's " Dictionary," we find that " swifters doe belong to the maine and foremast, and are to succour the shrowdes and keep stiffe the mast. They have pendants, which are made fast under the shrowdes at the head of the mast with a double block, through which is reeved the swifter." Mention must be made of the " forebolings " and main bowlines. Our ancestors made great use of these bowlines in order that these great square sails might set quite flat. Until the triangular head sails came in about the middle of the eighteenth century, the foremast was stepped very far forward, for the spritsail was only used off the wind and when getting under way. The manner in which the spritsail in this illustration of the *Ark Royal* is shown in the head stowed is quite correct.

The inventory mentions also the clew-garnets and

* Edited by Professor Sir J. K. Laughton, M.A., R.N., Navy Records Society, 1894.

martnets (leech-lines) of the foresail, and the "fore-puttocks" (*i.e.*, futtock shrouds) of the foretop-mast. The fall of the martnets of the topsails led down into the fighting-top where it was hauled, and the expression " top the martnets " was the order for hauling the martnets up. The yards were hoisted by jeers or halyards. Manwayring defines " jeere " as a hawser, made fast to the main or fore yard close to the ties of great ships only. It came through a block which was seized close to the top and led down to another block at the bottom of the mast close to the deck. Great ships had one on either side of the ties. Apart from the use of the jeer to hoist or lower the yards, it was especially serviceable for taking some of the weight off the ties, and to hold the yard from falling down if the ties should break. In fights, when the sickle-shaped shear-hooks already mentioned were used by the enemy, the opponent would sling his yards in chains " for feare least the ties should be cut, and so the yards fall downe, and these chaines are called slings " (Manwayring). The lateen yards on the mizzen and bonaventure-mizzen had parrals to secure them to the masts.

The *Ark Royal* carried three bower anchors of 20 cwt. as well as three others and a grapnel. She had fifty fathoms of 15-inch cable, three compasses, four running glasses, three flags of St. George and two of the Queen's arms, as well as a silk ensign. In the illustration before us the St. George's flags will be noticed flying at the fore and bonaventure mizzen ; at the main is the royal standard, and at the main-mizzen the Tudor Rose. From the spritsail yard flies a pennant surcharged with a St. George's cross, from the foretop a pennant bearing a foul anchor, being the pennant of the Lord High Admiral. This flag will also be noticed on the foremast of the ship of Charles II.'s time of the frontispiece. In fact, as the reader is probably aware, this is still used as the Admiralty's flag. From the fore topgallant yard is a streamer bearing a lion rampant, of Lord Howard of Effingham, Lord High Admiral of England; from the maintop another streamer, striped, whilst at the waist is a large banner with Howard's arms thereon. The inventory includes ballast baskets for carrying the gravel on board, or in which it would be stowed; netting for the forecastle, the waist and the half-deck, as well as cloths for the waist and top armours for the mizzen top, but we shall refer to these later.

Touching the sails of the *Ark Royal*, she had a bonnet to her spritsail laced on in the manner adopted to-day by the wherryman of the Norfolk Broads. The mainsail and foresail and main mizzen also had the bonnet, but the others had not, although a topsail bonnet was found rarely. The foresail had a double bonnet with a single drabbler, likewise the mainsail. In the case of the main mizzen the bonnet was a double one. The inventory only includes one topgallant sail, although three are shown in this engraving. This fact is certainly an argument for those who assert that the illustration represents not the *Ark Royal*, although the rest of the evidence is against this assertion. Much more likely is it that the other topgallant sails were added at a later date.

The inventory includes a sail for the ship's boat, and two for the pinnesse. A long boat with a brass sheave in the head and supplied with oars, a pinnesse and a " cocke " (derived from the French *coque*) which was a ship's boat, as well as an older pinnesse, were carried on board the *Ark Royal*. During the survey at Chatham it was decided to have her overlop in the waist made less curved and more level for the sake of placing the guns in better position, a lesson that had been impressed on them even more forcibly by the ill-success of the fire of the Spaniards. In our illustration it will be noticed that the curve has disappeared. I therefore conclude that this engraving was made after the ship had been altered at Chatham. It seems very probable that it was during this overhaul that the other topgallant sails were added, in which case the argument against the veracity of this engraving is rebutted.

Elizabeth's own royal ships were undoubtedly fine able vessels for their time. They were seaworthy, and at at any rate during the time of the Armada did not suffer from leaks. But the same statement cannot be made of the merchant ships that joined the royal fleet from the various English ports. These were far from sound and leaked badly. In a letter from Howard to Walsyngham * we find that the merchants besought the former that he and the rest of Her Majesty's fleet would carry less sail for they could not endure it, while " we," writes Howard, " made no reckoning of it." This inferiority is confirmed also by Seymour, who writes to say that the merchant ships in the English fleet were not as good seaboats as the Queen's.

Before we leave the *Ark Royal*, let us call to the reader's attention a detail that, if he is a sailorman, he will have already noticed. The furling of the sails, correctly shown here, is very clumsy and bungling. The custom was when the sails were furled to bind them to the yard with rope yarns, and these yarns were cut to loose the sail when getting under way. Thus Sir William Wynter, writing on February 28, 1587, concludes his letter : " Written aboard the Vanguard, being in the Downs, ready to cut sail." †

Centuries ago, when England had only her Viking-like craft, she had bravely claimed for herself the Sovereignty of the Seas. It was to the foreigner an insolent, arrogant boast. She had fought for the distinction many times. Spain had grown up to be the first maritime nation of the

---

* Given on p. 274 of " State Papers relating to the Defeat of the Spanish Armada," *vide supra.*

† *Ibid.* p. 82.

world, but just as in after years the Dutch and the French had, not without a severe tussle, to be prevented from usurping this distinction, so England had to smash the Armada—the greatest aggregation of naval power the world had ever seen on one sea—and with this defeat England was again, for a time at least, the mistress of the sea. Drake's voyage round the world with a squadron of five ships, the largest of which did not exceed 100 tons, set the final seal on the abilities of English seamanship and navigation. The victory over the Armada settled their superiority in ships, strategy and shooting.

Before we pass from the story of the fight that never grows old—and there is no more stirring reading than the plain narrative included in Hakluyt—let us not forget that capable as were the royal ships of Elizabeth, they could never have been victorious had not the West countrymen of England come to help with their ships and their crews. The former may have been leaky, the latter may have been not as skilled as Howard's men in the finer arts of war, but they did their duty, in spite of a thousand drawbacks, and did it well. Where had they learned their seamanship? How was it that they had even such good ships as they possessed but a hundred years after Henry VII. had come to the throne? As Mr. Blackmore points out,* ever since the discovery of Newfoundland the men of Cornwall and Devon had gone forth year after year to fish for cod off the Banks. Kipling, Connolly, and others, have sung the epic of the brave fishermen who to-day race out to the same banks from Gloucester, U.S.A. Most readers of fiction know that cruising about there is no latitude for a fair-weather sailor, yet three hundred years before them, when the arts of shipbuilding and navigation were not what they are now, Englishmen in ships built at Dartmouth and else-

* See "The British Mercantile Marine: a Short Historical Review," by Edward Blackmore, London, 1897.

where were making regular voyages across the broad Atlantic to those fishing banks. Big vessels and brave capable seamen were essential for these trips. Both, at the summons of necessity, had gradually evolved from the West Country, and, at the hour of need, placed themselves at the service and in the defence of their fatherland.

What were the kinds of ships that sailed in English waters during the reign of Elizabeth? As far as historical research will suffer us let us try and obtain a general idea as to their rig and appearance. Fig. 51, which is taken from the Rawlinson MSS. in the Bodleian, affords an excellent example of an Elizabethan man-of-war. The flags flying are the green and white Tudor colours on the ensign staff and the St. George at the main, which was the national flag, but it was men-of-war only that were allowed to fly it at the main. According to Manwayring the Elizabethan ships, when running before a wind or with the wind on the quarter in the case of a fair fresh gale, often unparralled the mizzen lateen yard from the mast, and launched out the yard and sail over the quarter on the lee side, fitting guys at the further end to keep the yards steady. A boom also appears to have been used in this case. If a ship gripe too much, says Manwayring, then the mizzen was stowed, for otherwise "she will never keep out of the wind." The mizzen was sometimes used when at anchor to back the ship astern in order to keep her from fouling her anchor on the turn of the tide.

Perhaps in the mind of the general reader the one type of ship of this age that he has any vague knowledge of is the galleon. He associates her with the Armada and with the Spanish nation exclusively. He has not forgotten that he learned in the days of his youth that the ships of the Armada were of enormous size, and that the English ships were victorious because they were small and nimble.

SAILING SHIPS

It is perfectly true to say that our vessels were light and comparatively handy, but we must not omit to throw into the balance the superiority of our seamanship and gunnery, as we pointed out just now. The English had a natural taste for the sea; the Spaniards, in spite of all their trading and exploring across the ocean, had for it an equal distaste. They were admittedly bad seamen.* I am not expressing an opinion but asserting a fact, and this was as much the cause of their defeat as anything else. But the English ships were not particularly small. At least seven were of between 600 and 1100 tons. There were in the whole Spanish Armada only four ships larger than our *Triumph*, whilst of the English merchantmen the *Leicester* and the *Merchant Royal* were each of 400 tons.

Nor did the word "galleon" necessarily denote a Spanish ship. It is perfectly true that the Spanish Armada contained a number of cumbrous galleons, but it must not be inferred from this that a galleon was necessarily clumsy. In point of fact, Spain was the last of the great maritime nations to adopt the galleon. In England the galleon denoted a vessel built expressly for war, as distinguished from the adapted merchantmen. She was essentially a ship built with finer lines, and in every way smarter than the ordinary vessel. The type had been first introduced into the English service by Henry VIII. long before Spain had adopted it, although, as we mentioned earlier, there was considerable confusion as to the actual names. Thus Henry VIII.'s ships were classed as "great ships," "galleasses," and "galleys," while for a long time, both in England and France, the galleon was called indifferently "galleon," "galleasse," "galley," and "galliot." By the outbreak of the Spanish war practically all the men-of-war in our country were galleons, and were thus described by foreigners. Nevertheless, as Mr. Corbett

* "Naval Tracts of Sir William Monson," edited by M. Oppenheim, Navy Records Society, 1902. See vol. ii. p. 328.

points out,* English seamen never took kindly to the word galleon. They continued to confuse "galleasse" and "galleon" in describing the ships of foreigners. But for all that English shipwrights understood perfectly the technical characteristics, and in official building programmes after the middle of Elizabeth's reign the three terms "galleon," "galleasse," and "galley" appear correctly. The galleon, as Mr. Masefield well describes her, was roughly the prototype of the ship of the line, the galleasse the prototype of the frigate, and the pinnace of the sloop or corvette. The galleon was low in the waist with a square forecastle and a high quarter-deck just abaft the mainmast, rising to a poop above the quarter-deck. Reckoning upwards, the two decks, according to Manwayring, were called lower orlop or first orlop, and the next the second orlop. But if a ship had three decks they never called the uppermost—the third—by the name of orlop, but simply "upper deck." The wooden bulkheads that separated the stern from the waist were pierced with holes for small quick-firing guns.

The length of the galleon was three times that of her beam, whereas the ordinary merchantman was only twice her own beam, thus preserving the old distinction that we saw in classical time existing between the long ship and the round ship. Yet the newer class of Elizabethan merchantman was getting longer, influenced by the experience gained on the long voyages across the Atlantic. It had been in Italy, the great home of maritime matters in earlier days, that the galleon had first been built. The galleon was in fact the child of necessity. The Mediterranean possessed the galley-type from very early times as

* "Papers relating to the Navy during the Spanish War, 1585–1587," edited by J. S. Corbett, LL.M., Navy Records Society, 1898: I wish to express my indebtedness to this volume, and to Mr. Oppenheim's "Naval Tracts of Sir William Monson," for much matter in regard to the different types of Elizabethan ships.

we have already seen; she had, as we have also seen, the
"round" merchant type. But as time went on a demand
arose for a compromise between the two. Able to hold
as much cargo, and more, than the old round ships, yet
not utterly helpless like them in calms and narrow waters,
the galleons were yet to be of such a kind as to be capable
of acting with the galleys in war time. So they were
made not as long but with more beam than the galleys,
with a built-up structure fore and aft and—let us note
this carefully—though they were sailing ships they had at
first auxiliary oar-propulsion. The smaller English galleons also retained their oars for a long time.

The immediate ancestor of the English galleon was the
Italian merchantman that traded between Venice and
London. This had three masts with a square sail on the
foremast, but lateen on the main and mizzen. She carried
also oars as auxiliaries. Afterwards, by degrees the oars
were dispensed with, so that by the end of the sixteenth
century the galleon was a purely sailing vessel with sometimes two and sometimes three decks, while the galleasse
had oars as well. Her special claim was that she was both
faster and more weatherly than the older type of warship.
English shipwrights understood a galleasse to be similar
to a galleon but with more length in proportion to her
beam, though strictly speaking the galleasse should desig-
nate a large ship with high freeboard, using oars as well
as sails. The ships, however, that fitted this description
were known to them by the name of "bastard galleasses."
The galleasse was sometimes flush-decked and minus both
poop and forecastle and never so highly charged (*i.e.*, with
such high decks at stern and bow) as the galleon. A good
illustration will be found in the foreground of Fig. 52,
which contains two of these with their oars out. This
picture represents the Spanish Armada coming up
channel when first sighted off the Lizard. The illustration has been taken from one of the plates in "The

Tapestry Hangings of the House of Lords," engraved by John Pine, London, in 1739. If the reader will pardon a short digression it may not be out of place to say a few words in explanation of these engravings.

After he had defeated the Armada in 1588, Lord Howard of Effingham, later raised to an earldom, determined to commemorate the victory by depicting the scenes he had so recently passed through. Accordingly Hendrik Corneliszoon Vroom, who had at this time obtained a European reputation as a marine artist, was invited from Haarlem to paint the pictures. From these Francis Speiring, an eminent craftsman, wove the designs into tapestry. Howard, or, as he now was, the Earl of Nottingham, sold them in his old age to James I., who hung them in the precincts of the House of Lords. When, during the Commonwealth, the House of Lords was abolished, the tapestries were fitted into brown wooden frames and hung on the walls of the chamber which had been used for the Upper House. Here they remained until the House was burned down in 1834, when the ten tapestries perished. Fortunately, however, even in the inartistic eighteenth century, an artist, John Pine, and a friend of Hogarth, had the inspiration to reproduce them by engraving, But for this we should lack what is a most valuable record. It is so easy to fall into inaccuracies a century after an event, but since Pine copied from the tapestries, and the tapestries were executed under Howard's own supervision, there cannot be much room left for anything incorrect in respect of the ships. Howard had fought against the Spanish ships night and day in that memorable month of July, and had every opportunity of noting the rigging and lines of his enemy's vessels, so that when he had left the sea and, not unnaturally, devoted his attention to his own memorial, he would be the ideal person to see that accuracy was insisted upon. These engravings are still to be picked up occasionally in some of the London print-sellers, but the illustration here given is from the collection in the Print Room of the British Museum.*

The reader who is familiar with Elizabethan literature must have found considerable confusion existing in his mind as to what a "pinnesse" really was. Let us say at once, then, that the name was indiscriminately given to two distinct classes of craft. One class was a kind of galleasse, only smaller; that is to say, she relied on both oars and sails. She was a sea-going ship and decked. Under this heading came also row-barges, and at various times also galleots, galleys, frigates, and shallops. The point to notice is that this class comprised really big craft. The other "pinnesses" were ships' boats. The modern use of the word pinnace expresses pretty clearly its relation to the mother ship. The greatest critics are unable to define exactly what a "bark" was, but from an early Venetian print I gather that she was smaller than the prevailing Mediterranean galley. At the same time the word seems to have included also vessels ranging from fifty, to a hundred and fifty tons. Thus they were sometimes small ships, and sometimes large pinnaces. Whilst Elizabethan seamen included all sailing vessels fit to take their place in the line of battle under the generic term of ship, the shipwrights divided them according to their design into "ships," "galleons," "galleasses"; "barks" being a convenient term for vessels of smaller ability.

The "brigandine" or "brigantine" was a Mediterranean type of small galley, rowed by its own fighting crew and without slaves. Sometimes she was classed as a "pinnesse" and sometimes as a bark, but never as a galley. Whether or not she possessed sails she was primarily a rowed boat. The illustration in Fig. 53 represents a big sea-going

* The reader who desires fuller information on the subject is referred to an interesting article "The Lost Tapestries of the House of Lords," in *Harper's Monthly Magazine*, April, 1907, from the pen of Mr. Edmund Gosse.

The Black Pynnes

FIG. 58. THE "BLACK PINNESSE," WHICH BROUGHT HOME THE BODY OF SIR PHILIP SIDNEY. *p. 208*

Fig. 54. A Galleon of the Time of Elizabeth.

p. 209.

pinnesse as distinct from the ship's boat. This was the vessel that carried home the body of Sir Philip Sydney, and is taken from " Sequitur celebritas et pompa funeris . . ." (of Sir Philip Sydney) by Thomas Lant, printed in 1587. The Elizabethan deep-sea pinnaces were from eighty to fifteen tons. The present illustration shows the vessel with her waist cloths rigged up to prevent boarding, and with nettings * drawn over the waist to intercept the missiles dropped from the fighting-tops of the enemy. Mr. Masefield says that this cloth was of canvas two bolts (three feet six inches) deep. It was gaily painted with designs of red, yellow, and the Tudor green and white. It was of no protection against the enemy's guns, yet it helped the sail trimmers on board from being aimed at. But against the enemy's arrows sent from the tops it was efficacious, for though they penetrated the texture they were caught. We have already called attention to the additional protection of the shields or pavesses that ran around the outside of the deck.

The illustration in Fig. 54 shows a galleon with decorated sails, a practice that died out about the close of Elizabeth's reign.† This decoration was effected by stitching on to the canvas cut-out pieces of cloth with twine. Most of the sails were woven in Portsmouth on hand looms, and the stuff was of good quality. But during the reign of James II. when the Huguenots took refuge in England, among the many new trades which the settlers brought over was that of the manufacture of sailcloth. A French refugee, Bonhomme, who had settled down at Ipswich, taught the secret of its manufacture. Previously, England had imported her sail-cloth from France. The new factory was assisted in every possible way, but was

---

* These nettings were at first made of metal chain, but in the time of Elizabeth they were of rope.

† The illustration is taken from a print in the British Museum made by an artist who was born in 1620.

finally destroyed by French agents, who bribed the artisans to return once more to France. Another factory was set up in London during the reign of William III., but as late as the time of George I. sail-cloth was imported from abroad.

As to the rigging of Elizabethan ships: the shrouds of the fore and main masts led outside the ship to chains to which they were made fast. The platforms in the " chains " of the ships of this time were of no small size as we shall see when we come to consider the Spanish vessels. The shrouds of the mizzen and bonaventure were set up usually from inside the bulwarks on deck. The fighting-tops were of elm, being entered through a lubber's hole in the floor. Contemporary prints show sheaves of arrows projecting from the tops. At a later date light guns were placed here, but as this necessitated the use of lighted matches there was always the risk of setting fire to the sails. The shrouds and stays were of thick nine-stranded hemp. We see from old prints of this time that those parts, as for instance where the foresail came into contact with the bowsprit, which were liable to suffer from chafing were protected by matting made of rope or white line plaited, and then tarred. Masts were made of pine or fir. In dirty weather the fore-yard and fore-topsail yard could be sent on deck. Parrals of course kept the yard to the mast. There is not so very much difference between the sailor language of Elizabeth's time and that in use on board a modern sailing ship. Mr. Bullen in an essay on " Shakespeare and the Sea " reminds us that " Elizabethan England spoke a language which was far more studded with sea-terms than that which we speak ashore to-day." In such plays as *Twelfth Night, Comedy of Errors, Macbeth, King Henry VI.*, and *The Tempest*, we have instances of this. Thus in Act III. Scene I. of the latter the first sailor commands the other to " slack the bolins there." Modern bowlines are slight ropes leading from forward to keep the leach or weather edge of the courses flat and rigid in light winds when on a wind. But in olden times the bowline was of far greater importance, as we have seen, and led well out on to the bowsprit. Not merely the lower course, but topsail and topgallant sails possessed them.

When the English fleet opposed the Armada it consisted of 197 vessels made up as follows: 34 of Elizabeth's own royal ships, 34 merchant vessels, 30 ships and barks paid by the City of London, 33 ships and barks (with 15 victuallers not reckoned in the total number), 23 coasters varying from 160 to 35 tons, 20 other coasters and 23 voluntary ships. Of the merchant ships the *Galleon Leicester* and the *Merchant Royal* are each given as of 400 tons and carrying 160 men. The smallest was the small caravel of 30 tons with 20 men. But we have spoken at some length of the English ships. Let us now turn to consider the ships of other nations of this period.

The Armada consisted of 130 vessels if we add up the list given in Hakluyt. This number was made up of the following types: galleons, patasses or pataches, galleasses, zabras, galleys and hulks. Besides these there were 20 " caravels rowed with oares, being appointed to Performe necessary services unto the greater ships," making a total of 150. The tonnage of the fleet came to 60,000. There were 64 galleons " of an huge bignesse " and " so high that they resembled great castles," but in attacking ability " farre inferiour unto the English and Dutch ships, which can with great dexteritie weild and turne themselves at all assayes." It was this " bignesse " and the high castles at bow and stern that caused the prevailing fallacy to arise that the Armada ships were far larger than ours. The former were very high but very short on the keel, and in consequence equally unseaworthy. Ours were, as we pointed out above, long on the keel and not highly " charged " with castles. The Hakluyt account says the upperworks of the galleons were so thick and strong as to resist musket shot. The lower part of the hull and its timbers also were "out of measure strong, being framed of plankes and ribs foure or five foote in thicknesse, insomuch that no bullets could pierce them, but such as were discharged hard at hand : which afterward prooved true, for a great number of bullets were founde to sticke fast within the massie substance of those thicke plankes. Great and well-pitched cables were twined about the masts of their shippes, to strengthen them against the battery of shot."

The galleasses "were of such bigness, that they contained within them chambers, chapels, turrets, pulpits, and other commodities of great houses. The galliasses were rowed with great oares, their being in eche one of them 300 slaves for the same purpose, and were able to do great service with the force of their ordinance.* All these together with the residue aforenamed were furnished and beautified with trumpets, streamers, banners, warlike ensignes, and other such like ornaments." The various vessels also carried 12,000 pipes of fresh water and plentiful supplies of bacon, cheese, biscuit, fish, rice, beans, peas, oil, vinegar and wine. Among their stores were candles, lanterns, hemp, ox-hides and lead sheathing to be used to stop the holes that should be made by the enemy's guns.

The Spanish ships had been built unnecessarily strong by very heavy scantlings. They were, according to Mr. Oppenheim,† of light draught with broad floors and were

---

* It is interesting to note that in the year 1903 some Armada relics, consisting of a bronze breach loader, found fully charged, and a pair of bronze compasses were recovered from the wreck of the Spanish galleon *Florencia*, in Tobermory Bay, Isle of Mull. She had formed one of the Spanish fleet which fled up the North Sea from the English Channel, round the north of Scotland to the west coast, where in August of 1588 this 900-ton ship was blown up.

† See "Naval Tracts of Sir William Monson," vol. ii. p. 318 *et seq.*

both crank and leewardy. The seams opened in spite of the strength with which they had been put together. They were bolted with iron spikes and it was not long before these ships became " nail-sick." Their masts and spars were too heavy and their standing rigging too weak ; in fact, whilst the demand had to be met for big ocean-going ships, the Spanish shipwrights and naval architects were not sufficiently advanced at this time to deal with such enormous masses of material.

We have mentioned above that Spain was the last of the great maritime Powers to adopt the galleon. In Fig. 55 the reader will see a representation of her galleons. It was not till about 1550, Mr. Oppenheim states, that the great galleon was introduced. The print here reproduced is in the British Museum, and the date the authorities assign to it is about 1560, so that we have every reason for supposing that this illustration is a correct one. The reader will at once notice the high-charged stern immediately abaft the mainmast. The Spanish ships were notorious for their wall-like sides ; and for the height to which the bowsprit was " steeved," both of which details will be noticed in the illustration before us. We mentioned in this chapter that in her origin the galleon owed something to the galley. Now, one of the chief characteristics of the galley type was the ram which was handed down from ancient times. Here, then, in this picture will be seen the survival of the ram affixed to the galleon. But it is here no longer entirely for the purpose of attacking the enemy's ships but for boarding the fore-tack when by the wind. The bowlines are clearly seen on the vessel to the right of the print, leading from both the foresail to the bowsprit and from the main-sail. On both the fore and main courses, the martnets or leach lines are shown very clearly in the print ; it is a little difficult to indicate these so clearly in reproduction. Notice, too, that both foresail and main have got both

bonnet and drabbler laced on. Below the bowsprit is
seen the spritsail. The main-mizzen topsail is stowed,
and the bonaventure does not carry a topsail above her
lateen. The under portion of the hull of these Spanish
ships was painted white, but ochre was frequently used
for the stern. They had lids to their portholes, nettings
and waistcloths, and "blinders" to avert the arrows and
musket fire. The armament of the Spanish merchantman
was, in the case of vessels of 100 tons, four heavy iron
guns and eight hand guns aside as well as eight other
hand guns ; but after about 1550 the armament became
heavier.

We pass now to speak of the Spanish treasure-
frigates. These were an important class of vessel during
the last quarter of the sixteenth century. The length on
their upper deck was nearly four times the beam, and they
possessed considerable speed. They were not properly
cargo ships, but built in order to carry the valuable
treasures from the Spanish Main across the Atlantic to
Spain. Specially designed by Pero Menendez Marquez
about the year 1590, to get across from the West Indies
with the utmost despatch, they carried 150 men with
soldiers and marines. Hakluyt * contains "certaine
Spanish letters intercepted by shippes . . . containing
many secrets touching" South America and the West
Indies. The extremely interesting drawing in Fig. 56
was sent home by an English spy and is now preserved in
the Records Office, by whose permission it is reproduced
here. This illustration shows very clearly that she had
evolved from a galley. She has three masts of which the
main and mizzen are seen to possess topmasts that lower.
These two masts also have topsails. The yards of the
mainsail and foresail have also affixed to their extremities
crescent-shaped shear-hooks for tearing the enemy's rigging.
The forestay and foretopmast stay are well indicated.

* See vol. x., p. 158, of Maclehose's edition of 1903.

214

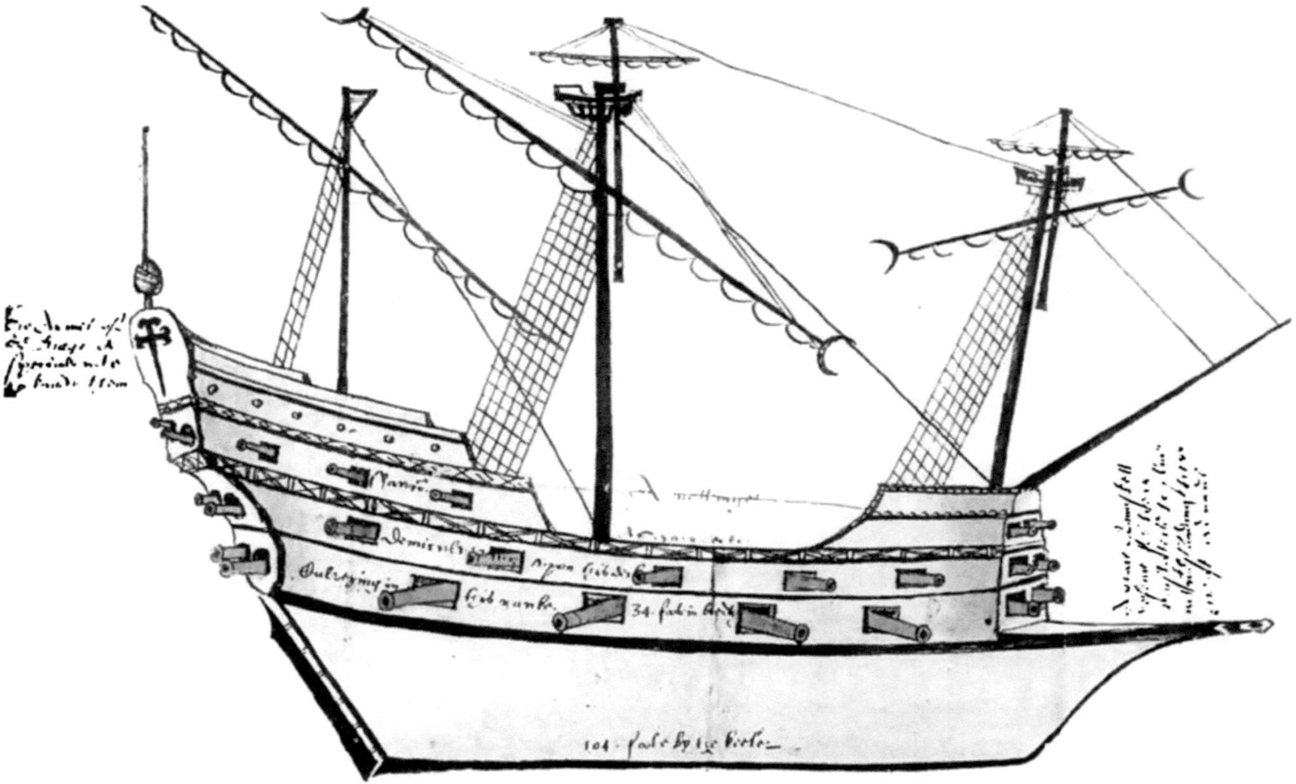

FIG. 56. SPANISH TREASURE-FRIGATE OF ABOUT 1590.

The mizzen has a lateen as usual, and the ram still survives. The artist has also shown the netting mentioned just now. As to the hull, we see from the spy's handwriting that she was "104 foote by the keele" and "34 foote in breadth." She has three tiers of guns, these being mounted also forward, so as to be able to fire straight ahead. She appears to have as many as six decks aft—main, upper, spar and four poop decks. The greatest precaution was taken by the Spanish government to ensure seaworthiness in the ships leaving their shores for the West Indies. Three times they had to be inspected before being allowed to set forth: once when empty, then when laden, and lastly, immediately before departure. No cargo was allowed to be carried on deck except water, provisions and passengers' luggage. In the huge "channels" which were mentioned above were stowed such commodities as wool, small casks of water, and straw. Mr. Oppenheim mentions that an ancient "Plimsoll" mark was ordered by the inspectors in the year 1618, although the Genoese statutes had ordained this as early as 1330.

When in 1592 the English captured the "huge carak ' called the *Madre de Dios* belonging to Portugal, there were found stowed in her capacious channels about 200 tons of goods. This will give some idea of the extent to which these channels grew in size. Hakluyt contains a long and detailed account of the capture and dimensions of this carack, which was the largest the English seamen had yet encountered. She was 1600 tons, having between 600 and 700 souls aboard, besides her rich cargo of jewels and spices and silks and other goods. She was eventually brought into Dartmouth, and is said never again to have left the harbour. When surveyed, Hakluyt says that she measured from beak-head to the stern, 165 feet, extreme beam, 46 feet 10 inches. Her draught when laden had been 31 feet, which, being about the draught of one of the largest modern liners, would seem exaggerated did not the account definitely state that the survey was exactly made by "one M. Robert Adams, a man in his faculty of excellent skill." When, after being lightened, she was taken into Dartmouth, she drew only 26 feet, which is still enormous. Her decks at the stern comprised a main orlop and three closed decks. At the bows she had a forecastle and a spar deck "of two floors apiece." The length of her keel was 100 feet, of the mainmast 121 feet, while the circuit at the partners was 10 feet 7 inches, the main yard being 106 feet long. The following year another enormous carack was fired and sunk by the English. Her name was *Las Cinque Llagas* ("The Five Wounds"), and she is said by some to have been bigger even than the *Madre de Dios*.

One of the most memorable of naval battles was that which was fought on the Adriatic Sea in 1571. On the one side were the allied forces of Venice, Spain, and the Papal States: on the other, the Turks who were defeated. Galleys and galleasses played an important part in obtaining this victory. To what development the galley had attained since the times of the early Greeks and Romans will be seen in Figs. 57 and 58. But in spite of all that history had added to them, it is surprising how little they differ in essentials. Fig. 57 has been sketched from a model in the South Kensington Museum. It is quite old, and is said to have belonged to the Knights of Malta. Her dimensions if built to scale would work out at about 165 feet long, by 22 feet beam, with extreme beam from gunwale to gunwale, 31 feet. The depth would be 9·9 feet, and the number of sweeps 44. In the United Service Museum there is also an instructive Maltese galley model of a large size which, though of the eighteenth century, differed so little as to be closely similar to the excellent illustration which we give in Fig. 58. This has been taken from an important publica-
216

tion, of the beginning of the seventeenth century, by Joseph Furttenbach, entitled " Architectura Navalis,' printed at Ulm in 1629. As will be seen, each oar is still worked by a gang of men. At the stern the captain sits

FIG. 57. MEDITERRANEAN GALLEY.

with his knights by his side, while at the extreme stern is the pilot. Along the *corsia* or gangway down the ship walk two men with long poles with which to beat the lazy oarsmen. The principal armament was carried in the bows and so was unable to be used for broadside fire. Notice also the survival of the trumpeters. The length of this vessel was 169 feet from beak to stern, with an extreme beam of about 20 feet. The word *antennæ* is still found at this time as applied to the yards. In spite

217

of the handiness of the galley and her consequent popularity in the Mediterranean, she was thoroughly despised by Elizabethan seamen. Much more after their own heart was the *nave* or ship shown in Fig. 59, and also taken out of Furttenbach. The reader will notice a wise restriction of high-charged structures. This vessel, in fact, shows a steady improvement in naval architecture. Thus, besides the lateen mizzen she carries a square topsail above, while in addition to the spritsail seen furled to its yard on the bowsprit, there has now been added a sprit topsail whose yard is seen to hoist up a sprit topmast. When we compare this vessel with the wooden walls of the eighteenth century, she will be seen to be wonderfully modern. The last traces of crude mediævalism are disappearing. Science in design has fast begun to supplant rule of thumb and guess-work based only on ignorance. Skill has taken the place of inexperience in the work of the shipwright, and both design and construction have been based on the knowledge obtained not only in long and tedious voyages, but in the brisk fighting between nation and nation and privateer against treasure ship and trader. In the same volume of Furttenbach a useful plan of the lines of this ship is given, from which we see that whilst the main mast is stepped at the keelson, the fore and mizzen are stepped on the main deck.

A favourite vessel with the Turkish pirates who infested the Mediterranean at this time was the *carramuzzal*, classed as a brigandine. Her sail, says Hakluyt, consisted of " a misen or triangle " sail, that is of course a lateen. She is shown in Furttenbach purposely without rigging or sails so as to indicate clearly her method of firing. The *tartana*, with her lateen sail, sometimes seen in contemporary prints, was a Mediterranean fishing vessel.

In spite of the great interest manifested by England and other nations recently in Arctic exploration, let us

218

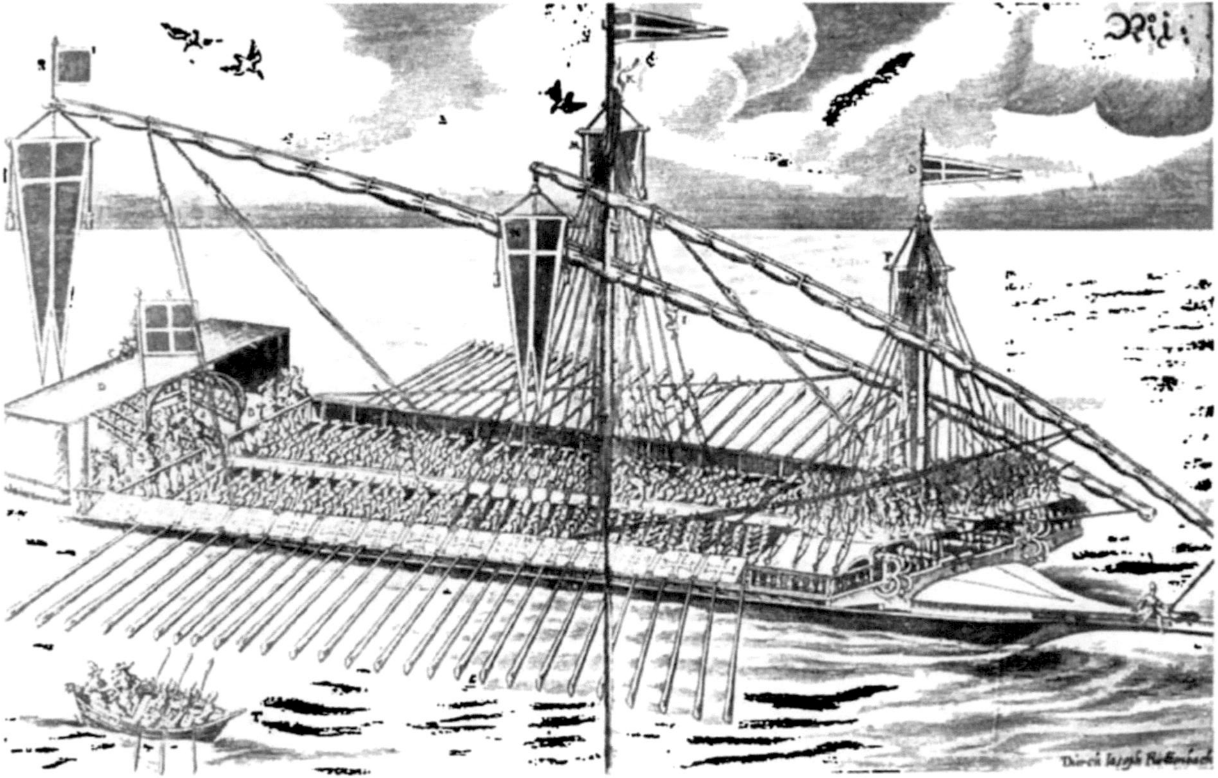

FIG. 58. AN EARLY SEVENTEENTH-CENTURY GALLEY.

Fig. 59. A Full-rigged Ship of the Early Seventeenth Century.

p. 212.

not forget that the first true polar voyage was undertaken during the reign of Elizabeth by Dutchmen. Their object was to find the North-East passage to China, and terrible were the privations and perils endured. The reader who has become familiar with Franklin's, McClintock's, Nansen's, Scott's, Shackleton's, and other explorers' travels to the poles, is advised to compare the experiences which these Dutchmen endured. Many of them have their counterpart in the accounts written by modern explorers. Thus one of the ships was tilted over to a dangerous angle, though ultimately righted. Once one of the ships was caught in a driving pack of ice, and suddenly freeing herself three of her crew who were on the ice had barely time to be drawn quickly up the ship's sides and saved from drowning. These and the other incidents mentioned here are all delightfully illustrated in " A true account of the three new unheard of and strange journeys in ships . . . in the years 1594, 1595 and 1596," by Levinus Hulsius, printed at Frankfort in 1612. The type of ship used for this expedition appears to be the galleon. The rigging and sails, the lacing holes for the drabbler and bonnet, the topsails "goared" out to the clews, and the bowlines, are all shown. One illustration proves that when close-hauled these ships stowed both spritsail and sprit topsail.

Unhappily for the navigators, but luckily for us, their big ship stuck fast in the ice and remained there. Anxious, therefore, to return to Holland with the approach of summer, they determined to attempt the journey in open boats. Now much as we sympathise with the sufferings of these brave men, this unfortunate incident of an abandoned ship has given us a picture of the men engaged in adding raised gunwales to their small boats and afterwards sailing across the sea. Hitherto in this history of the sailing ship, except when we spoke of the lateen, we have always had in mind the squaresail rig. Its virtues never grow old when utilised for big ships and deep-sea sailing. But for small craft and for handiness there is nothing to beat what is known as the fore and aft rig. Just exactly when the fore and aft rig originated is not possible to determine, although its rise and influence have been since very powerful, especially in the modern yacht and fishing vessel. But it may be taken as practically certain that the sloop rig (by which I mean a vessel with a peaked mainsail and a triangular headsail), like many other good points of ship development, came from the Low Countries during the first half of the sixteenth century. In a map* sent in 1527 from Seville, in Spain, by M. Robert Thorne to Doctor Ley we see a Dutch-like sloop depicted. A map of Ireland of 1567 contains two vessels of this rig. H. C. Vroom, whom we referred to above as the designer of the House of Lords tapestries, painted a picture entitled *The Arrival at Flushing of Robert Dudley, Earl of Leicester,* 1586. The date of Vroom's birth was 1566. Now this picture shows about half a dozen small vessels rigged exactly like the small boat given in Hulsius. This rig consists of a triangular sail hoisted up the forestay, and with a mainsail having no boom or gaff, but a large sprit across; in fact, exactly resembling the rig of the Thames "stumpey" barge to-day. It was only at a later date that the jib was added to the foresail and a topsail to the sprit mainsail. The other small boat given in Hulsius is shown square rigged, with one course on her main and the same on her fore, but the latter mast is stepped very far forward and right at the bows. The design of the latter boat's hull shows the remnant of the Viking influence, which is not obliterated even in the modern Dutch schuyt. It should be mentioned also that the cutter-rigged boat in Hulsius just alluded to has a yard-tackle coming down from the top of the mast to about the middle of the sprit,

* This map will be found reproduced at p. 171, vol. ii., of Maclehose's edition of Hakluyt, published in 1903.

while from the peak of the sail two vangs lead down aft, just as in the modern barge.

Before we close this eventful period we must not omit to mention the East India Company, which ranks after the Armada and the Battle of Lepanto as the most important item to be reckoned with in connection with the development of the sailing ship. Formed by a company of merchant-adventurers to trade to the East Indies, Elizabeth granted its charter in 1600 : its first fleet consisted of the *Red Dragon* (600 tons and 200 men), the *Hector* (300 tons and 100 men), the *Ascension* (200 tons and 80 men), and the *Susan* (240 tons and 80 men), together with a deep-sea pinnesse of 100 tons with 40 men.

The Tudor period had seen the most wonderful innovations and developments in connection with the sailing ship. Under no period had it altered so much or in so short a space of time. Not, indeed, until we come to the middle of the nineteenth century did the sea witness such original craft voyaging across its surface. But let us see now what happened during the reigns of the Stuarts and their successors.

CHAPTER VII.

FROM THE ACCESSION OF JAMES I. TO THE CLOSE OF THE EIGHTEENTH CENTURY.

 NE of the most lucrative, if exciting, professions which was far from unpopular during Elizabeth's reign was that of fitting out a small fleet of two or three ships, roving about the seas, especially off the coast of Spain, attacking and, when fortunate, capturing a ship homeward bound with treasure from the West Indies. In spite of the distinguished Englishmen who were engaged in this, in spite of the excellent training it afforded to our seamen, it can only be condemned as illegal and piratical, although for a long time it was winked at. James I., however, on his accession determined to take away from it any semblance of approval. He did his best to bring an end to these marauding expeditions, but for all that they went on persistently though not overtly. Captain John Smith, a distinguished sailor of this time, who was also the first Governor of Virginia, has left us a lively account depicting an imaginary engagement to illustrate the working of a ship of this date. It is to be found in " An Accidence or The Pathway to Experience necessary for all young

sea-men . . . written by Captaine John Smith sometimes Governour of Virginia and Admirall of New England," printed in London in 1626. As it shows in actual use the very details of the ship and equipment we mentioned in the last chapter, I cannot refrain from quoting at length the following graphic description. I give it just as it was printed, substituting only modern spelling and punctuation:

" A sail ! How stands she ? To windward, or leeward ? Set him by the compass. He stands right ahead, or on the weather bow, or lee bow. Out with all your sails : a steady man to the helm. Sit close to keep her steady. Give chase or fetch him up. He holds his own. No : we gather on him. Out goeth his flag and pennants or streamers, also his colours, his waist-cloths and top-armings. He furles and slings his mainsail. In goes his sprit sail and mizzen. He makes ready his close fights * fore and after : well, we shall reach him by and by. What ? Is all ready ? Yea, yea. Every man to his charge. Dowse your topsail. Salute him for the sea—hail him. 'Whence your ship ?' 'Of Spain : whence is yours ?' 'Of England.' 'Are you merchants or men of war ?' 'We are of the sea.' He waves us to leeward for the King of Spain and keeps his luff. Give him a chase piece, a broad side and run ahead. Make ready to tack about, give him your stern pieces. Be yare † at helm : hail him with a noise of trumpets.

" We are shot through and through, and between wind and water. Try the pumps. Master, let us breathe and refresh a little. Sling a man overboard to stop the leak. Done, done ! Is all ready again ? Yea, yea. Bear up close with him. With all your great and small shot charge him. Board him on his weather quarter. Lash

---

* That is to say he not merely covers with the canvas-cloth the whole length of the deck to prevent boarding, but the nettings would also be drawn over the waist to catch the falling wreckage of spars. (See Fig. 53.)

† Dexterous.

fast your grappling irons and sheer off. Then run stem-lines the midships. Board and board * or thwart the hawse. We are foul on each other. The ship's on fire. Cut anything to get clear, and smother the fire with wet cloths. We are clear, and the fire out. God be thanked. The day is spent, let us consult. Surgeon, look to the wounded, wind up the slain. With each a weight or bullet at his head and feet. Give three pieces for their funerals. Swabber, make clean the ship. Purser, record their names. Watch, be vigilant to keep your berth to windward, and that we lose him not in the night. Gunners, spunge your ordinances. Soldiers, scour your pieces. Carpenters, about your leaks. Boatswain and the rest, repair the sails and shrouds. Cook, see you observe your directions against the morning watch. Boy ! Hulloa, master, hulloa ! Is the kettle boiled ? Yea. Boatswain, call up the men to prayer and breakfast.

" Boy, fetch my cellar of bottles. A health to you all fore and aft. Courage, my hearts, for a fresh charge. Master, lay him aboard luff for luff. Midshipmen, see the tops and yards well manned with stones and brass balls. To enter them at shrouds and every squadron else at their best advantage, sound drums and trumpets and St. George for England. They hang out a flag of truce. Stand in with him, haul him amain, abaft, or take in his flag. Strike their sails and come aboard, with the captain, purser and gunner, with your commission, cocket or bills of loading. Out goes their boat. They are launched from the ship side. Entertain them with a general cry. God save the captain, and all the company, with the

* " Boord and boord "—*i.e.*, when two ships touch each other.

Manwayring advises against boarding the enemy at the quarter, which is the worst place, because it is high. The best place for entering was at the bows, but the best point for the play of the guns was to come up to her "athwart her hawes "—*i.e.*, across her bows. By this means you could then bring all your broadside to play upon her, while all the time the enemy could only use her chase and prow pieces.

trumpets sounding. Examine them in particular, and then conclude your conditions with feasting, freedom or punishment, as you find occasion. Otherwise if you surprise him or enter perforce, you may stow the men, rifle, pillage or sack and cry a prize."

Perhaps we may be allowed to add a word further in explanation of the duties of the officers taken also from this little book. The captain was not necessarily a seaman. His authority was to command the whole company and keep them in order. The lieutenant was to assist the captain and—hence the word—in his absence to take his place. The captain also directed a fight, while the master was really the sailing master and gave orders to the sailors, taking charge of the ship as long as she was on the high seas: but "when they make land" the pilot "doth take charge of the ship till he bring her to harbour." The duties of the sailors included hoisting sails, getting the tacks aboard, hauling the bowlines and steering the ship. The Yonkers were the young men whose work was to take in the topsails, furl and sling the mainsail, to do all the bowsing or tricing, and take their turn at the helm. In the setting of watches, the master chose one and the mate the other.

As to the ship herself we find that the planking of a vessel of 400 tons was to be four inches thick, ships of 300 tons to have three-inch planking, and small ships two-inch, but never less than this. Between the beams of the deck and the orlop there were to be six feet of headroom, and ten ports on each side upon the lower orlop. A flagstaff was over the poop. A jeer-capstan was only to hoist the sails of big ships, being raised by hand on small vessels. Smith mentions using in a "faire gaile your studding sayles," and confirms the use of the mizzen topsail. One interesting item that he enumerates is obviously what we now know by the name of drogue or sea-anchor. Smith calls it a "drift sail." Manwayring describes the drift sail as " a sail used under water, being veered out right ahead, having sheets to it, the use whereof is to keep a ship's head right upon the sea in a storme.   Also it is good, where a ship drives in fast with a current, to hinder her driving in so fast, but it is most commonly used by fishermen in the North Seas."   Smith mentions also the cross-jack yard as being now in use.

During James I.'s reign the East India Company, encouraged by the King, endowed with a new charter, began to flourish considerably.   An important new vessel was built for them called the *Trade's Increase*, but she was careened whilst abroad at the end of her first voyage, in order to have some repairs made to her hull.   She fell over on to her side and was burnt by the Javanese.   Her size was 1100 tons, and the loss of so large a vessel in those days was a severe blow.   This was not the only occasion in which an English ship was thrown away in this manner. Manwayring, writing of the contemporary practice of careening, says that if a ship wanted attention below the waterline, as for instance her seams to be caulked, when the vessel could not be conveniently put ashore and in ports where the tide does not dry right out, the method was to take out most of the ballast and guns.   Then by her side was brought a lower ship to which tackles were attached, by means of which the larger vessel was hauled down on to her side, care being taken at the same time not to strain the masts too much.   Some ships which were not naturally top-heavy did not careen without difficulty, but English ships, having still fairly high decks, careened somewhat easily.   The Dutch, through the shallowness of the water off their coasts, could not have a deep draught, and in consequence their decks were not built high.   And because they were the reverse of top-heavy it was with great difficulty that a Dutchman was careened.

In 1603 James built three new ships for the Navy, and five years later the *Ark Royal* of Elizabeth's reign was rebuilt and renamed the *Anne Royal.* In 1608 the keel was laid for the *Prince Royal,* a ship of 1200 tons, whose appearance will be found in Fig. 60. This illustration is from a picture in the Trinity House, and is here reproduced by kind permission of the Elder Brethren. She was the largest and finest ship that had ever been designed for the English Navy, and was the finest man-of-war of her time. She was both built and designed under the supervision of Phineas Pett, Master of Arts of Emmanuel College, Cambridge, a distinguished member of a distinguished family which, from the reign of Henry VIII. right down to William and Mary kept up a continuous line of naval builders and architects. An unsuccessful attempt was made to launch her on September 24, 1610, when it was found that the dock head at Woolwich was too narrow to allow her to get through. She was eventually launched successfully, however, at a later date. She was a three-decker in the sense that she had two full batteries and an upper deck armed. Gorgeously decorated with carvings and paintings the *Prince Royal* was double-planked, and with but slight modifications, chiefly in respect of her decoration, would not be dissimilar to the ships built at the beginning of the nineteenth century. Indeed so slight, comparatively, were the developments that took place between this and the time of the Battle of Trafalgar that the ships of the early Stuarts would not have looked out of place among the ships of Nelson's fleet. Between now and the close of the eighteenth century the similarity between men-of-war and merchantmen was so close as to make distinction practically impossible. That, too, will account for the fact of the English in the foregoing imaginary encounter by Smith asking whether the Spanish vessel were a merchant or man-of-war. We have made so many changes between the two classes of ships since then that it is a little difficult at first to realise this.

In the design of the *Prince Royal*, many of the old-fashioned conventionalities went by the board, and, as is always the case with a daring innovation, hostile criticisms were not scarce. Some of these, however, were justified, for when a Commission was appointed to report on the design, it was found that more than double the number of loads of timber were used than had been estimated for. The *Prince Royal* had a figurehead representing the King's son on horseback, after whom she was named. Her dimensions were : length of keel, 114 feet ; beam, 44 feet. She was pierced for 64 guns and carried 55. This number was restricted in order to guard against the excessive top-weight. In action the vacant port-holes would be filled by guns from the opposite side of the ship. The reader will notice how close the similarity is between the hull of this ship and that of the merchantman in Fig. 59, of this period, taken from Furttenbach. The disappearance of the high poop and forecastles is particularly obvious. Three lanterns were carried at the poop, and subsequently this vessel was cut down smaller. At the beginning of the seventeenth century the lowest decks of ships carried the bread and other store-rooms, the cables, the officers' cabins as well as some of the crew. The second deck was about 6 feet above and pierced with nine ports aside.

By 1624, James' navy contained four ships of the first rank, viz., the *Prince Royal*, the *Bear*, the *Merhonour* and the old *Ark Royal*, now called the *Anne Royal*. Besides these there were fifteen of the second rank, nine of the third, and four of the fourth, as well as some hoys. It is curious to find, too, the existence still, in the navy, of four galleys. They were a source of constant expense, being never used now that the value of big ships had been realised, and they were eventually ordered to be sold out of the service.

Charles I. took the liveliest interest in the Navy, and

FIG. 60. THE "PRINCE ROYAL."

Fig. 61. The "Sovereign of the Seas." Built in 1637.

under him naval architecture continued its progression. The first additions he was responsible for were not of big ships, but of the sea-going pinnesses of about 50 tons and under, equipped with both oars and sails. They were square-rigged, three-masted, and had two decks. They were, however, sparred and ordnanced far too heavily. In spite of the fact that England had built a few large ships during the last century, she had not been conspicuously active in this respect. Far easier and cheaper had it been to capture the pick of the enemy's fleet, and then to refit them and turn the prizes into English men-of-war. But this lethargy was beginning to disappear. Pett was one of the chief influences in regard to this, and it was he who, having closely studied the lines of a fine French ship lying in British waters, learned some of the improvements that afterwards were embodied in the ships of our country.

The *Sovereign of the Seas* in Fig. 61, reproduced from an engraving in the British Museum, after the picture by Van der Velde, owes her design to Pett also. The reader will see how much nearer his craft approaches to the old wooden walls of the eighteenth century. Built in 1637, this vessel was for the next generation the admiration and envy of foreign nations. Like the *Prince Royal* at a later date, she was cut down in 1652 to a two-decker, having been found somewhat crank. But as originally constructed, the *Sovereign of the Seas* was a three-decker— the first of her kind—and her measurements, probably taken on the gun-deck, were : 169 feet 9 inches long, by 48 feet 4 inches beam, the depth of her hold being 19 feet 4 inches. She had a tonnage of 1683 burthen, and her anchor weighed 60 cwt. Designed by one member of the Pett family, Phineas, she was built under the supervision of Peter Pett. In 1684 she was practically rebuilt and then renamed the *Royal Sovereign*, but twelve years later had the misfortune to be burnt accidentally at Chatham, yet not before she had done excellent service under Blake and others during the seventeenth century wars. Notice in the illustration that instead of the rare use of the topgallant at the main, she carries them on all three masts: further still, observe the fact that by now royals have come into use for the first time. The fore and main have them stowed with yards lowered.* Originally the *Sovereign of the Seas* had four masts. She carried over 100 guns; had a figure-head; and the beak-head, though somewhat similar to that of the *Prince Royal,* is placed lower, while the length of the ship is proportionately greater, and the original tubby appearance of the *Prince Royal* is improved upon. There is a medal of the time of Charles 1., commemorating the Declaration of Parliament of 1642. On one side is shown a conventionalised design of this or a similar ship, showing both top-gallants and royals, the latter stowed.

Comparing a ship of the seventeenth century with a modern sailing craft of the same tonnage, the most striking defects that would appear in the former were the clumsiness in proportions. The lowness of the bow and the height of the stern seem to us nowadays ridiculous: so they were. But it was just one of the stages reached in the transition from those lofty forecastles and stern-castles that we saw originate in early times. But masts and spars were now no longer the stumpy items they had been. There was an improvement, too, in

---

* I am far from convinced, however, that the drawing is in this respect correct. Edward Hayward in his book on "The Sizes and Lengths of Riggings for all His Majesties Ships and Frigates," printed in London in 1660, only twenty-three years after the *Sovereign of the Seas* was launched, makes no mention whatever of either her royals or of any mast or spar above topgallant, although he mentions in detail the masts and yards and rigging and sails other than royals. He does mention, however, that the *Sovereign* carried a bonnet to be laced on to her spritsail. It is possible, however, that the royals were added in 1684, when she was rebuilt.

the existing rule of tonnage-measurement, Up to 1628 it had been far from reliable, being reckoned by the capacity for storing so many tuns of wine. From the time of Henry V. and long after, ton as applied to shipping denoted the capacity to hold a barrel measuring 42 cubic feet in the hold below deck. Therefore a vessel of 900 tons was capable of holding 900 such barrels. As the barrels were circular and could not be packed close together, the tonnage was really greater than what was given.* But from 1628 it was to be estimated from the length of the keel, leaving out the false post (a piece bolted to the after edge of the main sternpost), the greatest breadth within the plank, the depth from that breadth to the upper edge of the keel, and then to multiply these and divide the result by one hundred.†

We have seen how, in the sixteenth century, the greatest rivals of the English were the Spaniards. Now, in the seventeenth century, it was the Dutch. Gradually they had been getting stronger and stronger until about the middle of the seventeenth century they had reached their zenith in prosperity and power. They had accumulated considerable wealth, were building fine, capable ships, and about the time we are speaking of had no equals in either of these possessions. Before the close of the sixteenth century we have seen them engaging on the first Arctic Expedition and inventing a new rig for small vessels. All through the reigns of James and Charles I. they had gone on developing. It was not until about the close of Elizabeth's reign that Holland had commenced to build ships purely for fighting purposes, but by the year 1624 their men-of-war were the superior of ours. They

* See Appendix II. of "Ancient and Modern Ships," by Sir G. C. V. Holmes.

† See "A History of the Administration of the Royal Navy and of Merchant Shipping in Relation to the Navy," &c., by M. Oppenheim, p. 268.

kept their ships well, and we find incidentally that it was the practice of the Dutchmen to tallow the bottom of their ships while the English had allowed their vessels to become overgrown with weeds and barnacles below the water-line. The competition between the two countries set ablaze so much jealousy that an explosion was bound to come sooner or later. It did come during the Commonwealth, but though the Civil Wars of Charles I. had the same ill effects on our Navy as the Wars of the Roses, yet under Blake the Dutch were beaten, our Navy became again the finest in the world, and settled for the future the position which English fleets should occupy in respect of other nations. Highly ruinous as this war was to Dutch shipping and commerce, it meant the rise of our own Navy and merchant service. True, our vessels were slower under sail than the Dutchmen, yet we were more solidly built and armed more heavily. One result of the war in 1654, not a little gratifying to our pride, remained in the acceptation by the enemy that henceforth all Dutch ships, whether men-of-war or of the merchant service, on meeting any English men-of-war in British seas should strike their flags and lower topsails. Another and more practical result was that many valuable Dutch ships passed into our Navy as prizes.

During the Dutch hostilities was employed, for the first time, by the English, a man-of-war named the *Constant Warwick*, which was the successor of the galleasse and the immediate precursor of the frigate of the eighteenth century. Originally the name " frigate " (French, *frégate*) was only known in the Mediterranean: it was then used as applied to the galleasse type of craft, having oars plus sails. But it was the English who were the first to appear on the ocean, says " Falconer's Marine Dictionary," with frigates denoting " a light, nimble ship, built for the purpose of sailing swiftly." The *Constant Warwick* was of 315 tons. Before the end of the Commonwealth the frigate was given finer lines to her underwater body, whilst the height of the hull above water was reduced and the keel lengthened. The rake fore and aft was lessened, so that the extreme length over all became diminished in proportion to the length of the keel. In spite of the obvious improvements which would ensue from this alteration, there was one vessel, the *Gainsborough*, which Mr. Oppenheim cites, that was unable to beat to windward. These new frigates were built at first without forecastles, but afterwards, except in the case of the fifth and sixth rates, they were added to the larger ships. They were somewhat under-canvassed rather than the reverse. The long boat was still towed astern as we saw in an earlier century, the pinnace and skiff being stowed on board. Although during the Commonwealth the ornate decoration of ships was restricted, gilding being entirely stopped, yet in 1655 Mr. Oppenheim states that this restriction was relaxed. The figurehead, the arms on the stern and the two figures on the stern gallery were to be gilt, but elsewhere the hull was to be black and picked out in gold where there was carving. In spite of all that we can bring against Cromwell it is only fair to say that he exercised a considerable amount of good on behalf of the Navy and English commerce. In addition to settling the Dutch troubles, there had been another matter affecting our shipping that needed attention. For some time the piratical people of Algiers had made the seas to be so dangerous as practically to have throttled overocean trade. Cromwell, however, in his own determined manner undertook an expedition to the Mediterranean under the command of Blake, and secured relief for our commerce from the attacks by which it had been harassed.

From "Two Discourses of the Navy: 1638 and 1659," by John Hollond,* we are able to gather some further

* Edited by J. R. Tanner, M.A., Navy Records Society, 1896, from the MSS. in the Pepysian Library.

information as to the material used for ships of the English Navy during the Commonwealth. Thus, the second of these discourses, written the year before Cromwell died, mentions that there were three kinds of hemp in use, viz. : Russian, which was the cause of considerable complaint because it lasted only a year, while home-made hemp endured for eighteen months ; Rhine band being another variety, and Riga band the third. But there appears to have been a good deal of trickery and dishonesty generally going on at this time in connection with hemp and cordage.

As to the timber, English oak was used for straight, curved (referred to as "compass"), and knee timbers. Ash was used for blocks and tholes, &c., while elm and beech were used for the planking below the waterline and also for the keel. There was in this century a great dearth of timber, and the royal forests had seriously deteriorated. As a result, foreign planking was imported in large quantities from abroad, and especially the Baltic. In this may be found the explanation for the speed with which our ships decayed. In Charles II.'s time the planks and timbers were fastened with tree-nails or hard wooden pins. Those who have not forgotten their undergraduate days will be interested to hear that the best trees for this purpose were grown at Shotover and Stow Wood, Oxfordshire.

With regard to the iron used, by 1636 there were as many as three hundred iron works in the country. Iron nails were stolen in such large quantities that the systematic marking of Navy stores was begun about the time of the Restoration. A proclamation of 1661 introduced the broad arrow, as a Government mark on timber and anchors.

We pass now to the time of Charles II.* Following up the zeal of the ancestors of his house, Charles showed

* I am indebted for many important details of this reign to "A Descriptive Catalogue of the Naval MSS. in the Pepysian Library at Magdalene, Cambridge," edited by Dr. J. R. Tanner, Navy Records Society, 1903.

a very real interest in the Navy. In spite of all his follies, in spite of his libertinism and effeminacy, Charles had one great outstanding series of good deeds to his name in having done more for the English Navy than perhaps any English rulers before him. Navigation and naval architecture went ahead rapidly: the Greenwich Royal Observatory and the Nautical Almanac were founded, the science of astronomy encouraged, and yachting in this country given such an impulse as is still felt to this day.

The total strength of the Navy at the Restoration was 156, this number being made up of the following entities : first rates, second rates, third rates, fourth rates, fifth rates, sixth rates, hoys (small sloop-rigged merchant vessels adapted for war purposes), hulks (for transporting horses, &c.), sloops, ketches, pinks and yachts. Sir Walter Raleigh refers * to "hoyes" of Newcastle as needing a slight spar-deck addition fore and aft. He speaks of them as being ready in stays and in turning to windward. They drew but little water, and carried six demi-culverin and four sakers. Manwayring defines the ketch somewhat vaguely as "a small boate such as uses to come to Belingsgate with mackrell, oisters &c." The ketch was a two-masted ship, not necessarily fore and aft rigged as we speak of them nowadays, but with the mainmast stepped well aft.† Descended from the Dutch galliot, the ketch was especially used at the end of the seventeenth century as a "bomb-ketch." The illustration in Fig. 62 is from an old French print in the United Service Museum, Whitehall, where it is called a "Galiote à bombe." Bomb ketches were first employed by Louis XIV. in the bombardment of Algiers with great success. They were about 200 tons burthen, and built very strongly, so as to bear the downward recoil of the mortars. The reason for the large triangular space left

* "Judicious and Select Essayes and Observations," p. 29.
† But see Chapter IX. of this volume.

between the mainmast and the bowsprit is to give plenty of room for the mortar to fire. The hold was closely packed with old cables, cut into lengths, the yielding elastic qualities of the packing assisting in taking up the force of the recoil.* The stamp used by the Hakluyt Society on their publications is ketch-rigged. About the time of the beginning of Charles II., the fore and aft ketch would be rapidly developing. The pink was also of Dutch extraction. She is—for the Dutch craft have scarcely altered since the seventeenth century—a cutter or yawl-rigged small open boat, and clinker built.

About 1660 Chatham was the most important of the royal dockyards, Pett being in charge there. Sir Anthony Dean made a report on the state of the Navy in 1674, at the close of the Third Dutch war. As a result the sum of £300,000 was voted by Parliament to build twenty ships as suggested by Sir Anthony. As to the comparative strength of the European nations at this time, the following list is instructive. On April 24, 1675, England had ninety-two ships carrying twenty to one hundred guns and upwards : France had ninety-six ships and Holland one hundred and thirty-six. As we mentioned just now, the shallowness of the Dutch waters prohibited the building of big ships, so that they were unable to build three-deckers, and the largest ships carried no more than eighty or ninety guns. In addition to the figures quoted above, we must add three fireships to the English, four to the French, and forty to the Dutch fleets.

The £300,000 voted by Parliament was really with a view of meeting the increase in the French Navy. It was during the first year of the reign of our Charles II. that young Louis XIV. took the government of the French into his own hands. There was then practically no French Navy in existence, if we except a handful of frigates. But three years before Sir Anthony Deane's

* " Ancient and Modern Ships," pp. 111, 112.

Fig. 62. Four Kettu

FIG. 63. THE "ROYAL CHARLES." BUILT IN 1672.

p. 283.

recommendation was approved by Parliament, France had increased her fleet to fifty ships of the line, besides a large number of frigates and small craft. It was during Louis' regime, in fact, that England had to look, not to Spain, nor to the Dutch for signs of possible trouble on the sea, but to France, which rose rapidly to a position of the first importance as a naval power. Thus, English first-rates were to be built not with a view of the shallow-draught Dutchmen but in order to be able to contend with the fine French fleet whose vessels were the superior to ours in size, though our first-rates were capable of standing an enemy's battery better than most ships.

English second-rates had the advantage financially of needing fewer men. They drew less water, carried a smaller weight of ordnance, but by reason of the fire from their three decks were able to render a good account of themselves in battle. Fourth-rates served only as convoys, and likewise the fifth-rates. In Pepys's time England had as many as thirty-six fourth-rates.

We are able to gather a good deal of information respecting naval matters of the time from Pepys's Diary. In the early part of the reign war with the Dutch had broken out again, and in 1667 the Dutch had actually sailed up the Thames estuary and burnt our ships in the Medway. In spite of the ultimate good results to the English Navy under Charles II., the daring and pluck which had been so conspicuous in the Elizabethan seamen appear to have been not always alive. But what worse evidence could be wished of the condition of the English character of the time when we remember that while a Dutch fleet of eighty ships burned the forts of Sheerness and ascended the Medway as far as Chatham, capturing and destroying our men-of-war, Charles II. " amused himself with a moth-hunt in the supper room, where his mistresses were feasting in splendour "? Under the date of July 4, 1666, Pepys writes in his diary :

SAILING SHIPS

" With the Duke, all of us discoursing about the places where to build ten great ships: the King and Council have resolved on none to be under third-rates; but it is impossible to do it, unless we have more money towards the doing it than yet we have in any view. But, however, the show must be made to the world. In the evening Sir W. Pen came to me, and we walked together, and talked of the late fight. I find him very plain, that the whole conduct of the late fight was ill; that two-thirds of the commanders of the whole fleet have told him so: they all saying, that they durst not oppose it at the Council of War, for fear of being called cowards, though it was wholly against their judgment to fight that day with the disproportion of force, and then we not being able to use one gun of our lower tier, which was a greater disproportion than the other. Besides, we might very well have staid in the Downs without fighting, or anywhere else, till the Prince could have come up to them; or at least, till the weather was fair, that we might have the benefit of our whole force in the ships that we had. He says three things must be remedied, or else we shall be undone by this fleet. First, that we must fight in a line, whereas we fight promiscuously, to our utter and demonstrable ruine: the Dutch fighting otherwise; and we, whenever we beat them. Secondly, we must not desert ships of our own in distress, as we did, for that makes a captain desperate, and he will fling away his ship, when there are no hopes left him of succour. Thirdly, the ships when they are a little shattered must not take the liberty to come in of themselves, but refit themselves the best they can, and stay out—many of our ships coming in with very small disableness. He told me that our very commanders, nay, our very flag-officers, do stand in need of exercising among themselves, and discoursing the business of commanding a fleet: he telling me that even one of our flag-men in the fleet did not know which tacke lost the wind,

238

or kept it, in the last engagement. He says it was pure dismaying and fear that made them all run upon the Galloper, not having their wits about them: and that it was a miracle they were not all lost."

From his entry made on October 20, 1666, we gather that the "fleet was in such a condition, as to discipline, as if the Devil had commanded it. . . . Enquiring how it came to pass that so many ships had miscarried this year . . . the pilots do say that they dare not do nor go but as the Captains will have them, and if they offer to do otherwise the Captains swear they will run them through. He [*i.e.* Commissioner Middleton] says that he heard Captain Digby (my Lord of Bristoll's son, a young fellow that never was but one year, if, that, in the fleet) say that he did hope he should not see a tarpawlin [*i.e.* a sailor] have the command of a ship within this twelve months."

And again on October 28:

"Captain Guy to dine with me, and he and I much talk together. He cries out on the discipline of the fleet, and confesses really that the true English valour we talk of, is almost spent and worn out."

It was Pepys who urged that ships should be built of greater burden, stronger and beamier, for at that time the men-of-war needed to be girdled round the hull. They were crank-sided, could not well carry their guns on the upper decks, especially in bad weather, and not enough room was left for the carrying of stores and victuals. He gives the following comparison between the two principal ships of the French, Dutch and English:

FRENCH

Soll Royall (more correctly *Le Soleil Royal*), 1940 tons.
Royall Lewis (*Le Royal Louis*), 1800 tons.

Besides these, two others were 140 feet long on the keel with 48 feet beam.

SAILING SHIPS

DUTCH

The White Elephant, 1482 tons.
Golden Lion, 1477 tons.
The former was 131 feet long on the keel, the latter
130 feet. Both had 46·9 feet beam, drew 19 feet 8 inches
of water, and carried three decks.

ENGLISH

The *Royal Charles*, "with the girdling of 10 inches
measure," was 1531 tons.

The *Prince* (says Pepys) "is full as big now girdled
and as long on the gun deck as the Charles, but having a
long rake they measure short on the keel or she would be
1520 tons."

It must be observed in reference to the above figures
that the Dutch ships had a greater rake forward and would
measure much bigger, being very beamy. Pepys mentions that "the excellent French and Dutch ships with
two decks are more in number and much larger than our
third rates."

The *Soleil Royal* mentioned above was a fine three-
masted ship of the line, carrying 108 guns. She was a
worthy example of the high state of excellence reached by
the French naval architects of this period. She was lost,
however, when the combined English and Dutch fleets in
1692 defeated the French off Cape La Hogue. This was
a decisive blow to another of those plans for the invasion
of England, and the naval battle in which the French fleet
was utterly destroyed has been regarded by historians as
the greatest naval victory won by the English between
the defeat of the Armada and the battle of Trafalgar.

We give in Fig. 63 an illustration of the *Royal Charles*
mentioned above. This delightful picture is from a photo-

graph of a model in the South Kensington Museum. Built at Portsmouth in 1672 to the designs of Sir Anthony Deane, she carried 100 guns: her length was 136 feet, beam 46 feet, depth 18 feet 3 inches, draught 20 feet 6 inches. The arms of England and the lantern that ornamented her stern are still preserved in the Rijks Museum, Amsterdam, for the *Royal Charles* was one of those vessels which were either captured or destroyed when the Dutch came up to Chatham in 1667. In the beautiful model before us the ports are correctly gilded. The rake and length of the bowsprit are in accordance with the information that has been handed down to us. At the extreme end of the latter will be seen the sprit topmast, up which the sprit topsail was hoisted. A jackstaff is at the top of the sprit topmast. The present model does not show topgallant yards, but as we know from Heyward they were found in the inventory of this ship. Below the sprit topmast and on the bowsprit will be noticed the spritsail yard now kept fixed to the bowsprit.

As to what vessels of the seventeenth century looked like under way the delightfully realistic picture which Mr. Charles Dixon has painted for our frontispiece will materially help our imagination. And here perhaps we may say a word regarding the subject of the flags carried at this period. After the union of England and Scotland in 1603 all British vessels flew the Union flag of the crosses of St. George and St. Andrew in the maintop for a time, English and Scotch ships also carrying their national colours in the foretop. Ensigns of red, white or blue with the St. George's Cross on a white canton next to the ensign staff were also commonly carried until the time of the Commonwealth. But on May 5, 1634, it was ordered that men-of-war alone were to fly the Union flag in future, and that merchantmen according to their nationality were to fly the St. George's or the St. Andrew's flag merely. This rule ended in February, 1649, when Parliament directed men-of-war to fly as an ensign the St. George's Cross on a white field.* The Union flag was carried on the sprit topmast as shown in the frontispiece, and to-day the Jack is still seen at the bows of our men-of-war, though they be built of wood no longer.

Edward Heyward in his book just mentioned gives still further details of contemporary ships. The rule which he mentions for ascertaining the length of the mainmast was that it should be half the length of the keel and once the length of the beam put together. The mainstay was to be in thickness half of the diameter of the mainmast. The shrouds were to be one half the thickness of the stay, and the topmast shrouds to be one half the main shrouds' thickness. One ton of hemp required three barrels of tar. As to the ship's boats of the *Sovereign*, her longboat measured 50 feet 10 inches long, $12\frac{1}{2}$ feet broad, and $4\frac{1}{4}$ feet deep. Her pinnace was 36 feet long, $9\frac{1}{2}$ feet broad, $3\frac{1}{4}$ feet deep. Her skiff was 27 feet long, 7 feet broad, and 3 feet deep. Fourth-rates only carried a long boat and a pinnace, fifth-rates carrying simply a longboat, while sixth-rates had only a 22-feet boat.

The *Prince* mentioned in the above list was the *Prince Royal* of James I.'s reign. Her career had been a distinctly varied one. As originally launched she was the *Victory* belonging to Elizabeth's reign. She fought against the Armada, having been turned into a galleon two years before the fight. In 1610 as stated she had been rebuilt and called the *Prince Royal*, but this "rebuilding" was during this period something far more than any moderate adaptation. After the death of Charles I. her name was called during the Commonwealth the *Resolution*, and at the Restoration this was changed yet again to the *Royal*

* "The Royal Navy," by W. Laird Clowes, London, 1898. See p. 25, vol. ii.

Prince. According to Le Sieur Dassie in his "L'Architecture Navale" printed in Paris in the year 1677, *Le Soleil Royal* had a tonnage of 2500 as well as 120 guns and 1200 men. *Le Royal Louis* had the same tonnage and the same number of guns, but only a thousand men. He gives also a very full and interesting inventory of *un vaisseau du premier rang* of 2000 tons. Every detail is mentioned even to the *ornements de chapelle.* Very confusing is the naming of the three masts as used by the French at this time and embodied in Dassie's work. Thus, as we hinted in a previous chapter, the foremast is the *misaine*, the main is the *grand mast*, while the mizzen is the *mast d'artimont*, or exactly the reverse of what we should have expected them to be named. From such a work as Dassie's and, some years later, of Jean Bernoulli in his "Essay d'Une Nouvelle Théorie de la Manœuvre des Vaisseaux," printed at Basle in 1724, we see how at last the scientific study of naval architecture had begun to make headway. The action of heavy bodies passing through the liquid sea, the relation of speed to design, were being slowly understood. Finally in 1794 the same scientific treatment was applied to sails. In "A Treatise Concerning the True Method of finding the proper area of the sails for Ships of the Line and from thence the length of masts and yards," by F. H. af. Chapman, printed in London, the area of the sails in regard to the stability of ships is thoroughly entered into.

The illustration in Fig. 64 is of a model of a Dutch man-of-war now in the Royal United Service Museum, Whitehall. It is supposed to be of contemporary date, belonging roughly to the period of Louis XIV's. rule, 1661–1715. The rigging may be relied upon, but the model is too broad in proportion to her length. The guns are also exaggerated in size, but for all that it may serve to assist the reader in visualising the ships of what was so important a maritime Power. The notable characteristic of the Dutch and French craft of the seventeenth century as opposed to the English was that the two former had their sterns terminating squarely, while the English rounded the lines of the stern above water more. This foreign characteristic of the square stern is everywhere noticeable in the contemporary paintings and engravings of Holland. Over and over again we see the overhanging stern gallery, with the transom stern below, going in (so to speak), for the gallery above to project out. We find it in the earliest yachts of Holland, in the Dutch East Indiamen as well as the ships of the line. The reader will recollect at an earlier period we referred to the "tumble-home" which had become a new phase in naval architecture consequent on the introduction of cannon on board ship. This during the ensuing two centuries had been overdone, so that the upper deck bore a ridiculously narrow proportion to the width of the ship at the water-line, but the Dutch in the height of their naval knowledge were the first of the nations to relinquish it. It is to the Dutch of the last part of the sixteenth and the first half of the seventeenth centuries that we owe the beginnings of the fore-and-aft rig and of yachting as we mentioned earlier. But in order that our attention may not be distracted from the history of the squaresail, it will be more convenient to deal with the development of the smaller craft in Chapter IX.

We have already referred to the great influence for good exercised on the English Navy by Dutch and French naval architects. Among the points of superiority which the smaller French craft possessed over ours was that their lower guns were as much as four feet above the water, an improvement that made for greater safety. They could also stow four months' provisions, whereas our frigates were narrower and sharper, and carried their guns little more than three feet clear of the water, having space only for ten weeks' provisions. It was as improvements on these defects that the *Resolution* and *Rupert* had been built by Sir Anthony Deane. During the reign of Charles II., also, Sir Philip Howard made an invention for sheathing his Majesty's ships with lead in preference to using wooden boards with a layer of tar and hair between the sheath and the ship, the whole having been covered outside with a composition of sulphur, oil and other ingredients. The old method of sheathing with elm boards had been introduced by Hawkins during Elizabeth's reign, but it does not appear to have been successful, for in a report dated October 12, 1587, the chief shipwrights state that the *Bonaventure*, which had been treated according to Hawkins' method, had decayed timbers under her sheathing. But the reader will recollect that as far back as the reign of Edward VI. the ships that voyaged to the North-East under Chancellor and Willoughby had part of their underbody covered with thin sheets of lead, while the ancients of the time of Caligula and even before, had also adopted this method of preserving the hulls of ships. So Howard was really a reviver rather than an inventor.

Still, since complaint had been made that Hawkins' method necessitated frequent cleaning, and the roughness of the wood-sheathed bottom interfered with the sailing abilities, Howard's plan was adopted. The first experiment of using his milled lead sheathing was made on the *Phœnix* at Portsmouth in 1670–71, and afterwards on the *Dreadnought*, the *Henrietta*, and others in 1672. The *Phœnix* was careened at Sheerness in 1673, after two voyages to the Straits, and inspected by the King himself. In the same year Howard's new method was finally adopted for the Navy by the Lords of the Admiralty. Considerable opposition was made by some critics, who rightly pointed out that the action of the lead was to corrode very rapidly the iron nails and rudder-irons of the ship, and eventually in 1682 the Navy Board reported against a further use of this sheathing.

SAILING SHIPS

An experiment of quite a different nature was made in 1674 in utilising cypress trees from the new colony of Virginia. They were said to be large enough for the masts of yachts, and both lighter and tougher than fir, which was then being used. It is curious how persistently the galley endeavoured, in spite of every discouragement, to make its reappearance in England. This, however, was owing to the success with which it had flourished in the Mediterranean. In 1666 the Duke of Florence presented Charles II. with two of the best galleys that could be built, one of which went from Leghorn to Tangier. Anthony Deane, the younger, subsequently built a galley called the *James* at Blackwall; another, called the *Charles*, was built at Woolwich, by Phineas Pett the younger, the date of both being 1676. They were classed in Pepys's "Register of the Royal Navy" as fourth-rates. From the naval papers of the period we find that 1000 loads of timber will build a third-rate of 1000 tons. A ship of 1000 tons costs £10 a ton to build, and the life of a ship was about thirty years. Great merchant ships cost from £6 to £8 2s. 6d. to build, but merchantmen of 250 tons cost from £5 to £7 a ton.

By the end of the seventeenth century the sailing ship had reached a stage in development which, till the close of the eighteenth century, altered but little. Naval architecture, thanks to French influence, was progressing. Eddystone lighthouse was built, and Dampier had undertaken his famous voyage to Australia. The naval authorities had by now become firmly convinced of the folly of the high-charged decks, with the enormous rake ascending from the low bows to the lofty stern. But another change was also beginning to take place. For some time it had been customary when a fleet of ships voyaged in company to have them rigged as nearly as possible with spars and sails of the same size, so that in the event of anything carrying away, each ship would be

FIG. 64. A DUTCH MAN-OF-WAR OF ABOUT THE END
OF THE SEVENTEENTH CENTURY.

p. 246.

Fig. 65. The "Terrible," a Two-decker captured from the French in 1747. p. 247.

able to supply the other with a sail, or spar, or rope of the proper dimensions. Later, as ships became bigger and carried more sails and spars, this idea had been extended to the individual ship. Thus, soon after the Revolution, Cloudesley Shovel advocated the supplying of two spare topmasts to every ship, and fitting spritsails in such a manner that when necessity arose they might serve as main topsails. The yards, too, of spritsail, topsail, mizzen topsail, and main topgallant were to be made so as to be interchangeable. By about the beginning of the eighteenth century, the triangular headsails are seen on full-rigged Dutch ships, whilst the lateen mizzen still continues. The reader will recollect that this shaped headsail had first been introduced on the Dutch sloops of the sixteenth century, with their foresail working on a stay as to-day, having a sprit mainsail, resembling that of the modern Thames barge, but with no jib for the present. Now, in the century we are discussing, the Dutchman uses the same shaped headsail for his big ships, the spritsail underneath the bowsprit still remaining. In course of the first half of the eighteenth century this innovation spread to France and to England. At the beginning of the eighteenth century, also, besides the fore staysails, main and foretopmast staysails and main topmast studding sails were in use in our ships. The cables were each 100 fathoms long, made of 21-inch hemp, and the bower anchors weighed 74 cwts. for a first-rate. The length of the longboats was 36 feet, the pinnaces 33 feet, and the skiff 27 feet. The heaviest guns were 42-pounders.* By the middle of the eighteenth century the staysails and triangular headsails had become quite common, and two instead of one spritsail are found under the bowsprit. The sprit topmast disappears, but the jackstaff is used in its place to fly the Union Jack when at anchor, being taken in when under way, otherwise it would hinder the working

* " Life of Captain Stephen Martin, 1666–1740," edited by Clement R. Markham, C.B., F.R.S., Navy Records Society, 1895. See p. 24.

of the triangular headsails. An important change now takes place in the mizzen. The reader will recollect that for several hundred years it had been used in its Mediterranean triangular shape on European ships. Instead of the yard coming quite low down, as in Fig. 63 of Charles II.'s ship, the angle the yard makes with the mizzen mast is nearer to a right angle. Thus, instead of the sail being triangular it is rectangular, having four sides instead of three. The next stage is to cut off that part of this sail which projects forward of the mast, though the yard itself is still allowed to extend ahead of the mast without having any canvas on its forward end. The luff of the sail is laced to the mast, hoops not being used. Finally, by at least 1768, the portion of the yard still found without any canvas is lopped off, and the vangs which had been used all the time for the mainsail of the sloops are seen coming down from the peak to the stern. Also, following the example of the contemporary Dutch fore-and-afters, there is no boom. If the reader will now look at the mizzen of the corvette model in Fig. 69 he will see this penultimate stage clearly shown. The final stage comes later when a boom is added, and that, too, may be traced for its origin to the Dutch fore-and-afters, which, discarding the sprit extending diagonally across the mainsail, added a tiny gaff and a much longer boom, the sail being loose-footed. Instead of the long bowsprit of the early Stuarts, the middle of the eighteenth century saw this mast-like projection cut into two pieces, so as to make bowsprit and jib-boom. Topgallants now become far more frequently used.

After the Revolution, at the end of James II.'s reign, the three ranks of Admiral, Vice-Admiral, and Rear-Admiral, were established, and the practice of having red, blue, and white ensigns, which had been introduced during the time of Charles I., continued. These ensigns were shown on an ensign staff, each having a cross of St. George on a white field in the upper canton. The Jack flown on the staff on the bowsprit was blue with a white saltire and a red cross with white fimbriation over all. Signals were made, not by a combination of flags, but by changing the position of flags.

When Queen Anne died in 1714, there were in our Navy seven first-rates, thirteen second-rates, forty-two third-rates, sixty-nine fourth-rates, forty-two fifth-rates, and twenty-four sixth-rates. As to the meaning signified by these classes, the first-rates were vessels of one hundred guns, or upwards, carrying them on three decks. Second-rates carried from ninety to one hundred guns on three decks : third-rates had from sixty-four to eighty-four guns on two complete decks : fourth-rates had from fifty to sixty guns on two decks: fifth-rates had from thirty to forty-four guns, whilst sixth-rates carried only twenty to thirty guns. There were also in the service smaller vessels classed as sloops, and others classed as gun-brigs and bombs. The progress which had been going on in rigging, during the early years of the eighteenth century, continued in respect of size of tonnage and also in the weight of armament now carried. Regard, too, was paid to the proper seasoning of timber. The action of the Navy Board in 1719 established a scale of dimensions and tonnage for the construction of ships of the six separate rates, and this influence was felt for nearly a century after, although the establishment was not always strictly adhered to. Improvements went on with regard to internal structure and ventilation, and in order to counteract the injurious effects of bilge water. The result was that both the health of the ship herself and of her crew were improved when once the foul gases accumulating below had been overcome. Collaterally with the progress of the science of naval architecture in England was the development in France. Ever since the time of Jean Baptiste Colbert, during the reign of Louis XIV., France had stood superior to any European Power in ship-designing. Nor were English naval architects and ship-wrights slow to avail themselves of whatever opportunity presented itself for studying the lines and structure of the foreigner. Whenever one of the crack ships of the enemy became an English prize it followed that within the next few years an improved English man-of-war, based on the design of the foreigner, would be launched. As an example of the beautiful vessels which France was capable of building, about the middle of the eighteenth century, the illustration in Fig. 65 will at once be evidence. This is the *Terrible*, captured from the French in 1747, and afterwards passed into the English Navy. She was a two-decker with three masts, and carried 74 guns. Her gun-deck was 164 feet 1 inch long, and her beam was 47 feet 3 inches, while her depth was 20 feet $7\frac{1}{2}$ inches. Her tonnage worked out at 1590. The illustration has been taken from a contemporary print in the Royal United Service Museum.

Fig. 66 represents H.M.S. *Royal George*, of 100 guns, one of the most famous ships of the eighteenth century. Her size—2047 tons—alone makes her remarkable, apart altogether from her good looks. Her length on the keel was 143 feet $5\frac{1}{2}$ inches, beam 51 feet $9\frac{1}{2}$ inches, depth 21 feet 6 inches. Built at Woolwich she ended her days as tragically as another vessel we mentioned before, and owing to a similar cause. While she was being careened as she lay at anchor in Spithead for some repairs to her hull below the waterline, she sank on August 29, 1782. To-day she is still famous as the ship in which Rear-Admiral Kempenfelt, together with nine hundred men, women, and children, went down to their graves. The illustration is taken from an engraving, by T. Baston, in "Twenty-two Prints of several of the Capital ships of his Majesties Royal Navy," in the Print Room of the British Museum.

Still another experiment was made in 1761 in order to find some suitable method for sheathing ships' bottoms.

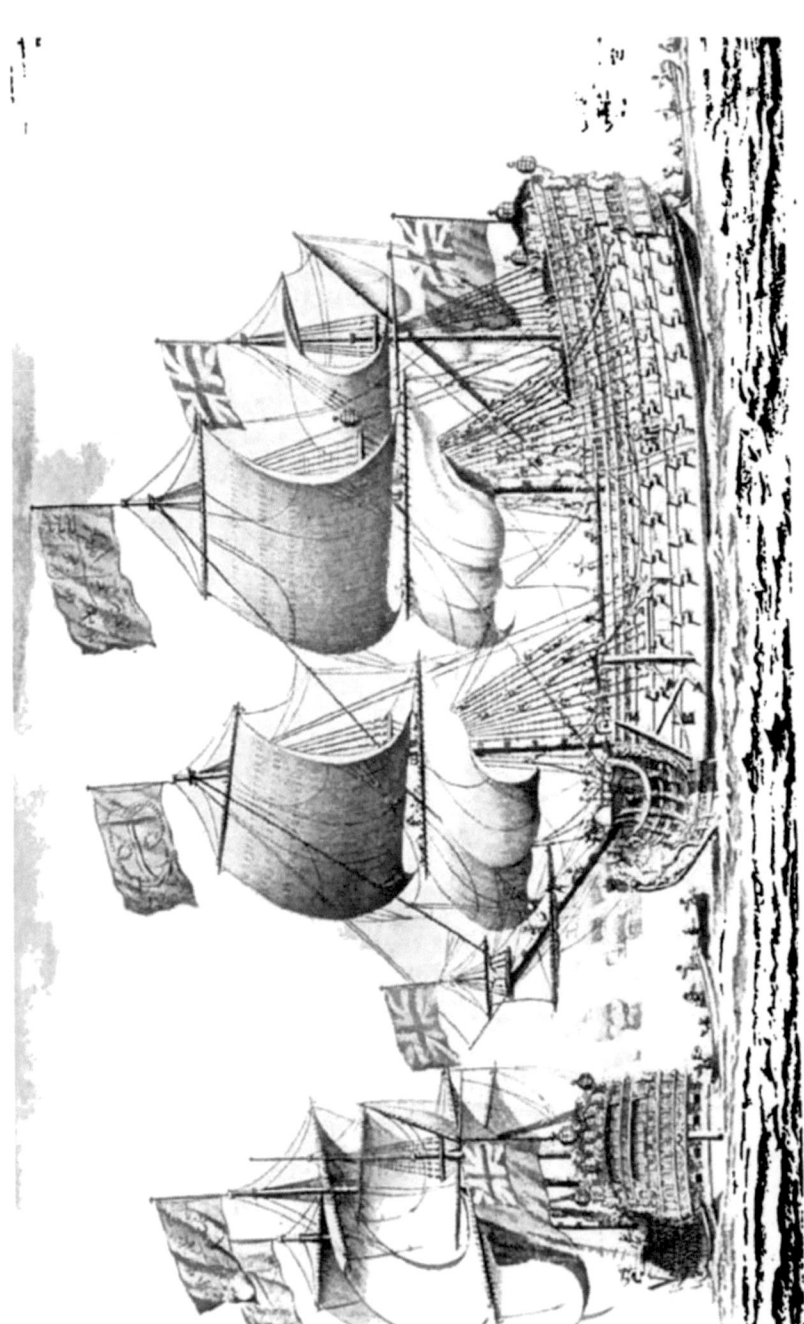

Fig. 66. H.M.S. "Royal George." 100 Guns, 2017 Tons. Foundered in 1782.

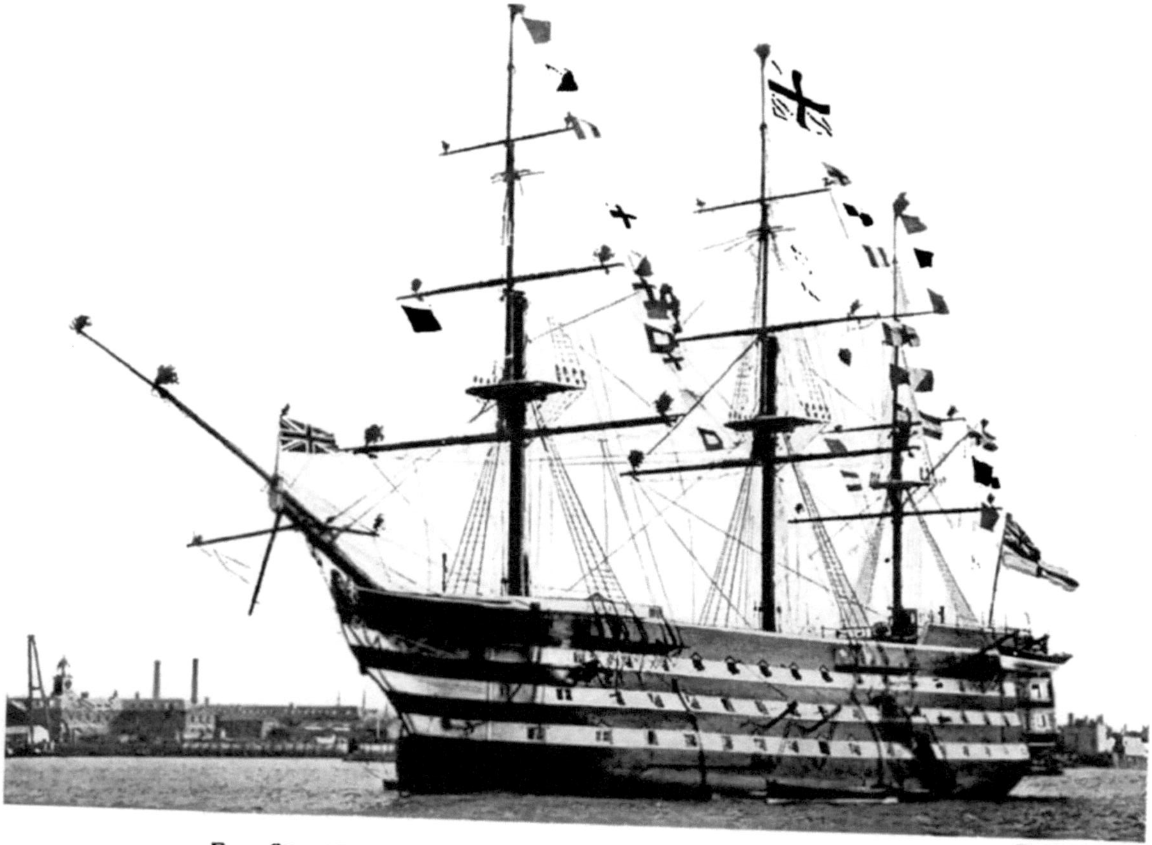

Fig. 67. Nelson's "Victory." 2162 Tons. Built in 1765.

Photo. S. Cribb.

At last lead had been finally discarded. But now the sensible plan of using copper was tried on the *Alarm*, a 32-gun frigate. Finding that not only did this preserve the ship's planking, but also increased the speed of the ship through the water, vessels of all classes were subsequently covered in the same way. The plates of copper were affixed to the hull, tough sheets of paper being placed in between the sheathing and the hull.

Nelson's historic flagship, the *Victory*, of 100 guns, was built in 1765. Her immediate predecessor of the same name was launched in 1735, being the finest first-rate of her time, until she was lost in a terrible storm off the Alderney Race, every one of the 1000 souls on board perishing with her. The illustration of Nelson's *Victory* in Fig. 67 was taken recently in Portsmouth Harbour where this fine old ship still swings to the tide. Her length is (measured on the gun-deck) 186 feet, beam 52 feet, depth of hold 21 feet 6 inches, whilst her tonnage is 2162, or slightly larger than the *Royal George* previously mentioned. The reader will notice the Jack flying in the place previously referred to. Very interesting to us who have traced its development is the stage at which the bow has arrived. Gone is the towering forecastle, though the name still survives as designating the fore-part of even small cabined craft. Even the diminished rake of the seventeenth century from bow to stern has disappeared too. In order that the reader may also obtain some idea of the stern, and the three lanterns which would have been part of the ship's inventory when she set out for the Mediterranean on her last voyage with Nelson, the illustration in Fig. 68 may be worthy of notice. It is only quite recently that the Admiralty have added these replicas, which look not a little incongruous as they tower above submarines and torpedo-boats churning up the water below. The flags flying in Fig. 67 were intended to represent Nelson's immortal signal. It was quite recently discovered, however, that the wrong signals had been flown on Trafalgar Day each year, for the code of a far too modern date was relied upon. This mistake has been rectified, and the correct flags are now flown on October 21.

The illustration in Fig. 69 represents a corvette of about the year 1780. Corvettes were vessels having far less freeboard and without the high quarterdeck. They were ship-rigged and carried less than twenty guns. Those carried on the ship before us would be six-pounders. Her crew would number 125, her tonnage would be 340, her length on the gun-deck, 101 feet, length of keel, 85·5 feet, beam 28 feet, depth of hold 12·5 feet. As to her canvas carried, the triangular head-sails with the two spritsails will be seen. In addition to her courses, she carries topsails, topgallants, and royals on the fore and main masts. The converted lateen has already been referred to, but it should be noticed that while she has on the mizzen a topsail, topgallant and royal, and also a crossjack yard, yet no sail is set on the latter, as it is to-day on a full-rigged ship. This yard had been in use since the beginning of the seventeenth century, and it was not until 1840 that a Yankee skipper took it into his head to introduce the sail which is known as the cro'jack. The French, since from this spar no sail was set, called it the " barren yard "—*vergue sec.** It was during this century that the frigate proper as a fast cruiser was introduced into the English Navy. Still stirred to energy by the activity displayed by the French, the dimensions of English ships were constantly being increased during the last years of the eighteenth century. The capture, in 1792, of the fine three-master *Commerce de Marseilles*, with a tonnage of 2747, and a length of over 200 feet, came as a welcome prize to our fleet which had

* " Old Sea Wings, Ways and Words in the Days of Oak and Hemp," by Robert C. Leslie, London, 1890.

nothing to equal her in respect either of size or armament. Again the design embodied in her was carefully studied by our experts, and before the close of the century two important improvements were made in English men-of-war. The first was to cease placing the lower battery so low down to the water. The reader will readily see that if the enemy were to leeward--as in all probability he should be—our lower ports must necessarily be kept closed unless there were only such a faint draught of wind as scarcely caused the ship to heel over. The French were thus at a great advantage in being able to fire from every one of their guns down to the lowest tier. The second improvement consisted in giving our newer ships a length far greater in proportion to the beam.

CHAPTER VIII.

THE DEVELOPMENT OF THE SAILING SHIP IN THE NINETEENTH AND TWENTIETH CENTURIES.

I SHALL endeavour in this chapter to conclude the narrative of the large sailing ship, all of whose sails, excepting her triangular headsails and the staysails and the new shape which we have seen the mizzen take, are square, and carried athwart the mast. Neither the fore-and-aft rig, nor those hybrid developments of squaresail and fore-and-aft rig, will be considered until the following chapter, in order that our attention may not now be distracted from the older form, and also that we may be able presently to consider, without break of continuity, the story of that newer rig which had its origin during the sixteenth century.

In 1801 the Union Jack was modified by the introduction of a saltire for the Union of Ireland with Great Britain. The white, red and blue admirals, with their corresponding ensigns, continued. Thus the Red Ensign had not become yet the exclusive use of the Merchant Service nor the White Ensign of the Navy, but all three colours were in use to indicate the rank and place of flag-officers. At Trafalgar we fought under the White Ensign solely.   After the practice had grown up of the whole fleet, for the sake of convenience, flying one colour, the three were in 1850 abolished, and the White Ensign became the colour of the Royal Navy.   -

One of the first war vessels to be laid down in the new century was the *Caledonia*, 205 feet long and of 2616 tons. This was in the year 1802, but she was not launched until six years later.   Carrying 120 guns she was a first-rate, and was based on the design of the *Commerce de Marseilles*, which we mentioned in the last chapter.   There is a model both of the *Commerce de Marseilles* and of the *Caledonia* in the Royal Naval College Museum, Greenwich.   The latter was broken up only as recently as 1907.   Up to the beginning of the nineteenth century ships of the Royal Navy were painted with blue upper works, bright yellow sides, and broad black strakes at the waterline.   The interior was generally painted red.*   But Nelson had the hulls of his ships painted black with a yellow strake along each tier of ports, but with black port-lids, and this chequer painting distinguished all men-of-war, both at Trafalgar and after.   White was soon introduced as a substitute for the yellow.   This white band has survived to this day on many of our biggest sailing ships, and is well seen in Mr. Charles Dixon's sketch of the four-masted barque reproduced in Fig. 78.

Among the innovations which came into use during the early years of the nineteenth century were the lifeboat and the prototype of the modern rocket life-saving apparatus.   In 1774 Captain (afterwards Admiral) Schank, while stationed at Boston, built the first craft that ever possessed a sliding keel.   This invention was put into actual use by the English fleet during the wars in which our country was engaged at the beginning of the century. By its means those ships thus fitted were able to sail

* For the purpose of not showing too prominently the blood shed in casualties.

255

closer to the wind without making so much leeway. They were made better on the helm, and they could take the ground with less possibility of damage. There is in the Greenwich Museum an excellent model of the 50-gun frigate *Cynthia*, fitted with these sliding keels in 1795.

The strenuous years that formed the beginning of the new century in which England was constantly at war, gradually increased the size of her Navy to the enormous total of 644 ships which was reached in 1813. When we mention that at the beginning of the present year, 1909, the British Navy, including certain ships not yet completed, did not exceed 517 warships of all kinds, one can readily realise how great had been the extension of the fleet, and, in consequence, how great an incentive to shipbuilding and the seafaring life had been given. But this number had as quickly diminished to 114 four years later, when the outlook of peace seemed bright and hopeful. In 1812 the unfortunate war broke out between the United States and Great Britain, and for another two years naval activity was renewed. What the immediate result of the American war had on the development of the sailing ship is not difficult to estimate. As regards English shipbuilding, owing to the great success of the American frigates and their superiority to our own vessels, a sudden wave of enthusiasm swept over the British naval authorities for frigates. In the panic, this was pushed to foolish extremes, and bigger ships were cut down and converted into frigate-shape. In America, the building of frigates of such unusual size first called the attention of naval architects to the advantages and possibilities of large vessels. It was thus that the way was paved for the coming of the early clippers in 1851.*

* For further matter regarding the American frigates, the reader is referred to " American Merchant Ships and Sailors," by William J. Abbot, New York, 1902

Fig. 68. The Stern of H.M.S. "Victory,"

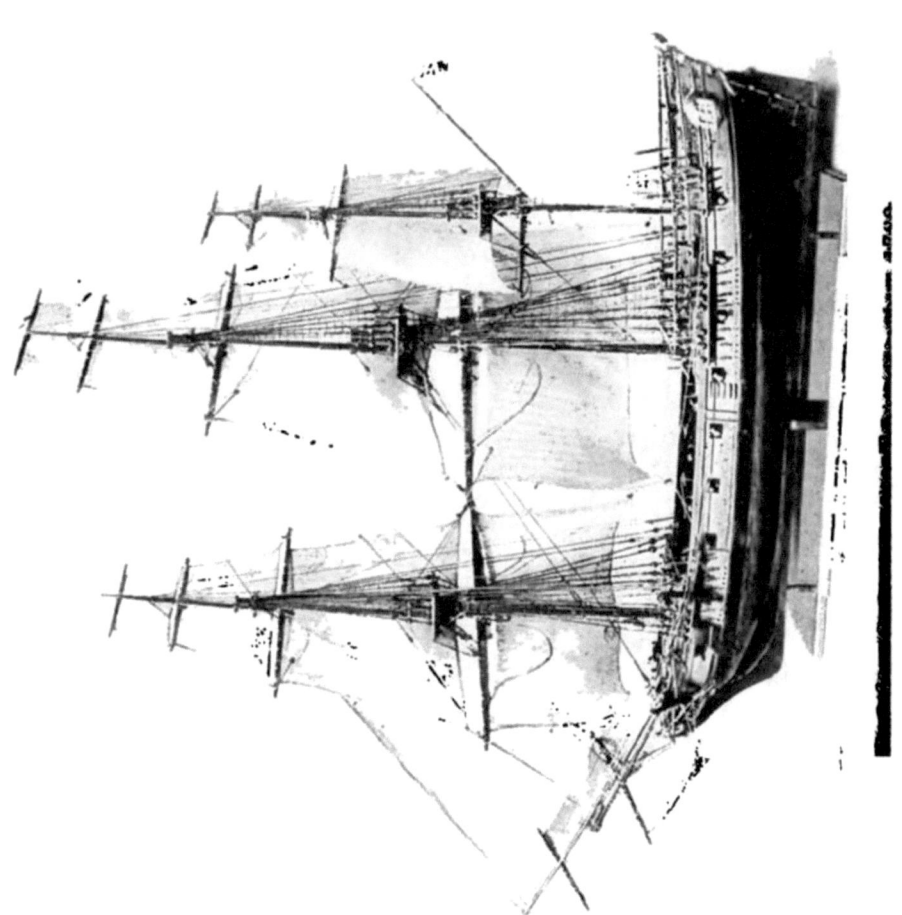

It is time now to refer to the powerful influence exercised over our naval architecture by Sir Robert Seppings. It was he who in 1804 introduced the round bow in place of the straight wall-like structure which had been inherited from the previous centuries. Similarly, instead of the square stern, he gave his ships a circular one. But more important still was the diagonal method of placing the timbers of a ship which he introduced in 1800. The advantage of this was increased strength and ability to resist the hogging strains, which the Egyptians also had to overcome.* A large model showing Seppings' method of construction will be found in the Greenwich Museum. The system, while no doubt being efficacious in preventing the " working " of a ship's component parts, must necessarily have added very considerably to her weight. It was about this time, too, that teak was used occasionally for the construction of ships. During the first quarter of the century whatever improvements were made in British naval architecture owed their origin almost entirely to the knowledge gained from the numerous prizes captured from the French. One of the finest ships ever built in France was the *Sans Pareil*, which we had taken from the enemy in 1794. She was of 2242 tons and carried 80 guns. (The reader will find a block-model of this ship in the Greenwich Museum). The influence which this vessel exercised over our naval architecture was not inconsiderable. So much admiration did she receive that as late as 1845 there was designed on similar lines and laid down at Devonport a British ship. She was never launched, however, as another *Sans Pareil*, but while on the stocks was altered, her length was increased, and she was eventually given the addition of a screw propeller, and thus launched in 1851.

The progress which had been made in the ships of the Royal Navy had its counterpart in the mercantile marine.

* See pp. 36–37.

SAILING SHIPS

Gradually through the centuries since the Crusades had opened up the Mediterranean to English trade our ancestors had acquired bigger and bigger ships for the purpose of carrying merchandise. The discovery of the West Indies, of North America, the Newfoundland Fisheries, and subsequently the founding of the East India Company, had step by step developed the ships which were used for purposes of commerce. Especially favourable for merchant shipping had been the East and West Indian trade. The voyages and discoveries made by Dampier, Anson and Cook increased still further the scope of English trade, and, consequently, the need for both ships and seafaring men became greater. War obviously arrested the progress already made, but by 182 the tonnage of the shipping of the British Empire amounted to the significant sum of 2,560,203, in spite of the keen competition now made by the United States. The East India Company at the beginning of the nineteenth century occupied the position now held in the twentieth century by the principal companies owning the biggest liners to day; that is to say, the largest and finest merchant ships belonged to them. And profiting by the monopoly which they owned, paying very handsome profits, they could afford to build their ships well and strong. Consequently it is not to be wondered that the East Indiamen from the commencement of the century down to the last of their race became historical for their building and capabilities Fig. 70 shows the *Newcastle*, a well-known East Indiaman of the early part of the nineteenth century.

During the eighteenth century brigs of about a couple of hundred tons had been used for coasting trade, and especially for carrying coals from Shields and Newcastle but with the advent of the steam collier the days of these ships were numbered. The illustration in Fig. 71 is from the painting by Turner in the National Gallery entitled *Spithead: Boat's Crew recovering an Anchor*. It was exhibited in the Royal Academy in 1809, and is here included in order to provide a contemporary picture of the full-rigged ships of the beginning of the nineteenth century.

Not till about 1810 was iron introduced for knees, breast-hooks and pillars, although the use of iron had been tried for the whole structure in a small boat as far back as 1787. The real introduction of building ships of iron occurred in 1829, yet it was not till the 'forties that opposition was entirely swept aside and iron came to be recognised as a suitable material for ships.

But we have digressed from the period before us. If the East India trade was a monopoly, commerce with the West Indies was unfettered by any such condition. Not unnaturally, therefore, competition was keen on this route, and as a result a number of excellent cargo-carrying ships were built, able to endure the trying conditions of the Atlantic without being deficient in the virtue of speed. The illustration in Fig. 72, taken from a print dated 1820, in the British Museum, will give some idea of the appearance of a contemporary West Indiaman. Gradually the similarity between purely mercantile and exclusively naval ships was disappearing, and we shall see presently how this gulf was widened still further.

Sir Robert Seppings was succeeded by Captain Sir William Symonds, R.N., who was Surveyor to the Royal Navy from 1832 to 1847, years full of importance in the history of the sailing ship. We have referred more than once to the slavish copying of French models which had been a feature of our naval architecture. This was now to end. Just as before, and many times after, England had shown herself to possess a genius not so much for inventiveness as for improving on the ideas of others, so now she began to design and build vessels that could not be surpassed even by the French themselves. During Symonds' *régime* the golden age of the wooden walls of

England was reached. It was he who was responsible for the design of such ships as the *Vernon* (fifty guns), the *Queen,* and about one hundred and eighty others. Seaworthiness combined with speed were their outstanding virtues, and these he obtained by improving their underwater lines and making them less heavy and clumsy.* Internally the ships were constructed so as to provide more room and air. Symonds completed the work of Seppings in getting rid of the mediæval stern which had lingered with certain modifications for so long a period. Instead of the circular, he gave his ships an elliptical stern, and devised a system whereby not only were the different spars of one ship interchangeable, but the spars of different ships and different classes of ships. There is a very fine large model of his *Queen* in the Greenwich Museum which has been rigged with the greatest regard to accuracy in every possible detail, so perhaps in studying her we shall get as good an example of Symonds' ships as we can desire. Built in 1839, this 110-gun ship had a tonnage of 3104. Her length was 204 feet 2½ inches, her breadth 60 feet 0½ inch, her depth 23 feet 9 inches, and she carried a crew of 900. She had been laid down as early as 1833, and her name had originally been the *Royal Frederick*, but after the accession of Queen Victoria she was named *Queen* at her launching. Later, in 1859, she was given the addition of a screw propeller.

In the Greenwich model she is seen as a sailing ship pure and simple, with three decks. As to her rigging I have had the pleasure of talking with more than one of those who served in this, the first three-decker that was launched during the reign of Victoria. One of the first points that strikes one is that the *Queen* is seen to have relinquished the historic hempen cable for the chain. The

* For some of the facts in connection with this period I am indebted to articles by the late Sir W. Laird Clowes in his monumental history of "The Royal Navy," and in Traill and Mann's "Social England."

rounded bow instead of the square shape already alluded to is immediately obvious. The yard of the spritsail athwart the bowsprit still remains, although this sail remained longer in the merchant service than in the Navy, being used but rarely in the latter at this late period. She possesses a bowsprit in three parts, *i.e.*, bowsprit proper, jib-boom and flying-boom. To encounter the downward strain the ship by now has also a dolphin-striker. The *Queen* carried stun'sails (studding-sails) of course, square in shape, which were often weighted down by shot at the outboard end. Many merchant ships of that time, however, had them cut not square but triangular, and these were then set, not as the modern yacht sets her spinnaker with the apex of the triangle at the top, but at the bottom. In the edition of " Falconer's Marine Dictionary " revised by Burney, and published three years before the *Queen* was laid down, he speaks of and illustrates stun'sails only for the courses, topsails, and t'gallant sails. Royal studding sails most probably never were seen, although I notice that E. W. Cooke, R.A., whose life was covered by the period between 1811 and 1880, who was one of the most faithful marine artists of the time, whose father was well known as an engraver of Turner's pictures, who himself was also at one time largely engaged on similar work, has an illustration showing a British frigate with both t'gallant and royal stuns'ls. It seems unlikely that so accurate an artist as Cooke should make such a mistake, although the weight of evidence is decidedly against him.

Falconer says that lower studding sails were used on the main and fore. The booms were generally hooked on to the chains by a gooseneck, and kept steady by a guy. Topmast and t'gallant studding sails were spread along the foot by booms which slid out from the yards. This is well seen in the *Queen* and many another model which the reader will no doubt have examined. In a similar manner the head of the sail had small sliding yards for the same purpose. The sail on the mizzen mast now called a driver or spanker was chiefly used when on a wind, being usually stowed when running. The boom will be found to project very far over the stern, even to an almost incredible extent, yet this is quite accurate for the period. As is still the custom, the gaff was kept up when the sail was not in use, contrary to the practice on a modern cutter-rigged vessel. The origin of this sail we have seen develop from the old lateen, and modified in its transition by Dutch influence. Now, one characteristic of the Dutchman was his love of brails, and even when the boom was added and the diagonal sprit taken away from this sail on the little fore-and-afters the brailing system clung tenaciously to the sail. We have a very good instance of this in the mainsail of the bawley (see Fig. 86), which has neither boom nor sprit, but which can be brailed up all the same. The barge has a sprit but no boom, and stows her sail by brailing. When this sail came to be used as the driver on square-rigged ships and the boom was also added, using a loose-footed sail, the brails still survived as we see them on the *Queen*. In furling the driver, therefore, the brail hauled the sail to the mast: then in order to make a neat job of it a kind of clew garnet drew the leach end of the foot diagonally across the sail to the mast also. This will be noticed in many contemporary prints of this period and earlier. I have talked with one old sailor who remembers, when the ship had got into the favourable trade-wind, not merely setting every stitch of canvas the vessel had to put up, but even stepping the masts of the ship's boats lying on deck and hoisting the sails of these boats to drive the ship along yet faster still. The reader may remember that Nelson's *Victory*, one of the fastest line-of-battle ships of her day, went into action at Trafalgar with studding sails set.

We have already shown that it was not long in the

new century before iron was introduced in connection with shipbuilding, though it was some time before it was able to take the place of wood for the hulls of ships. By the 'thirties steam was becoming gradually to be reckoned with as a serious menace to sail, and in the Navy the *Tartarus*, of four guns and a tonnage of 523, was classed as a paddle sloop. Nevertheless, paddle-wheel steamers attached to the fleet were regarded with scorn and spoken of as "dirty old smoke-jacks." As a distinguished naval officer and explorer, happily still with us, Admiral Moresby, says : "There was obviously no future for this type in the service, and sails would continue to waft us as they had done from the beginning. So we thought ; but one day a long, low craft, barque-rigged, and possessing no outward sign of a steamer but the funnel, joined the fleet. She was the *Rattler*, the first man-of-war screw-ship. We viewed her with interest but did not realise her significance. Pitted against her in every trial was the *Alecto*—a paddle-sloop of equal tonnage and horse-power—the *Rattler* an easy first in all circumstances. Finally they were lashed stern to stern in a 'pull devil, pull baker' grip, and ordered to put forth all their strength to see which could tow the other—a strange scene which I well remember. It was a calm day, with a long, heaving swell. *Alecto's* paddles were revolving and churning the foam like a whale in a flurry, while a slight ripple under the *Rattler's* stern alone showed that there was power at work. . . . *Alecto*, in spite of frantic struggles, was dragged slowly astern, and the era of the screw had begun."* The same author relates an amusing instance as showing the manner in which steam was contemplated by the old school. A certain captain was bringing his ship into harbour under steam and sail. As he ran up he shortened sail and came to anchor in handsome style, but unfortunately forgot that

* "The Navy Sixty Years Ago," by Admiral Moresby, in the *National Review* of December 1908.

his engines were still going, with a result that could only spell disaster !

There was between the naval ships of the 'forties and those of the time of Charles II. a similarity a hundredfold closer than that which can be found to exist between the former and those of King Edward's ships to-day. With a change in ships came a change in personnel. "The officers of the early 'forties," writes Admiral Moresby, "with few exceptions, were content to be practical sailors only. They had nothing to do with the navigation of the ship or the rating of the chronometers. That was entirely in the hands of the master, and no other had any real experience or responsibility in the matter. For example—I recall a captain, whose ship was at Spithead. He was ordered by signal to go to the assistance of a ship on shore at the back of the Isle of Wight. In reply he hoisted ' Inability. The master is ashore.' He was asked, ' Are the other officers aboard ? ' and signalled ' Yes.' But to the repeated order, ' Proceed immediately,' he again hoisted ' Inability,' and remained entrenched in this determination until a pilot was sent to assist him."

But to come back to the merchant service, to the old East Indiamen " with their stately tiers of sails and splendid crews of trained seamen," although they were much finer in their lines and less unhandy than the vessels in the Royal Navy of this period, their rig was in most respects akin to the latter.* They carried three courses—foresail, mainsail and cro' jack, three topsails (in each of which there were three or four reefs), and three t'gallant sails and royals, or twelve sails on the three masts. The fore-and-aft sails were : on the bowsprit and jib-boom, a fore topmast staysail, an inner jib and outer jib and flying jib. Below the bowsprit was set on the spritsail yard,

* See an interesting article by Mr. Frank T. Bullen on " Deep-Sea Sailing " in the *Yachting Monthly* of August 1907, to which I am indebted for some details of information.

what the reader has been accustomed through these chapters to know as the " spritsail," but which in the nineteenth century, even though triangular headsails were more in evidence than before, still continued, though known as a " water sail," or " bull-driver." Leslie, in his " Old Sea Wings, Ways and Words in the Days of Oak and Hemp," says that spritsails were not only used when going free but when on a wind. The reef points were placed diagonally so that when reefed that part of the sail nearest to the sea was narrower than the upper part. Two circular holes were cut, one in each corner, so that when the ship plunged her bows into a sea the water could run out and not split the canvas. Mr. Bullen says that this sail was not of much use, nor could he understand why it was carried at all, as it always had to be furled as soon as the ship began to pitch a little. However, this last and final relic of mediævalism has at last departed for good, although it dated back for its origin to the artemon of classical times. Even when the sprit topmast had disappeared, the sprit topsail was retained for some time by placing it below the bowsprit instead of above, but further forward of the spritsail proper.

Between the fore and main masts of the East Indiamen were the main topmast staysail, main topgallant staysail and main royal staysail. Between the main and mizzen were the mizzen topmast staysail, and mizzen t'gallant staysail, but a royal was seldom set on this mast. Abaft came the spanker or driver, often with the addition on the after-leach of a ring-tail. Stun'sles, too, were used. But in those days although these East Indiamen carried more hands than a sailing ship of like size does to-day, yet every night at sunset all light sails were taken off her and the ship was snugged down for the night. Still the old bluff-bowed East Indiaman had had its day when the young Republic of the United States, encouraged by the opportunity which freedom from war now afforded, introduced on the sea ships with clipper bow that literally cleft the waves instead of hitting them and retarding the passage of the hull through the water. With a freedom of mind which has ever characterised the American, both as a nation and an individual, the marine architects on the other side of the Atlantic threw convention still further to the winds by modifying the design of the stern in such a way that instead of squatting and holding the dead water the ship slid through it cleanly with a minimum of resistance. Possessing unlimited supplies of timber, they were in a position to build ships at a far lower rate than we in this country. In fact, so much was this the case that in England between the years 1841 and 1847 no fewer than forty shipbuilders went bankrupt in Sunderland alone. The one object of the American designer was to build a ship that should sail every other craft off the seas and so obtain the maximum of trade-carrying. Besides the improvement in bow and stern they lengthened the ship till she became five and six times longer than in breadth. This gave an opportunity of adding a fourth mast to the ship and to carry more sails. The sails themselves were improved in cut, being no longer mere bags to hold the wind, but of a " close-textured, dazzlingly-white canvas." In exact contradistinction to the East Indiamen, these Yankee ships did not reef down in anticipation of the gale that was to follow hours after, but took in sail reluctantly. The part played by the American clippers during the period that saw the close of the great wars and the beginning of the American Civil War is one of vast importance to the development of the sailing ship of any size. Even when steamers began to cross the Atlantic in 1840, these wonderful clippers were able to cross in about a fortnight. In every way superior to the old cotton-ships running between New York and Havre in the early 'thirties, the clippers of the 'forties and 'fifties were seaworthy as well as fast. One of the most famous was the *Flying Cloud* built in 1851, which performed the sensational run of 427 knots in twenty-four hours when on a passage from New York to San Francisco. The *Sovereign of the Seas* did even better still.

But yet again the English genius for improving on other peoples' ideas showed itself at a critical point in the history of shipbuilding. Shipbuilders and architects put their heads together and decided to meet the American on his own terms. If he had built clippers that had flown across the sea, it was their duty to build something that would fly faster still ; so a new chapter in British shipping begins, and headed by Mr. Richard Green, the famous Blackwall shipbuilder and shipowner, England built for herself the real thing in clippers, quite early in the 'sixties. The *Challenger* was in 1850 laid down in Messrs. Green's yard to sail against the American *Challenge*, in an ocean race from China, and won. Besides Messrs. Green, other British firms entered the contest and built splendid clippers, amongst whom may be mentioned Messrs. J. Thompson & Co., of Aberdeen, who founded the well-known line of Aberdeen clippers ; Messrs. Steele, of Greenock, and Messrs. Scott, of Greenock. Built of teak planking with iron frames, these new vessels were made to last, unlike the American ships, whose life was quite short, built as they were merely out of soft stuff. The enormous spars which the new British ships were given caused no little surprise at that time, but they managed to carry them none the less. The *Great Republic*, launched in the early 'fifties, was the first vessel to carry double topsails. Owned and built in America, she was 305 feet long, 53 feet broad, 30 feet deep, and had a tonnage of 3400. She carried also double t'gallant sails as well as staysails, and was barque rigged, having 4500 square yards of canvas. So perfectly was she rigged that she was handled by a crew of 100. She was chartered by the French Government to carry troops to the

Crimea,* had four decks and was strengthened with iron lattice-work.

But about the year 1853, we enter upon the final and most perfect stage of the sailing ship. Spurred on by competition and necessity, builders and architects had been compelled to put forth their best and to get right away from the old-fashioned ruts. So now wood at last was to give place to iron as the material for constructing sailing ships as well as steamers. In this year Messrs. Scott of Greenock built the iron sailing ship *Lord of the Isles* which, three years later, beat two of the American crack clippers, though nearly double her size, in the race from Foo Choo to London. The adoption of iron meant a saving of about a third of the weight of the hull; moreover, as ships became longer, increased structural strength was found to be lacking in wood.† As we saw in the time of Charles II., English oak had been getting gradually so scarce as to put us at a serious disadvantage in competition with such a well-wooded region as North America. The gold rush to California in the 'fifties, and to Australia, gave a tremendous impetus to shipping. The reader must recollect that by this time there were no railways across the American continent, and so when the inhabitants of the Eastern States of America decided to go west, they could only go *via* Cape Horn. This was the chance for the clipper ship to show her superiority to her predecessors, and in these voyages she soon showed that speed meant money.

But we must come now to the influence which the China tea trade had on the sailing ship. I understand that tea is a commodity which, as long as it is kept in a

---

* See " La Navigation Commerciale au XIX⁰ Siècle," by Ambroise Colin, Paris, 1901.

† " Ancient and Modern Ships," part ii., " The Era of Steam, Iron and Steel," p. 24, by Sir George C. V. Holmes, K.C.V.O., C.B., London, 1906.

ship's hold, quickly loses its delicate flavour and quality. Consequent on this, and the desire on the part of London merchants to obtain each year the first portion of the new tea crop at the earliest possible moment, it was to their interest to encourage a quick passage. Therefore enormous prizes were held out as an inducement, and the keenest rivalry existed between different ships in the race home. Solent regattas, the international race from Dover to Heligoland, even the famous race a few years ago across the North Atlantic look ridiculous when one thinks of the excitement that reigned on board during a race all the way from China to the River Thames. For a long time the American ships had been successful. Before the introduction of iron such craft as the *Sea Witch*, a clipper built in 1842, of 907 tons register, and carrying 1100 tons of China tea,* caused tremendous jealousy among the British skippers. In 1853 the *Challenge* had sailed from Canton to Deal in 105 days, though in the same year the English *Chrysolite* clipper sailed from Canton to Liverpool in 106 days. For a few years the Americans had the best of the competition ; but before the 'fifties had ended the China trade had been won by British clippers, and the American Civil War of 1861–1865 dealt a fatal blow to their clippers as rivals to ours. But none the less those keen races to England did not diminish. The rivalry which had existed between nation and nation now continued between ship and ship, between skipper and skipper, shipowner and shipowner. This led to the finest development of sailing ships, and as long as the word remains in the English language, so long will these clipper races remain famous alike for the skill as for the sporting instinct in the crews that got them home in record time.

Among the most celebrated ships of the 'sixties were

* "The British Mercantile Marine," by Edward Blackmore, London, 1897.

the Black Ball liners *Flying Cloud* and *Scomberg*; the Aberdeen clipper liners *Thermopylæ, Thyatera;* whilst among the China clippers were the *Sir Lancelot*, which was lost in the Bay of Bengal in a cyclone in 1896, the *Black Adder* and the *Cutty Sark*. Other famous tea clippers were the *Ariel, Taeping, Serica, Fiery Cross* and *Taitsing*. The first two of these will be found in Fig. 73, in which they are seen off the Lizard on September 6, 1866. They started together with *Serica* from Foo-choo on May 30, and lost sight of each other till they reached the English Channel. *Taeping* arrived in the London Dock (the same day she had passed the Lizard) at 9·45 P.M., while *Ariel* arrived at the East India Dock at 10·15 P.M., or with half an hour's difference after racing for over three months on end. *Serica* arrived only a few hours later. In the thrilling picture before us, these two ships are seen with stun's'ls and staysails set. The foretopmast staysail in both ships is stowed since the foresail with its projecting stun's'l would otherwise blanket and render it useless. The improved lines at bow and stern to which we referred just now are here seen at their best. Two of the fastest sailing vessels ever built were the *Thermopylæ* and the *Sir Lancelot*. The former especially, had a marvellous capacity for speed. In one day, in the year 1870, she made a run of 330 knots, or 380 statute miles, being an average of 16 miles an hour. The *Sir Lancelot*, for seven consecutive days, kept up an average of over 300 miles a day. It was the *Thermopylæ*, which in 1869 was the first tea ship home, having made the passage in 91 days, but the *Sir Lancelot* presently eclipsed even this wonderful passage in 89 days, being the fastest clipper ever built.

The *Cutty Sark* was not as fast as the *Thermopylæ* and *Sir Lancelot*, but in 1872, although she had her rudder carried away on the voyage, she ran home from Shanghai in 122 days. The *Thermopylæ* was a composite clipper of 947 tons register. She was 210 feet long by 36 feet beam and 21 feet deep. She was designed by Mr. Waymouth for Messrs. Thompson & Co. The *Sir Lancelot* was, like the *Thermopylæ*, a composite ship, and was built by Messrs. Steel, of Greenock, for Mr. James McCunn. She was 886 tons register, 197 feet long, 33 feet 7 inches broad and 21 feet deep. When fully laden with 300 tons of ballast and 1430 tons of tea, she drew 18 feet 7 inches of water forward and 2 inches more aft. Her complement was 30, and when in racing trim she spread more than an acre of canvas. Her best run in twenty-four hours was of 354 miles. The article contributed recently by Mr. Bullen to the periodical already mentioned set on foot an interesting correspondence, in which some valuable facts were brought out by those who had actually served on these clipper ships. And since the days of man are but three score years and ten, and before many more decades have run all those who went to sea in these magnificent ships will have passed away, I have thought it worth while to preserve here some of their recollections. The authors having adopted pseudonyms, I am unable to give their names.

One correspondent states that he remembers to have sailed 368 miles in one day, and 1000 miles in three days. One ship made a passage from the Start to the Ridge Lightship (30 miles from the mouth of the Hooghly) in 86 days. This was the *Northampton*, owned by Messrs. Soames and Co., of London. But other ships, including Messrs. Green's *Alnwick Castle*, did it in 69 days. On September 23, 1863, the *Hotspur* arrived at Madras in 79 days.

The illustration in Fig. 74 is taken from a model in the South Kensington Museum, and represents the iron clipper *Stonehouse*. It will be noticed she is ship-rigged; she was launched at Pallion in 1866. She has a full poop and topgallant forecastle, with considerable accommodation for carrying first-class passengers and cargo. Her displacement at load line is 2600 tons; her actual tonnage worked out at 1298; her length 220·5 feet, breadth 37 feet, depth 22·66 feet, and her load draught 19·25 feet. It will be noticed that she has double topsails, and her lines will give one an adequate idea of the famous clippers of the 'sixties.

The effect of the opening of the Suez Canal in the year 1870 was to place most of the trade to the East into steamers, which by now had become the deadliest enemy of the sailing ship. It would have been impossible to have carried on the trade in frozen food to-day in these fine old ships, and sentiment had necessarily to give way to the exacting dictates of commerce; but for a long time before 1870, and for some time after opening the canal, the traffic to India, Australia, and New Zealand was carried on in sailing ships, and the same keen rivalry to make the best passage continued. The Atlantic emigrant traffic also continued to be carried in sailing ships; but the ceaseless progress of the big steamship lines, and the competition which lowered the fares for steerage passengers, drove still another nail in the sailing ship's coffin. And yet, in regard to speed, these ships would sail to the east or the west with a regularity equal to most modern tramp steamers.

The beautiful illustration in Fig. 75 is from a photograph of the celebrated *Macquarie*. She is an iron barque, and was built in 1875 by Messrs. R. & H. Green of London. Her registered tonnage is 1977, her length 269·8 feet, her beam 40·1 feet, and her depth 23·7. In her day she was a famous beauty, but now she has changed her name and nationality. Known as the *Fortuna* she is registered at Sandefjord and flies the Norwegian flag. The reader will remark the old-fashioned white band introduced soon after the Battle of Trafalgar, and mentioned early in the present chapter.

The *Desdemona*, seen in Fig. 76, was built in 1875 by

FIG. 75. THE IRON BARQUE "MACQUARIE." BUILT IN 1875.

p. 272.

FIG. 76. THE "DESDEMONA."

Photos. Hughes & Son, Ltd.

FIG. 79. THE "QUEEN MARGARET."

Messrs. W. H. Potter & Co. of Liverpool. Constructed of iron, she is ship-rigged and has a registered tonnage of 1564, and is British owned. Her length is 242 feet, beam 87·7 feet, and depth 22·9 feet. As she is running before the wind, her head-sails have been stowed. As the reader is probably aware, ships usually when "running their easting down" haul up a point or two, so as to bring the wind on the quarter, in order that all sails may be allowed to draw and none allowed to blanket the other. Thus after running a certain distance with the wind on one side they gybe her and bring the wind on the other quarter. The photograph was taken recently off Cape Horn.

As the largest British sailing ship of the year 1890 we may mention the *Liverpool*, of 3330 tons register. Ship-rigged and built of iron with steel beams she was given two decks, whilst her length came to 333·2 feet, breadth 47·9 feet, and depth 26·5 feet. The five-master *France*, built on the Clyde for a Bordeaux firm in 1890, with the large tonnage of 8784, must also be mentioned as a famous barque of the 'nineties. Her length is 344 feet, beam 49 feet, and she was built of steel throughout, masts and yards as well. So great a capacity do her holds possess that she is capable of carrying 6100 tons of cargo. Another large French sailing vessel is the *Dunkerque*, measuring 105 metres long and 13·9 metres wide. Her sail area is no less than 4550 square metres. The illustration in Fig. 77 is from a photograph of the *Olive Bank*. Here she is seen with the following sails reading from forward to aft: On the bowsprit she carries flying jib, outer jib, inner jib, and fore topmast staysail. On her foremast she has foresail, lower and upper fore-topsails, lower and upper fore t'gallant sails, and fore royal. On her main she has mainsail, lower and upper main topsails, lower and upper main t'gallants and main royal. On her mizzen she has besides her course, double topsails and double t'gallants, the royal being seen half furled. On the jigger she carries a driver (or spanker) with topsail. She is a four-masted barque, and her registered tonnage is 2824. Built in 1892 of steel by Messrs. Mackie & Thomson at Glasgow, she is 326 feet long, 43 feet broad, $24\frac{1}{2}$ feet deep, and is British owned. The illustration in Fig. 78 and in colour on the cover is at once realistic and symbolical, with the four-funnelled *Mauretania* four miles astern chasing the poor sailing ship from the seas which for so long a time she has adorned as a creature of infinite beauty and an eternal joy to those who have eyes to see and emotions to be thrilled.

Our last illustration before we say good-bye to the large sailing ship is the *Queen Margaret* in Fig. 79. This is a steel, four-masted barque. She was built in 1893 by Messrs. A. McMillan & Son, Ltd., at Dumbarton. Her registered tonnage is 2144, her length 275 feet, her beam 42·2 feet, and her depth 24 feet. The photograph was taken only the other day from a passing vessel off Cape Horn. Most modern sailing ships of any size are now four masters; but, omitting entirely the large seven-masted schooners of America, there are a few square-rigged ships with five masts. When that is so they are named thus, reading from forward to aft: foremast, mainmast, middle, mizzen, and jigger. It is a circumstance all too true that, owing to the enormous advance of steam, both seamen and seamanship are nowadays hard to find in our country. The best deep-sea sailing-men are the Germans, who own the biggest five-masted sailing ships afloat. The *Potosi*, for instance, with five masts and belonging to Hamburg, is one of the very largest sailing ships ever launched. It is an undeniable fact that this ship has made eleven consecutive voyages between Hamburg and Peru in the average time of five months and twenty days, including stay in harbour, making an average rate of travel while at sea of eleven knots per hour, and it is not surprising to hear that this now stands as the world's record

274

for the deep-sea sailing ship. The largest sailing ship afloat is also a German five-master, the *Preussen*. Built of steel in 1902 by Messrs. J. C. Tecklenborg at Geestemünde, she is 407·8 feet long, 53·6 feet broad, and 27·1 feet deep, and is ship-rigged. Between this ultra-modern craft and that quaint prehistoric specimen we saw from the Egyptian jar in Fig. 3 what little connection is there, save for the one solitary fact that both depend on water for their buoyancy and on wind for their propulsion! For not only has wood disappeared as the material for ribs and skin, but chain is now used for topsail sheets and slings. (Slings are used to suspend the lower yards, the upper yards being sent down when necessary.) Spars and masts are made of steel, wire has taken the place of much of the rope that was used. Shrouds and stays are of wire, rigging screws are used instead of lanyards and of deadeyes. All the brace-pendants except the lower ones are of wire, even to the royal and skysail braces, so that the greater part of the rigging of a ship is now done in harbour ashore by skilled mechanics. The result is that "marlinspike seamanship" is fast disappearing and getting under way to join the spritsail, oak and hemp of other days. Only among the somewhat diverse class of fishermen, yachtsmen, and the seafaring men from Scandinavia and up the Baltic, does it survive with any outward signs of life at all.

We have seen the beginning of the bowsprit with its enormous rake to carry the artemon; we have watched it continue through the Tudors and Stuarts as practically an additional mast steeved at a considerable angle. Gradually the angle has got smaller and smaller until now in the twentieth century in the latest ships, it is much more nearly horizontal. We saw this spar become divided into two, and later into three parts—flying jib-boom, jib-boom, and bowsprit. To-day, though it is made of iron or steel, it has gone back to be of one piece. We witnessed the introduction of bonnets; they also have gone except in Norway, Norfolk, and the Thames barge. The studding sails which Raleigh spoke of are scarcely ever seen, although in the 'sixties they were prominent features of the clippers when getting every ounce of power out of the ship. No doubt their awkwardness, and the necessity of having a first-class helmsman to prevent the ship swerving suddenly off her course, had most to do with their departure. Convenience, too, in handling so much canvas up the mast led to the introduction of the topsails and topgallants, being cut in half and used double, though on the mizzen a single topsail is frequent. The gradual introduction of skysails during the last hundred years has continued till they are found often on fore, main, and mizzen, while the staysails, which were such characteristic features of the eighteenth century Dutchmen, are now used freely on most of the stays. Nor has the change been confined to the spars, sails, and rigging. Some of the Gallic vessels of Cæsar's time—so he records—were fitted with iron cables. Then, as the reader knows, rope came in, and hemp remained for centuries until, roughly, 1800. The introduction of the chain, then, has been merely a revival. Lead sheathing was used by the ancients, forgotten for many centuries until the Spanish restored its use in the fifteenth century, and the English in the sixteenth. It was forgotten again until the seven-teenth century, when it was introduced afresh. That was another revival. The Romans used bronze nails, and we have revived those again. The Greeks invented the schooner bow, as we saw in Fig. 13. It was forgotten for centuries again and re-introduced, as we saw in the seal of Dam in Fig. 40. Still another revival. In yachts, the last few years have seen the introduction of a reefing gear for furling both mainsail and headsails. The Chinese have had the former for centuries. Quite lately the fashion has come in to build yachts with double-ended " canoe " sterns. That, too, is but a revival of the old Viking shape—

Fig. 77. The " Olive Bank."

Steel Four-masted Barque. Registered Tonnage, 2824. Built in 1892.

p. 276.

Fig. 78. A Modern Four-masted Barque, with the R.M.S. " Mauretania " coming up astern.
From a painting by Charles Dixon.

p. 277.

roughly. The reader will remember that in the years following the coming of William the Conqueror the tendency was for the ship to have terrific sheer, so that instead of being long and straight she was almost semi-circular. Gradually, century by century, this absurd sheer has disappeared, though reluctantly, until to-day the most modern deep-sea sailing ships have practically no sheer considering their length, as the reader will see from the photographs of the modern ships in this chapter.

What and where the next revival will be—who knows? Perhaps some day, when all the coal has been burnt and all the oil extracted from the ground, both engines and motors will be banished, and a revival of sailing power will be made. One cannot tell. But as to the immediate future of the big sailing ship two considerations arise on two widely different points, each of which demands attention. The first is the Panama Canal, to be opened in 1915, though this actual date may be delayed. Will it deal the last and most cruel blow of all by driving away those fine white-hulled sailing ships one sees sometimes bound from South America? Like the opening of the Suez Canal, will the piercing of the Panama Isthmus mean that, by enabling steamships to shorten their voyage and its cost to South America, Cape Horn will no longer be rounded by the sailing ship? That is one subject for consideration. The other is the effect that the installation of the motor will have. Coasters with auxiliary power are now becoming common. In the opinion of experts, ocean-going vessels of 700 tons can be fitted with motors of sufficient power. A three-masted fore-and-aft schooner was recently built in North Wales for the coasting trade fitted with an auxiliary motor. The vessel has a dead-weight carrying capacity of 200 tons, and the experiment has been found eminently successful. In towing charges and independence of weather she will be found to be cheaper even than a small steamer. A company was formed last autumn in London for the purpose of building barges propelled by paraffin oil motors with auxiliary sails, and such barges having a capacity of carrying 300 tons of cargo have been used on the Continent for some years. Time alone, therefore, can tell whether we have seen the last and final stage of the sailing ship, or whether we are about to see the dawn of a new development of her usefulness.

CHAPTER IX.

THE FORE-AND-AFT RIG AND ITS DEVELOPMENTS; COASTERS, FISHING BOATS, YACHTS, ETC.*

SO far we have, with the exception of the primitive lateen, dealt exclusively with the square-rigged sailing ship. We have seen that this was the earliest and has continued to be the most universal sail of the ship. The Egyptian and other early races possessed it, and likewise the Greeks, Romans and Vikings. In the most modern full-rigged ship it is to-day seen as conspicuous as ever. For ocean, deep-sea sailing it has no peer, but in course of time with the growth of the coasting and fishing shipping, of pilotage and yachting, a rig that was suitable for deep-sea sailing was found to be not altogether ideal for the new demands. And so, gradually, side by side with the squaresail, has grown up another development which we may divide into two sections: first, the fore-and-aft rig, and secondly, the compromises that have been made between the fore-and-aft and the squaresail.

* In connection with this chapter, I wish to acknowledge my indebtedness to certain matter contained in the following :
"Architectura Navalis Mercatoria," by F. H. Chapman, Holmiæ, 1768; "The History of Yachting," by Arthur H. Clark, New York, 1904; "Yachting," by Sir Edward Sullivan, Bart., Lord Brassey, &c., 2 vols., London, 1894–95; "Mast and Sail in Europe and Asia," by H. Warington Smyth, London, 1906; "Lloyd's Almanac"; "Lloyd's Yacht Register," &c.; the Yachtsman; the Yachting World; the Yachting Monthly.

It would be quite impossible here to trace in such complete detail the history and development of the fore-and-afters as we have done of the larger sailing ships ; that, indeed, demands a separate volume to itself. But we can show here, what, as far as I am able to ascertain, has never been attempted by any previous writer, in outline, at least, the story of the rise of the fore-and-after, and link it up to that larger ship that sets her sails at an angle athwart the keel instead of parallel with it. We shall thus complete our study in connecting the present with the past, and in showing how the latest *Shamrock* is related to the early Egyptian ship, and how on the one hand she has inherited certain family characteristics of her fore-parent, yet on the other hand, through coming under new influences and acquiring new habits, she has altered some of the features by which her ancestors were especially distinguished.

In an earlier chapter we mentioned that it was in Holland during the sixteenth century that the fore-and-aft rig originated. At first it was only used for quite small sailing boats, but it was not long before craft of fifty tons and more adopted it. We must remember that about this time the Dutch were more advanced in maritime matters than any other nation. With them shipbuilding and naval architecture were much nearer to being an art and a science than elsewhere. The vast number of miles open to inland navigation, the shallowness of their channels and coasts naturally encouraged and stimulated them to study the problem of smaller ships. What the Tigris and Euphrates and Nile had been to the ancients the inland waterways were to the Dutch. The squaresail rig was out of the question. It was far too clumsy for tacking in and out of the small harbours of the Zuyder Zee and German Ocean. It would not sail close enough to the wind to allow the little craft just to lay her course in a straight narrow channel, while at the same time the Mediterranean lateen rig with its enormous yard was not suitable for the boisterous, squally North Sea. So the Dutchman, appreciating the virtues which the lateen shape possessed, just preserved this same triangular form, but cut it in two for convenience and handiness, though at the sacrifice of speed. Let the reader take his pencil and draw a vertical line to represent a mast. Across this let him draw a triangle with the apex well over to one side of the mast and the rest of the triangle and base to the other. This is roughly the shape of the Mediterranean and Eastern lateen as one can see by comparing Figs. 102 and 103. Now rub out from the drawing that part which is forward of the mast, and there remains a rectangular figure which is the germ of the first mainsail the cutter, or, more properly, the sloop-rigged boat had. In actual practice the sail was made much squarer at the top. A sprit was then stretched diagonally across the sail, with the peak on nearly the same level as where the throat now is. This sprit was supported just as in the Thames barge to-day, by a yard-tackle coming down from the throat to the sprit. It was thus, as we see from the engravings of the contemporary record of the first Dutch voyage to the North Pole in 1599, that the little craft that brought the ill-fated members home was rigged. Similarly the staysail, working on the forestay, as to-day, was in shape and size roughly equivalent to that part which in the triangular sketch just now would project forward of the mast. Vangs came down from the peak, and a bonnet being in use on the contemporary full-rigged ships, was naturally enough used for the smaller ships, too. Thus the sprit is really the old lateen yard modified, and the fore-and-aft rig is in its earliest days but the dhow rig cut in two. I have made a close study of the earliest Dutch engravings and paintings, and have little doubt in my mind as to the stages of development here indicated.

The next change came when the last relic of the lateen yard disappeared, for in place of the sprit a tiny gaff was added at the top and a boom at the bottom of the sail. The sail was, of course, loose-footed and very baggy, and was kept to the mast by lacing, wooden hoops being still unknown. Then a long clumsy bowsprit was given, so that forward of the staysail a jib might be introduced. Thus it is not the foresail that was added to the jib, but *vice versā*. Originally the foresail was the *fore* sail in fact as well as in name, until the jib was introduced. Then top-sails were added. These were copied from those on the contemporary full-rigged ships, were square in shape, were set athwart the ship and not parallel like the modern topsails. Before long, we find that not content with one square topsail, some of the bigger craft set a square top-gallant sail also. The topsail was goared out considerably and the foot was cut in a deep curve upwards, but a " barren " yard like that of the old cro'jack was retained. In light winds, the triangular spinnaker not being yet invented, the Dutchman set a large squaresail for running. This was similar to the lower course of the full-rigged ship and was set below the topsail when the ship was large enough to carry the former. This lower course extended from the hounds, was hoisted *outside* the forestay and, if she was a large sized ship and possessed a bowsprit, the sail extended right down to the furthest end of the latter. If she had no bowsprit then it came down to the stem. This latter instance will be seen in Fig. 82, which has been sketched from the picture by Van der Cappelle in the National Gallery (No. 964; Van der Cappelle painted from 1650 to 1680). We find in the paintings and engrav-ings of this time that the Dutch were immensely fond of booming out these sails with a light spar. One is seen in this illustration, but sometimes, besides such a one as this, they would set another boom one-third of the way up the sail, so that it might catch every breath of wind. In the present illustration the staysail is seen set, but one often finds it rolled round and round the forestay. So, too,

Fig. 80. A First-rater of 1815, showing Details of Spars and Rigging.

p. 284.

with the mainsail, if it should happen to be a spritsail, then the foot was boomed out, in running, with a light spar also. It was thus, I believe, that the introduction of a boom and gaff mainsail came—the boom first and the necessary spar at the top to correspond thereto. Then,

not infrequently, one finds in the Dutchmen of about 1700 that they dispense with the boom but retain the gaff. The brails, in the case of the sprit sails, were plentifully used, sometimes with the addition also of reef points. As to the hulls, they were tubby, bluff-bowed, but excellent sea boats, if slow. Being of light draught, they had leeboards. Until about 1840–1850, we in this country continued to model our fishing and small sailing craft generally upon the lines of these Dutchmen (notice the cutter shown in Turner's painting reproduced

Fig. 82. From " River Scene with Sailing Boats," by Jan Van der Cappelle.

in Fig. 71). But whilst we have gone ahead from improvement to approximate perfection, from ignorance to knowledge, the ships of the Low Countries remain but little altered since the days of Tromp, when the Dutch were at the height of their maritime progress. The Dutch schuyt, such as may be seen any day lying at her buoy off Billingsgate, is shown in Fig. 83. The Viking influence is written largely over the ships of Holland, but breadth has taken the place of the length beloved of the Northerner.

If we compare the last-mentioned sketch of a modern Dutchman with that in Fig. 84, which has been copied from the exquisite little Van der Velde in the National

FIG. 83.   A MODERN DUTCH SCHUYT

Gallery, we shall see how little the hulls of their ships have altered. Van der Velde (the younger) lived from 1633 to 1707, so that he saw the Dutch ships at their very best. As Macaulay says, the Van der Veldes, father and son, produced, when they came over to Greenwich as

Fig. 84. "A Fresh Gale at Sea."
After the painting by W. Van der Velde, No. 150 in the National Gallery.

painters to Charles II., some of the finest sea-pieces in the world. The title given to the present picture is *A Fresh Gale at Sea* (No. 150). It is extremely interesting to us for its indication of the rig. The ship in the foreground on the port tack will collide with the other if both stand on. But to avoid this she has resolved to bear up. The reader will notice the helm has been put hard over as the other ship is seen staggering out of the squall and mist. Easing off her sheet she has also lowered her peak by slacking off the tackle at the foot of the sprit. In another of Van der Velde's paintings in the same gallery (No. 149, *A Calm at Sea*) the same peculiar method of lowering sail is seen. We see a ship at anchor in a calm. She has slacked off the tack in the same way, so that the spar

287

Fig. 85. "River Scene"

comes right across the mast. English ships of the eighteenth and nineteenth centuries possessing this characteristic will be found in the paintings of Turner and other contemporary artists.

For many years, though the Dutch had changed their rig for small craft, yet they still felt the influence of the bigger squaresail ships, notably in the design of the sterns. Thus the familiar decoration and the sheer to a high poop will be noticed in the vessel that occupies the centre of Fig. 85, which is rigged with a spritsail. This has been copied from another Van der Velde in the same gallery (No. 978). I have selected this picture expressly for the purpose of indicating, as Van der Velde has done, as many of the prevailing types of Dutch seventeenth-century craft as possible in a small space. The short gaff, the spritsail furled by means of its brails, the large squaresail for spinnaker work seen on the ship to the left of the picture, the high stempost (relic of the Vikings) on the ship to the right—these will all be found deserving of notice. It was no doubt a ship very similar to the high-pooped yacht in the centre of this picture that was sent to Charles II. in 1660 by the Dutch. The vessel was called the *Mary*, and was the first yacht ever owned in this country.

In England the revenue and other sailing cutters of the seventeenth and eighteenth centuries were rigged with the square topgallant sail and " goared " topsail below, with a hollow foot. Old prints of the beginning of the eighteenth century (1717) show British cutters sailing with the jack flying from the staff at the end of the bowsprit just clear of the jib. The bowsprit is steeved remarkably high and is very long. In a like manner were rigged also the yachts of this period. So the cutters continued until the 'forties and 'fifties, when the bluff bows and rough rig gave way to a larger, cleaner lined, and more scientific production than the slavish copying of a seventeenth century Dutch type could produce. Now the old-fashioned square topsail has utterly disappeared in fore-and-afters, and one of more or less triangular shape has taken its place. But since it is in the building and rigging of yachts that the most complete changes have occurred during the nine-

FIG. 86. THE BAWLEY.

teenth and twentieth centuries we shall postpone the further progress of the cutter until later in the chapter.

No modification of the cutter rig in England is so thoroughly Dutch as the bawley (Fig. 86). Not even the least observant of passengers on the Margate steamer can have failed to notice these little ships off the Nore or cruising somewhere up and down the Thames estuary. Off Southend and Whitstable they are as common as flies in summer, and bigger children of the same family are to be seen brought up in the Stour abreast of Harwich. The bawley inherits the Dutch ancient mainsail, with brails that can speedily shorten canvas, and without a boom to be kicking about from side to side as the ship rolls in the trough of the nasty seas that can get up off the entrance to our great waterway. With their transom stern and easily brailed and triced mainsail these bawleys are excellent bad-weather boats.

Some of the finest cutters in the country are the Brixham Mumble Bees, trawlers of about 27 tons. They have their mast stepped well aft, so that they are able to set an enormous foresail. Here especially the long bow-sprit has survived, and without a bobstay to support it. The Plymouth hooker, with her mast stepped well amid-ships, with her square stern, no boom to her mainsail, and pole mast, cannot be said altogether to have escaped Dutch influence, although it is said that the Devon shire men in Elizabeth's time possessed cutters of their own.

The illustration in Plan 1 shows the sail and rigging plan of the *Gjöa*. The vessel is shown here because in combining much that is old and new she is one of the most interesting cutters afloat. Her tonnage is 70, length over all 69 feet, beam 20·66 feet, depth 8·75 feet, draught 7·5 feet. In June 1903 she set out from Christiania, and three and a half years later she had navigated the North-West Passage and reached San Francisco. Obviously built for the hard service of the Arctic regions, her hull is bluff and strong. The bowsprit is more that of an old-fashioned full-rigged ship than of a modern cutter, and the squaresail, whose yard and braces will be noticed, has come back from the times of the old Dutchmen, being, as already mentioned, of inestimable value for running across vast expanses of ocean. But in spite of her old-fashioned bow and stern and rigging she is fitted with a heavy-oil motor, as will be seen from Plan 2. This was found very useful, giving the ship a speed of 4 knots per hour; and it was the first time a motor-propelled ship had been so far north.   Plan **8** gives an adequate idea of *Gjöa's* deck arrangement.

Pass we now to trace the progress of the schooner.   It is a common error to suppose that this rig was derived direct from the cutter by merely adding another mast and sail of the same shape as the mainsail.   Such a statement is pure guesswork, and entirely contrary to fact.   The schooner originated quite independently of the cutter and much later, though the shape of her mainsail and foresail was obtained from the former.   About the beginning of the seventeenth century a craft far from uncommon among the Dutch was the sloop.   Now in order to clear the ground, let us carefully separate the three distinct kinds of craft to which this name belonged at that time. The word sloop, or more properly *sloepe,* was applied less to the rig than to the size of the craft, denoting a somewhat small tonnage.   Thus it was primarily applied to a ship's big boat, such as was used to run out the kedge anchor and for fetching provisions and water from the shore.   The same name was also given to the Dutch vessels of about 55 feet long and 12½ feet beam which sailed to the Cape Verde Islands.   More familiar to us was the custom of applying it to the early cutter-like craft which carried a triangular foresail yet no jib.   But not one of these is the sloop we are looking for.   This is found in that kind of sailing craft which was about 42 feet overall and with 9 feet beam.   She was rigged with two pole masts, the mainmast being 24 feet long.   On each she had just such a sail as we see in Fig. 83 of a modern schuyt, with loose foot and with both gaff and boom, but the most important fact is that she had neither bowsprit nor headsails of any kind, while her foremast was stepped right as far forward as it could get.   There are plenty of contemporary prints and paintings in existence to show such a vessel, which usually had an enormous sheer coming up from bow to stern.   This, then, was not a schooner but a

292

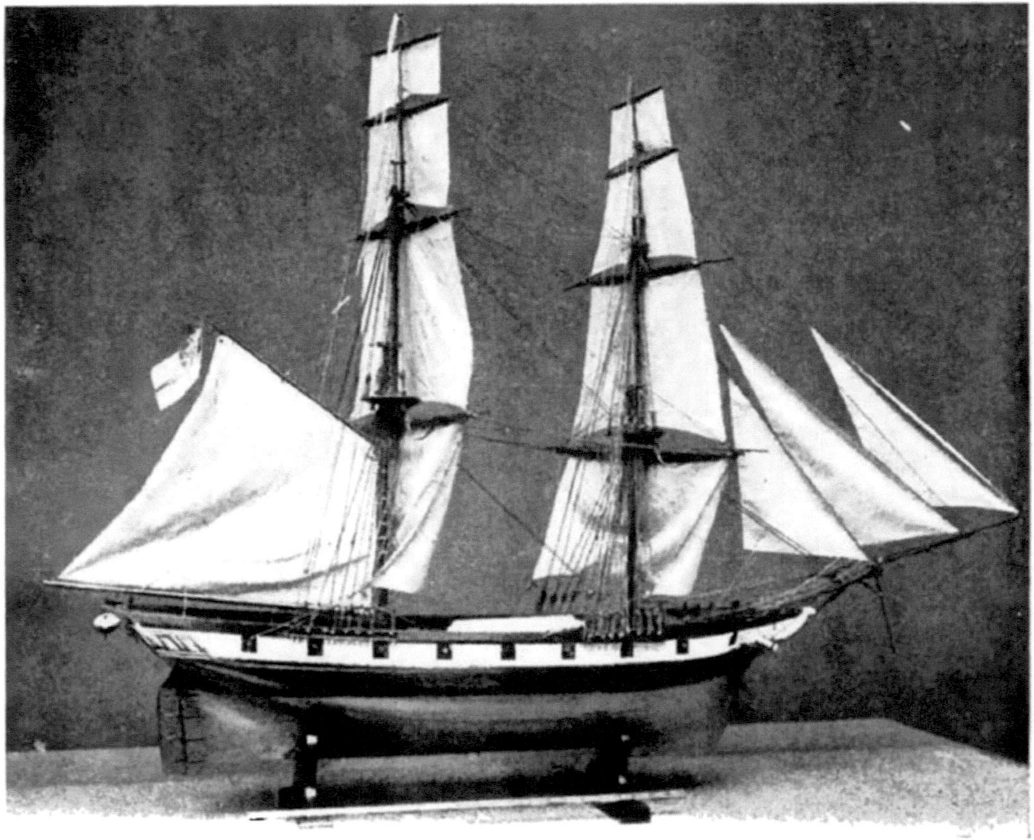

FIG. 94. THE "FANTÔME," 18-TON BRIG. LAUNCHED 1838.

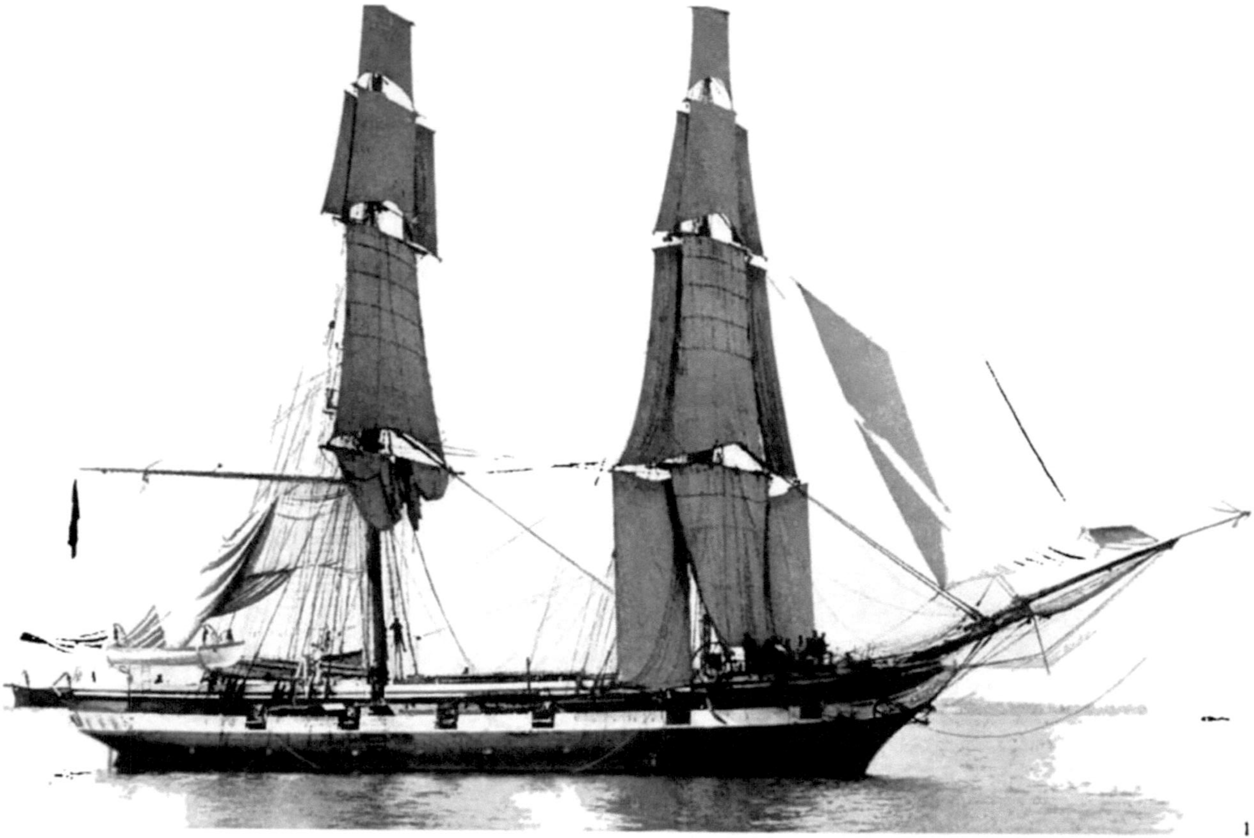

FIG. 95. H.M.S. "MARTIN." TRAINING BRIG. LAUNCHED 1836.

sloop, and you may search high and low in all the seventeenth century dictionaries, marine and otherwise, but you will not find such a word as "schooner" in existence. We come, then, to the early part of the eighteenth century, and we cross to North America. When in 1664 the British, during the war with Holland, seized the Dutch colony of the New Netherlands and changed the name of New Amsterdam to New York in honour of Charles II.'s brother, most of the Dutch settlers who had come out from Europe remained. So, like those early people who trekked westwards across the Syrian desert to Egypt, the Dutch had also brought with them their ideas and practical knowledge of ship-building, included in which was that of making sloops. It was at Gloucester, Massachusetts, still to-day famous for the finest schooners and the very finest schooner-sailors that ever tasted brine on their lips, that in 1713 the first genuine schooner with a triangular headsail was built. To add the latter to the two-masted sloop was but the easiest transition. Not till the first vessel of this now enormous class was actually making its first contact with water was the name schooner bestowed on it. As she was leaving the stocks some one remarked "Oh, how she scoons." "Very well, then," answered her proud builder, "a scooner let her be." And so she has remained ever since.

For the next century and a half Gloucester went ahead building these beautiful creatures, more stately than a cutter, less ponderous than a full-rigged ship, until 1852, when the famous *America* still perpetuated in the America Cup came across to the English waters and so wiped the slate that every rich owner of yachts desired to turn them into the same rig as this Yankee. We will say no more about her at present as we shall presently make her acquaintance anew when we come to deal entirely with yachts.

But to return to the more commercial schooner; for

whatever else Gloucester, Massachusetts, may yet become famous, it will always be associated with that wonderful fleet of fishing schooners which those who have read Kipling's "Captains Courageous," and Mr. J. B. Connolly's "The Seiners," already know. The origin of this wonderful

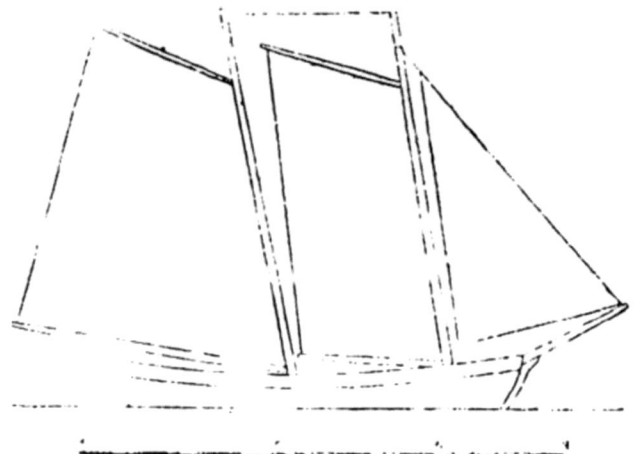

FIG. 87. THE SCHOONER "PINKIE" (1800-50).

Gloucester breed may be traced to the Dutch fly-boat, or *flibot*, of the eighteenth century. The next step in the evolution of the Gloucester schooner is seen in Fig. 87, the *Pinkie*, engaged in the fishery industry between 1800 and 1850. Although the sail plan belongs to a smaller boat than the one just indicated, yet we see the first step in the introduction of the single headsail to the old two-masted "sloepe," with the foremast even now stepped very far forward. Impelled by the demands for a ship that would be able to carry its fish to market with the utmost despatch, but which would be able to endure being caught in the terrible seas off the Newfoundland Banks; and subsequently encouraged to progress through the popularity which such craft were obtaining among the American pilots who used to come out enormous distances into

294

the Atlantic in those days to meet the incoming liners, the builders and designers went on improving the design and rig, giving them fine hollow lines, adding jibs and standing bowsprits, greater draught and speed, larger spars with a vast square measurement of canvas. The *Fredonia*,

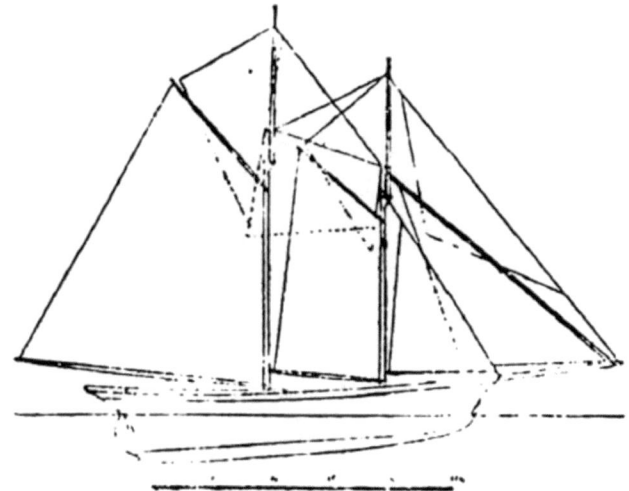

FIG. 88. THE " FREDONIA." BUILT IN 1891.

seen in Fig. 88, was one of the famous schooners of the 'nineties and is so still. She was designed by W. Burgess in 1891, and with her cut-away fore-foot and finer lines is a great improvement on the old Dutch models. This vessel measures 114 feet 2 inches long, with 25 feet beam, drawing 12 feet 8 inches. Her displacement is 188 tons, and her sail area is the enormous extent of 7542 square feet. Fig. 89 represents one of the earliest of the twentieth-century productions, and is designed by the famous Crowinshield. Her fore-foot is cut away more like that of a Solent racing schooner-yacht. Indeed, many of these Gloucester schooners are far more entitled to be called yachts than any other name. I have watched them turning up the Hudson in the winter, threading their way through the ice-blocks and the crowd of fussy tugs and mammoth liners in New York harbour with the handiness of a small rater. The most modern example of this ideal ship is that seen in Fig. 90. She is only a 53-tonner with an over-all length of under 70 feet, and is fitted with a

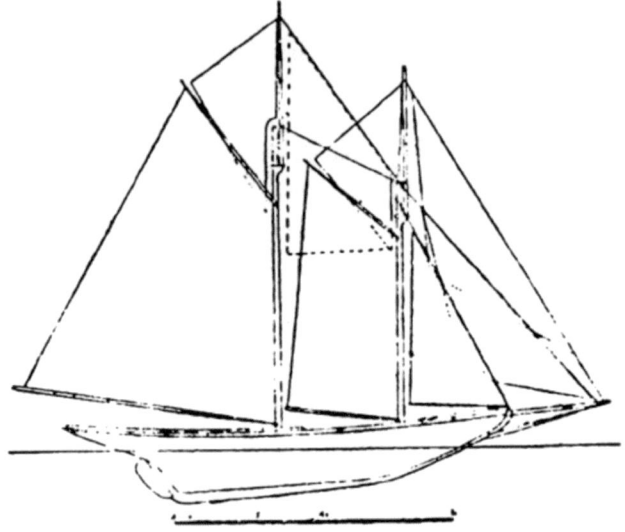

FIG. 89. GLOUCESTER SCHOONER, A.D. 1901.

25-horse-power motor. But in many cases the internal combustion engine has been adopted by the American sailing ships only to be rejected as not worth while.

The coasting trade of the United States of America is not done in the ketches and topsail schooners and barquentines that we use. It is done exclusively, where sailing ships are used, in fore-and-aft schooners which have arisen directly or indirectly from Gloucester. Two masts have become three, three have become five, and even as many as seven have been used. Perhaps the most notable of these was the seven-masted *Thomas W. Lawson*, which foundered off the Scillies on December 14, 1907. Remarkable for the ease with which it can be handled,

THE FORE-AND-AFT RIG, ETC.

a three-masted schooner of about 400 tons requires only a dozen hands aboard. In tacking, a couple of hands work the head-sheets, and these with a man at the wheel can work her in and out of narrow channels, for which the rig is more suited than any modification of the squaresail.

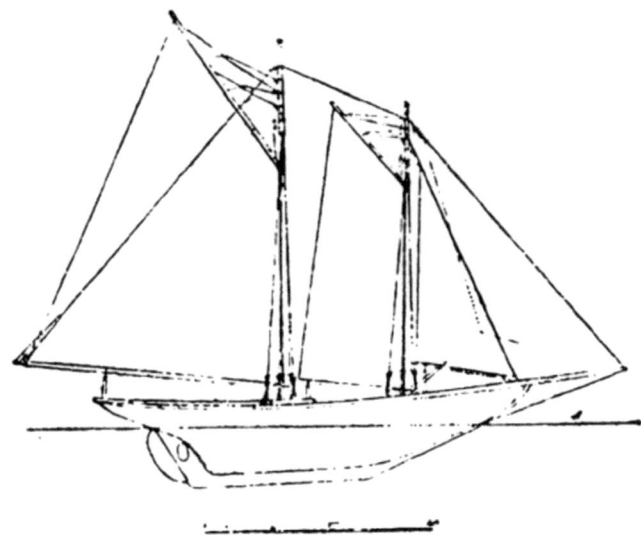

FIG. 90. GLOUCESTER SCHOONER, A.D. 1906.

For labour-saving "gadgets" the American schooner has reached the furthest limit. Thus the anchor and sails are raised by steam force; there is steam steering gear as well as steam capstan, and the biggest ships of all have been fitted even with electric light. The illustration in Fig. 91 of a four-master will give one some idea of the extent to which the American schooner has developed.

Coming back to European waters, besides the pure fore-and-aft schooner we have also the topsail schooner and the two-topsail schooner. No better instance of the former could be found than in the illustration in Fig. 116 of Lord Brassey's famous auxiliary yacht the *Sunbeam*, of which we shall give further details on a later page, among

297

the yachts. But we may now call attention to the square fore-topsail and smaller t'gallant sail on this ship. Some times, too, one finds a royal added also to the foremast. The braces, clew-garnet, lifts, and other rigging are so well shown in this photograph as to require no further comment

FIG 91. AN AMERICAN FOUR-MASTED SCHOONER.

A two-topsail schooner carries a square topsail and t'gallan sail at the main *as well as* the fore. The topsail schoone is perhaps the best known of our coasting types. Most o our trading schooners are " butter-rigged," that is to say that whereas the topsail schooner has a standing t'gallan yard set up with lifts, the butter-rigged sets her t'gallants' flying by hoisting the yard every time.

The illustrations in Figs. 92 and 93 represent barquen tines, although one of them is seen with the now obsolet stun's'ls. A barquentine is square-rigged on the fore masts, but fore-and-aft rigged on the main and mizzen The difference between the barquentine and the three masted schooner is that the former has a regular brigan tine's foremast. The three-masted schooner does not carr a fore-course, but in place of it a large squaresail, onl

used when running free in moderate weather, only differ
ing from the fore-course in that it is not bent to the yard.

The illustration shown in Fig. 94 represents the 18-ton
brig *Fantôme*. She was designed by Sir W. Symonds and
launched about 1838. Her armament consisted of eighteen

FIG. 92. A BARQUENTINE OFF THE SOUTH FORELAND.

32-pounders, and her complement was 148 officers and men.
Her tonnage was 726, her breadth 37·7 feet, length 120 feet,
and depth of hold 18 feet. This is from a photograph of
the model in the South Kensington Museum. Fig. 95 is
a photograph of the training brig *Martin*, actually afloat.
The brig was the last sailing ship to disappear from the
British Navy, and her final abolition is so recent that her
picturesqueness still lingers in the imagination of Solent
yachtsmen and others. The *Martin* was launched in 1836.
As will be seen from the photograph, which obtains even
greater interest when compared with the model just mentioned, she carried single topsails, t'gallants and royals.
Stun'sails will be noticed on the foresail, foretopsail, fore-
topgallant sail as well as on her main-topgallant sail. As
we shall never see these sailing brigs again, the photograph
is of more than ordinary interest.

In olden days the brig was a favourite rig for small coasters. In the marine paintings of Turner and the early part of the nineteenth century one sees them frequently. In the eighteenth century, and even as late as the nineteenth, the brig was used for the coal-carrying trade. The

FIG. 93. BARQUENTINE WITH STUN'S'LS.

nineteenth-century brigs often carried, besides the sails seen in the two illustrations, an enormous fore-topgallant staysail. But both the handiness of schooners and ketches began to oust her, and the coming of the steam collier finally did for her in the mercantile marine as, at a later date, she was abolished from the Royal Navy.

I have intentionally introduced the brig at this point notwithstanding that she is essentially a square-rigged ship, in order that we may compare her the more easily with that compromise between the square rig and fore-and-aft vessel, the brigantine. Strictly speaking, the brigantine is square-rigged at her fore-mast, but differs from the Hermaphrodite brig in carrying small squaresails aloft at the main. She differs also from the full-rigged brig in

FIG 101. DHOW-RIGGED YACHT. *p.* 300.

Fig. 111. The Yacht " Kestrel," 202 Tons.

p. 361

iving no top at the mainmast and in carrying a fore-
id-aft mainsail and sometimes a main-staysail instead
? a square mainsail and trysail. (The fore-and-aft sail
. a brig's mainmast is called a trysail.) The illustra-
on in Fig. 96 represents a Hermaphrodite brig, com-

FIG. 96. A HERMAPHRODITE BRIG, COMMONLY BUT
ERRONEOUSLY CALLED A BRIGANTINE.

only and erroneously called a brigantine. The Her-
aphrodite brig, or brig-schooner, is square-rigged at her
remast like a brig, but without a top forward, and carry-
ʒ only a fore-and-aft mainsail and gaff topsail on the
ainmast. And here it may not be out of place to mention
other subtlety: while a barque has three masts, being
uare-rigged at her fore and main like a ship, and differ-
ʒ from a ship-rigged vessel in having no top at her
izzen, but carrying a fore-and-aft spanker and gaff top-
il, yet what is known among sailormen as the " Jackass "

301

barque resembles a barque proper, but has no crosstrees, does not spread lower courses and has no tops. (Tops are the platforms placed over the heads of the lower masts, while the crosstrees are at the topmast heads, being used for giving a wider spread to the standing rigging).

The illustration seen in Fig. 97 shows one of the smallest schooner-rigged craft that ever sailed the ocean. This is the famous *Tillikum*, adapted from a "dug-out," in which Captain J. C. Voss, F.R.G.S., sailed round the world to England. The sketch which we give here of this odd ship was made in November 1906, while she lay off the Houses of Parliament. She has since changed ownership and been fitted with a motor, and in her green paint

FIG. 97. THE "TILLIKUM," SCHOONER-RIGGED "DUG-OUT," WHICH SAILED ROUND THE WORLD.

is a familiar sight to those who bring up in the Orwell off Pin Mill.

The origin of the ketch is also Dutch, although the word is in old French *quaiche* and in Spanish *queche*. We frequently find the influence of the bomb-ketch in old pictures and engravings, in which the mizzen is close up against the mainmast, and the latter is stepped well abaft of amidships, so as to allow the shot fired to clear the rigging, leaving a large fore-triangle. (See Fig. 62, the *galiote à bombe*.) This influence is felt even as late as the second half of the eighteenth century. The ketch is descended from the Dutch galliot, which, besides having a gaff mizzen, had a sprit mainsail like the barge, and with no boom, but three brails and one row of reef points. The usual vangs led down aft from the peak, and she also had lee-runners. But, besides her triangular headsails, consisting of a fore(stay)sail and a couple of jibs, she carried also a small t'gallantsail, with big topsail below, and often a large lower course below that—all these last three being square, as on a full-rigged ship, and to this day many Baltic ketches continue to be rigged in like manner. At the close of Charles II.'s reign we find that among the 173 ships in the British Royal Navy there were three ketches, but before this date, in his " Seamen's Dictionary " of 1644, Sir Henry Manwayring defines them simply as " a small boate such as uses to come to Belinsgate with mackrell, oisters, &c." From the time of Charles I. the Dutch have had the privilege of mooring three of their fish-carrying craft off Billingsgate in recognition of " their straightforward dealings with us," and any day the reader likes to go down in the vicinity of London Bridge he will see two or three Dutch schuyts swinging to their moorings. In an eighteenth century work on naval architecture it is curious to see the galliot also called a galleasse. In this case the mainsail has discarded the sprit and taken on a small gaft with boom and loose foot. Two rows of reef points are also added, and the squaresails are still there. An old English engraving also shows a close similarity to the former bomb-ketch. But in the course of time all the square-sails were abolished, the mainmast brought further forward, and the mizzen sail enlarged so as to be not much smaller than the mainsail. Nowadays nowhere is the modern ketch rig so prominent as on the east coast of England, from as far north as Whitby to as far south as Ramsgate, and even Brixham. The billy-boy, with her long raking bowsprit, setting almost as many jibs as a full-rigged ship,

and whose general design bears the most remarkable likeness to the ship in the seal of Dam in Fig. 40, is the
Yorkshire adaptation of the old Dutch galliot, and, with
her lee-boards and ketch rig, is well known in the North
Sea. In the 'seventies our East Coast fishermen were

Fig. 98. Lowestoft Drifter.

almost all rigged with the lugsail, but now some of the
finest ketches will be found in the fishing fleets of Yarmouth, Lowestoft, and Ramsgate. For powerful, seaworthy
craft, able to heave-to comfortably, and with the capacity
of riding out gales that few modern yachts with their cut-
away bows could survive, there is nothing on the sea, size
for size, to beat these ketches. In Fig. 98 we give an
illustration of a Lowestoft "drifter." With her boomless
mainsail and raking mizzen, setting a jackyard topsail
over both main and mizzen, she sets also in light winds a
large reaching jib.

We come next to the yawl. Correctly speaking this
word has reference not to rig but to shape. The Scandinavian *yol* was a light vessel, clinker-built and double-
ended, like the Viking shape. The Yarmouth yawls that we
shall consider presently, were correctly called yawls with their
bow and stern alike. But the word has now come to refer
to a later adaptation of the ketch, in which the mainsail
304

has grown bigger and the mizzen smaller. In a ketch the mizzen mast is stepped forward of the rudder-head; in the yawl the mizzen mast is abaft the rudder-head. The *Jullanar*, for instance, in Fig. 117, is a yawl. But to the Londoner no more familiar example could be found of a

FIG. 99. THAMES BARGE.

yawl than the Thames barge, of which the illustration in Fig. 99 is a fair specimen. Still inheriting her Dutch-like spritsail and brailing arrangement, she has also the vangs that were first attached to the peak in the sixteenth century. The old-fashioned topsail is a cross between a modern jackyarder and the old Dutch square topsail. Aft she carries another small spritsail on the diminutive mizzen. Smaller types of barge, called "stumpies," have only pole-masts and neither bowsprit nor jib nor topsail. But the larger type of barge, carrying topmast and setting a big jib-headed topsail, known as topsail barges, with their red-ochred canvas and the untanned jib, always known by bargemen as the "spinnaker," have grown to such sizes that they go right down to the west end of the English

FIG. 100. NORFOLK WHERRY.

Channel. Yet these are rather ketches than yawls. But even in the Thames barges developments have not ceased. Obviously Dutch, as they strike one in a moment, the old Dutch bluff bows have been replaced by the straight bow as seen in the sketch. A whole book could be written about the barge and her ways, her history, her leeboards,

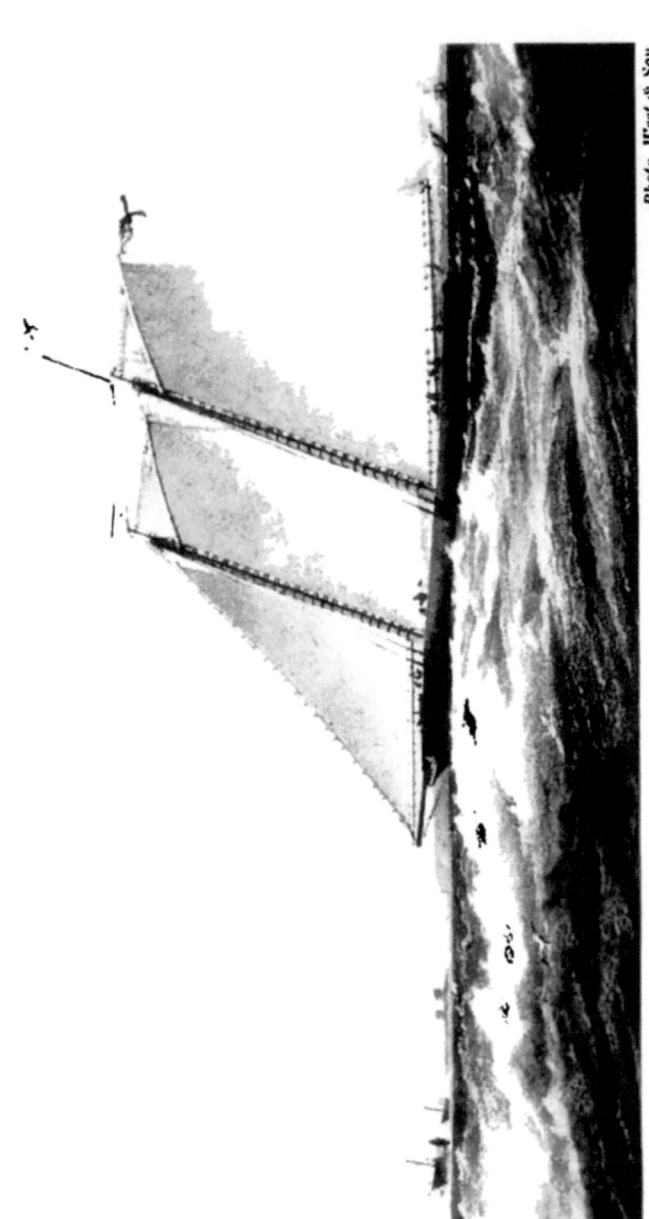

FIG. 113.   THE SCHOONER "ALARM" AS SHE APPEARED WHEN REBUILT IN 1852.   p. 307.

Photo, West & Son.

Reproduced by kind permission of the Royal Victoria Yacht Club, Ryde.

her lengthy topmast, and the wooden horse on which the staysail works; but we must pass on.

Curiously Dutch-like, too, is the Norfolk wherry seen in Fig. 100, with her one enormous sail, her mast fitted in a tabernacle for ease in lowering, unsupported by shrouds or rigging of any sort other than the forestay by which the mast is eased down. Only one halyard is required for both peak and throat, which are raised by means of a winch forward of the mast. She has no leeboards, nevertheless she draws under three feet of water: although I have heard her sweepingly condemned as defying all existing rules, yet the way she can sail right close into the wind is incredible to those who have not seen her. In running with her bonnet off and her sail close reefed she gripes badly and is a veritable handful as she comes sailing into Great Yarmouth from across Breydon Water or tearing through the rushes of Barton Broad and down the tortuous and narrow Ant. Within recent years, now that the Norfolk and Suffolk waterways have become a tourist resort, the wherry has changed her face a little and become smarter, and the tanned sail is often allowed to remain white, while the hatches have been taken away and a cabin roof, allowing plenty of headroom with ladies' saloons, pianos and other luxuries, have come in. But all the time the wherry remains as a useful cargo boat for bringing coals and timber from the ports of Lowestoft and Yarmouth inland to Norwich and the East Anglian villages, returning with eels, or marsh hay for thatching. Sometimes one notices them, in settled weather, with a fair wind steal quietly out from Lowestoft harbour and make a sea passage round to Yarmouth, but as Mr. Warington Smyth well says in his "Mast and Sail," "in the smallest wind and sea the wherry loses her head entirely and develops a suicidal tendency to bury herself and crew."

After the squaresail had for so many centuries held sway among the earliest dwellers of the earth, the lateen

FIG. 102. SUEZ DHOWS, WITH A SIBBICK RATER.

began stealthily to assert itself as we saw in the first chapters. Although Holland set the example in the sixteenth century of cutting up the lateen shape into the cutter rig, yet in the Mediterranean, along the East Coast of Africa and in the Indian Ocean generally, the lateen has refused to be made obsolete. The illustration in Fig. 101 represents a Bombay yacht of the second half of the nineteenth century rigged with a couple of lateens, and masts that rake forward at a considerable angle. Every tourist to Egypt is familiar with the picturesque lateens and lofty yards of which Fig. 102, showing a fleet of these with a small Sibbick rater in between, affords a study in contrast between the conservative East and the progressive West. The sketch was made at Suez. The felucca in Fig. 103 is a well-known lateen type in the Mediterranean, with her

FIG. 103. MEDITERRANEAN FELUCCA.

From the model in the South Kensington Museum.

white and green, her square stern and single deck. The sketch here shown has been made from a charming little model in the South Kensington Museum, and represents one of the familiar two-masters seen off the Spanish coast. The tack and sheets and rigging are shown so clearly that we need not stop to indicate them. In old paintings and prints we see that the felucca type in the Mediterranean developed into vessels of considerable tonnage with three masts. The Venetians and Greeks and Genoese, as well as the piratical Moors and the other Mediterranean inhabitants, used them both as cargo carriers and ships of war. They are in fact the lineal descendants of the ancient galleys. Further modifications include the addition of a jib, though the Southerner has not followed the universal Northern practice of transforming his lateen into a mainsail. Sometimes we find old prints showing a felucca with the addition also of a mizzen spritsail similar to that on the modern barge. The French signified by the word *brigantin* a two-masted lateen-rigged galley with oars as auxiliary. But there came into use that compromise between lateen and squaresail that in Northern Europe we have seen to exist between the pure fore-and-after and the square-rigger. Thus, for instance, one finds ships rigged with a large lateen on the foremast, the mainmast being square-rigged with mainsail, topsail and t'gallant, while the mizzen has a lateen with square topsail. The reader who wishes to see the different varieties of lateen and lateen-plus-square rig is referred to Mr. Warington Smyth's interesting volume " Mast and Sail," while for details as to design and rigging he will find some valuable information in Admiral Paris' " Souvenirs de Marine."

The Chinese in their own independent way went on developing from the early Egyptian models and have been not inaptly called the Dutchmen of the East in their nautical tendencies. They developed quickly but then remained at a standstill, whilst the European has gone on by slow steps of progression. Adopting rather the sail of the lugger than the old Egyptian squaresail, the Chinese made it into a balance-lug and stiffened it with bamboo-battens. The illustration in Fig. 104 was sketched by Mr. Warington Smyth (through whose courtesy it is here reproduced) near Kaw Sichang, and represents a Hailam junk. The sail of the Chinaman is hoisted up a pole-mast, the halyard passing through a large double block attached to the yard and a treble block at

310

the masthead, a hauling parrel keeping yard to mast and helping to peak the sail when reefed. Reefing with the Chinese consists simply in letting go the halyard, when the weight of sail and battens brings the sail into the topping lifts : two or more battens are bunched together along the

FIG. 104. HAILAM JUNK.

boom. The illustration in Fig. 105 will show in further detail the rigging of a Chinese junk. This has been specially sketched from a fine model in the South Kensington Museum. Built of soft wood, she has a full bottom and water-tight compartments. The mizzen mast will be noticed to be in duplicate, one on each quarter, only the leeward one being used under way, the sails being of matting. The rudder is remarkable, unwieldy, and projecting deep into the water, but capable of being raised by means of a windlass when in shallows. The windlass in the bows raises the three anchors, which are made of hard wood, the flukes being tipped with iron, whilst the stock is in the crown instead of in the top of the shank as in European anchors. Very similar to this model was the famous Chinese junk *Keying*, which caused some sensation by sailing from Canton to the Thames in 1847–8. These craft, owing to their light draught and bulky tophamper, are not much good going to windward, so that one is not surprised that the *Keying* took 477 days on the voyage to England. In crossing China seas they usually take advantage of the favourable monsoons. Their enormous crescent-shaped sheer makes them excellent bad weather ships. Their tonnage varies between 300 and 800. The *Keying* came round the Horn, and her rudder, when let down, drew 22 feet of water. It hung loose, as seen in the model, and was perforated, weighing nearly eight tons. Under way it necessitated fifteen men, as well as a luff-tackle purchase, to work the helm. She had no keelson, and the mast, instead of being stepped, was supported by a toggle. The seams of the vessel were paid with a kind of putty-cement made out of burnt pounded oyster shells and oil from the chinam-tree. The mainsail weighed no less than nearly nine tons, and took the crew two hours to hoist. Towards the end of last year (1908) the Australian Customs officials saw with amazement the arrival in their waters of another Chinese junk, the *Whang-Ho*. This craft, which was over a hundred years old, and was previously a pirate ship, set out from China for a voyage to San Francisco. Afterwards she sailed for the eastern side of America, but in making an attempt to round the Horn was less fortunate than the *Keying*, a wave carrying away her huge rudder; but she eventually reached Australia. She had previously touched at Tahiti, and nothing was heard of her until she reached Thursday Island, 100 days out.

Returning now to Northern Europe, we find the lug-sail surviving especially in fishing craft for which it possesses certain peculiar advantages. In Fig. 106 we have the sail plan of a Blankenberg boat. Those who are acquainted with the coast-line around Ostend cannot have failed to notice these craft with their leeboards raised, hauled up the sandy beach. Here the standing lug is set after the French style, the old mediæval bowline being

FIG. 105. CHINESE JUNK

still preserved from the squaresail to set the lug straight when on a wind. Notice that the foresail is right in the eyes of the ship, so that the rig looks as if it was no

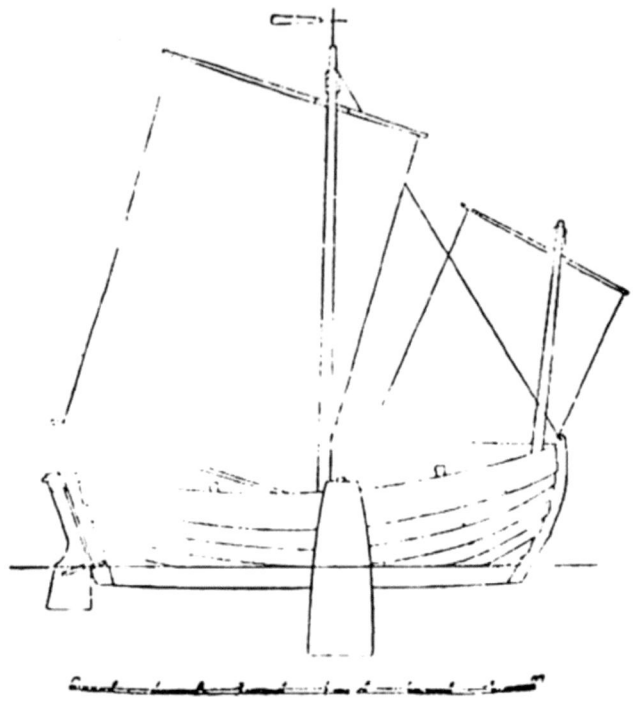

FIG. 106. BLANKENBERG BOAT.

distant relative of the vessel with the artemon that carried St. Paul on his voyage.

Every one who has cruised down Channel is familiar with the French *Chasse-Marée*, a curious figure on the sea-line, with her lug-sails and three crazy-looking masts. Over the mainmast she sets a square topsail, while forward she carries a long bowsprit with a small jib, the latter being in shape more of an equal-sided triangle than the modern English jib, while the French lug-sail is sheeted very high, as will be seen from the sketch (see Fig. 107).

814

THE FORE-AND-AFT RIG, ETC.

At one time Norfolk was famous for its beach yawls. Those who have visited Great Yarmouth will have noticed these very large open boats painted white with (if I remember correctly) a riband of green running along the gunwale. Double-ended, they are now usually rigged

Fig. 107. French "Chasse-Marée."

cutter fashion and used as pleasure boats. Clinker-built, they have a very fine entrance and a clean run, and sometimes measure 50 feet in length and 10 feet beam. They used to carry three lug-sails and jib owing to French influence. In the days when sailing ships were more frequent than to-day, Yarmouth Roads were usually a crowded anchorage, and these yawls would be launched almost every day during the winter to assist a vessel that had been picked up by the shoals. Nowadays one still sees them used for bringing pilots ashore, but it is at the Yarmouth and Lowestoft regattas that one is able to realise alike their enormous speed on a reach and the dexterity of each crew, numbering about twenty. The three-masted lug rig of olden days has now given way to

315

FIG. 108. SCOTCH "ZULU."

a two-master with a dipping lug for the main and standing mizzen, besides a small jib forward.

Until about 1860 the Scotch fishing boat was entirely influenced by Norway, and even to-day no one could deny that this influence is altogether wanting. But at

Fig. 109. Penzance Lugger.

last the fisherman began to seek the herring further out to sea, and so a bolder, decked ship was evolved, and clinker build gave way to carvel, and the design was given finer lines and greater draught. I have watched a fleet of such vessels as in Fig. 108 running into Scarborough Bay with an onshore breeze in the soft light of a September afternoon, with their yacht-like lines and their fine massive hulls suggesting an ideal combination of strength and beauty. Most of these large "Zulus," as they are called, carry steam capstans for getting in the heavy nets, hoisting sail and warping into harbour. Within the last few years they have been fitted with steering wheels instead of helms. They are good boats to windward, and are able to carry their enormous lugs longer than most vessels could keep aloft a similar area of sail.

The Cornish lugger is able to carry a larger mizzen but a smaller lug forward than his Scotch cousin. Fig. 109 is an example of a Penzance lugger. She draws also more water aft than the " Zulu." The Penzance luggers are famous all over England for their seaworthiness and easy lines. They are usually about fifteen or twenty tons, have in proportion to their size very high bulwarks to encounter the Atlantic

FIG. 110. DEAL GALLEY PUNT.

seas, and an exaggerated outrigger over the stern unsupported by stays and cocked up at an angle to clear the sea when the ship is pitching. Her mizzen is longer than her mainmast, and rakes forward at a great angle. Sometimes they set a topsail, as seen in the sketch over the mizzen: and at times they also run out a bowsprit and jib.

We could not close our list of characteristic luggers without including that brave little ship the Deal galley-punt (see Fig. 110). Chapman in his " Architectura Navalis Mercatoria," published in 1768,* shows a Deal lugger (or as she is called then a Deal cutter) with three spritsails,

* " Architectura Navalis Mercatoria," by F. H. Chapman, Holmiæ, 1768.

318

FIG. 115. THE "BLOODHOUND."   BUILT IN 1874.

Fig. 116. The Auxiliary Topsail Schooner-Yacht "Sunbeam."
Registered Tonnage, 227. Owned by Lord Brassey.

Photo. West & Son.

p. 319.

the mizzen having a bumpkin, whilst a jib is set on a bowsprit forward : but this type has become obsolete. In those days they were engaged in taking out from the shore heavy anchors and cables to vessels in the Downs which stood in need of them. With the advent of steam and improved holding gear their days of usefulness departed. But a smaller type, the Deal lugger, of which we now speak, is still a feature of the sailing craft at the eastern end of the Channel as she goes about her business " hovelling " or hovering on the look-out for such odd jobs as taking pilots ashore or attending on shipping between Dungeness and the North Foreland. Never a ship gets picked up by the treacherous Goodwins but the Deal lugger comes running out in any weather, ready for a salvage job and a third of its value as a reward. Even whilst these lines are passing through the press, they have been busy standing by the *Mahratta* liner stranded on the Goodwins, and hurrying ashore with the passengers and cargo of tea salved from the hold of the big steamer. These little craft sail very close to the wind and are out in the worst of weathers, and require considerable skill in handling. The one lug-sail has to be lowered and hoisted at each tack, but they are wonderfully quick both under sail and when rowed. Any sailing man will tell you how excellent a sail for lifting a boat the lug-sail is, and well the little Deal galley needs it. The yard of the sail hooks on to a traveller and is hoisted by halyards up the mast, a purchase being used to " sweat " it down taught. The rudder is made easily detachable, supported on pintles with a rope-strop attached. It is her length in proportion to her beam that gives her such speed. Clinker-built, the Deal lugger is about thirty feet long. Her mast is placed some distance from the bows, and is very stumpy, but in spite of this the Deal galley punt is a wonderful little ship on a reach.

Having shown the directions in which the development of smaller ships has taken place, and especially in the trading and fishing craft, let us now turn our attention to that very modern development, the yacht. As we set out not to write a history of yachting but of sailing ships, we shall consider not the marvellous growth of the queen of sports, but the influence which that has had in developing a particular species of ship used entirely for the purpose of pleasure and racing. We alluded in an earlier chapter to King Edgar, whose "sommer progresses and yerely chiefe pastimes were the sailing round about this whole Isle of Albion." He at least showed the real spirit of a yachts-man, and had he lived in later times he might have established the sport on a sound footing many years before it began to prosper.

But let us make no mistake about this word yacht. Of Dutch derivation, and related to the Norwegian *jaegt*, the word in the seventeenth century signified a transport for royalty or some individual of distinguished rank. In that way we could include those esneccas mentioned earlier in this volume which were prepared for carrying British royalty across from these shores to France. But it was not until the early part of the seventeenth century that the yacht as a special type of vessel, distinct from one temporarily adjusted for a short voyage, was produced. As other fore-and-afters first saw light in Holland at this time, so it was but natural that the yacht should originate there. From old paintings and prints we see them rigged after the manner of those Dutch fore-and-afters which we mentioned as to be seen there in previous pages of this chapter. Especially popular for yachts was the sloepe rig with the two masts and sails but no headsails, although the boom-less but gaff mainsail, fitted with brails not unlike the rig of the bawley, was also found. The high sterns, square and much decorated with carving and gilt, the compara-tively low bluff bows and the pair of leeboards were the most conspicuous features. The rig was usually cutter or sloop (in the sense of having one mast mainsail and foresail, but without jib). Later on we find ketches being favoured.

In 1660 the Dutch presented Charles II. with a yacht called the *Mary*, "from whence," writes Sir Anthony Deane to Pepys, "came the improvement of our present yachts; for until that time we had not heard of such a name in England." This *Mary* was of a hundred tons and was the first yacht to appear on our Navy list. She was lost in 1675 near Holyhead. From this model Christopher Pett in 1661 built the *Anne* at Woolwich, her tonnage, beam, and length of keel being the same as those of the *Mary*, but she drew three feet less water. In the same year Charles was presented with another but smaller yacht of only 35 tons, called the *Bezan*, which also came from the Dutch. From the arrival of the *Mary* various sized yachts began to be built in England, of which the tonnage gradually increased. The *Katherine*, built in 1661, was captured by the Dutch in 1673. So far had this new departure progressed in our country that in 1674 a design was made for two yachts to be built at Portsmouth for the King of France in imitation of Charles II.'s. But the largest built about this time was the new *Mary*, to replace the first one lost. Of 166 tons, she was launched in 1677. The smallest yachts were the *Minion* of 22 tons, and the *Jemmy* of 25 tons, and the *Isle of Wight* of a like tonnage. Incidentally we find in the Naval MSS. of the time that the dimensions of the biggest yacht's mast of the year 1683 were: length 20 yards, "bigness" (*i.e.*, thickness) 20 inches.

It was during the reign of that apostle of hedonism, Charles II., that the yacht became not merely the vessel of state but of pleasure. He introduced into England yacht racing, although the Dutch had for a long time delighted in regattas and naval sham fights with yachts. In 1661 Charles sailed in a match from Greenwich to Gravesend and back. One impulse that had been given to the Dutch to build so-called yachts with finer lines and high capabilities of speed was the trade carried on to the East by their Dutch East India Company, and it was this company that had made Charles the present of the first yacht he ever possessed. During the eighteenth century yachting began to be a new sport for noblemen and wealthy gentlemen, especially in the neighbourhood of Cork. By the end of the century the Solent was becoming the cruising ground for a large number of English yachts, and in 1812 a yacht club was started at the Medina Hotel, East Cowes. In 1817 this newly-formed yacht club was joined by the Prince Regent, who used to cruise between the Wight and Brighton in the *Royal George.** George III. had also patronised yachting, and the illustration in Plan 4 gives some idea of his yacht the *Royal Sovereign*. Launched at Deptford in 1804 she drew 9 feet forward and a foot more aft. She was copper-bottomed with a streak of yellow painted above, with another streak of blue above that, while her stern was ornamented with medallions of the cardinal virtues. Neptune presided over the stern, while the figurehead represented her Majesty. It will be seen at once how similar in colouring and decoration she was to the type of ships prevalent in Charles II.'s time. She was said to have been very fast and beautifully decorated, as well inside as out. She was 96 feet 1 inch long on deck with a breadth of 25 feet 7 inches. Her tonnage was 280$\frac{18}{94}$. She was ship-rigged and carried royals and stuns'ls, judging from a print of 1821. In the external decoration of this yacht we can see the influence which is still manifested in the royal steam yachts of this country to-day. The lavish display of gold leaf, the heavy stern and general clumsiness—all vile inheritances from the days of Charles II. when naval architects knew no better —were all reproduced in the old *Victoria and Albert* and

* This vessel was until recently in Portsmouth Harbour.

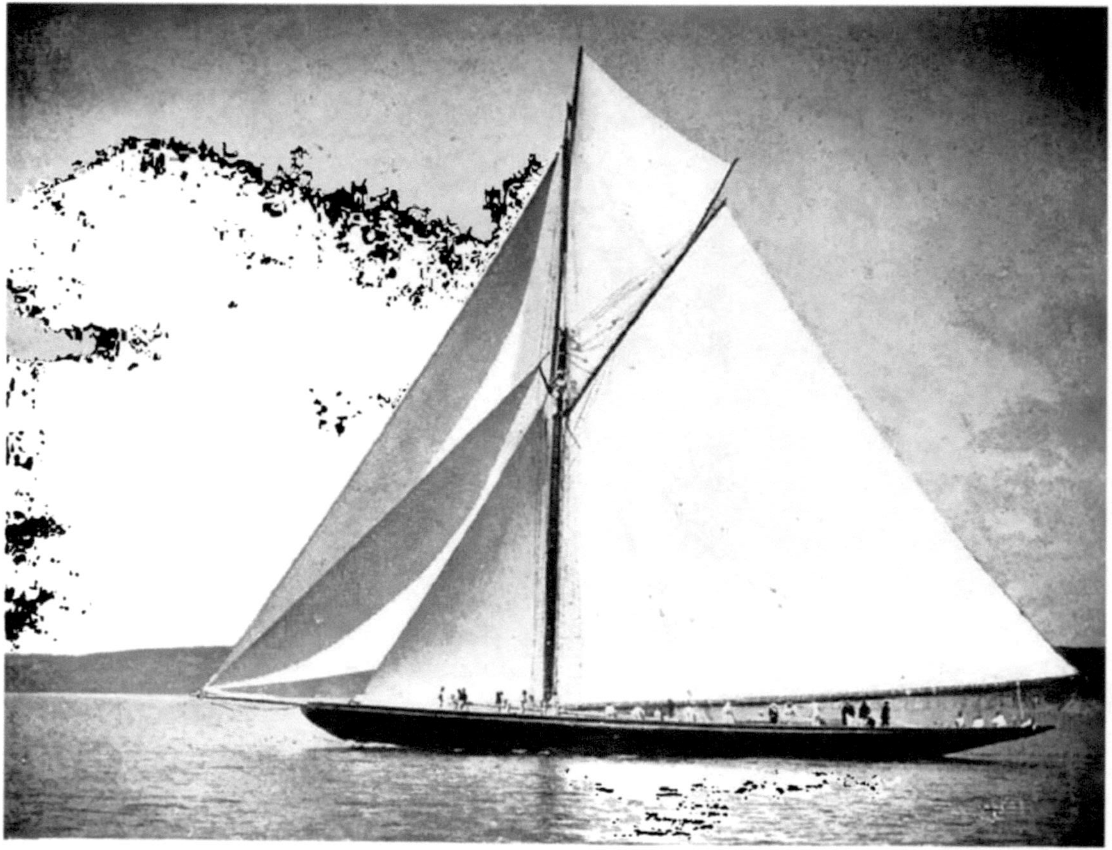

Fig. 113. The "Satanita." Built in 1893.

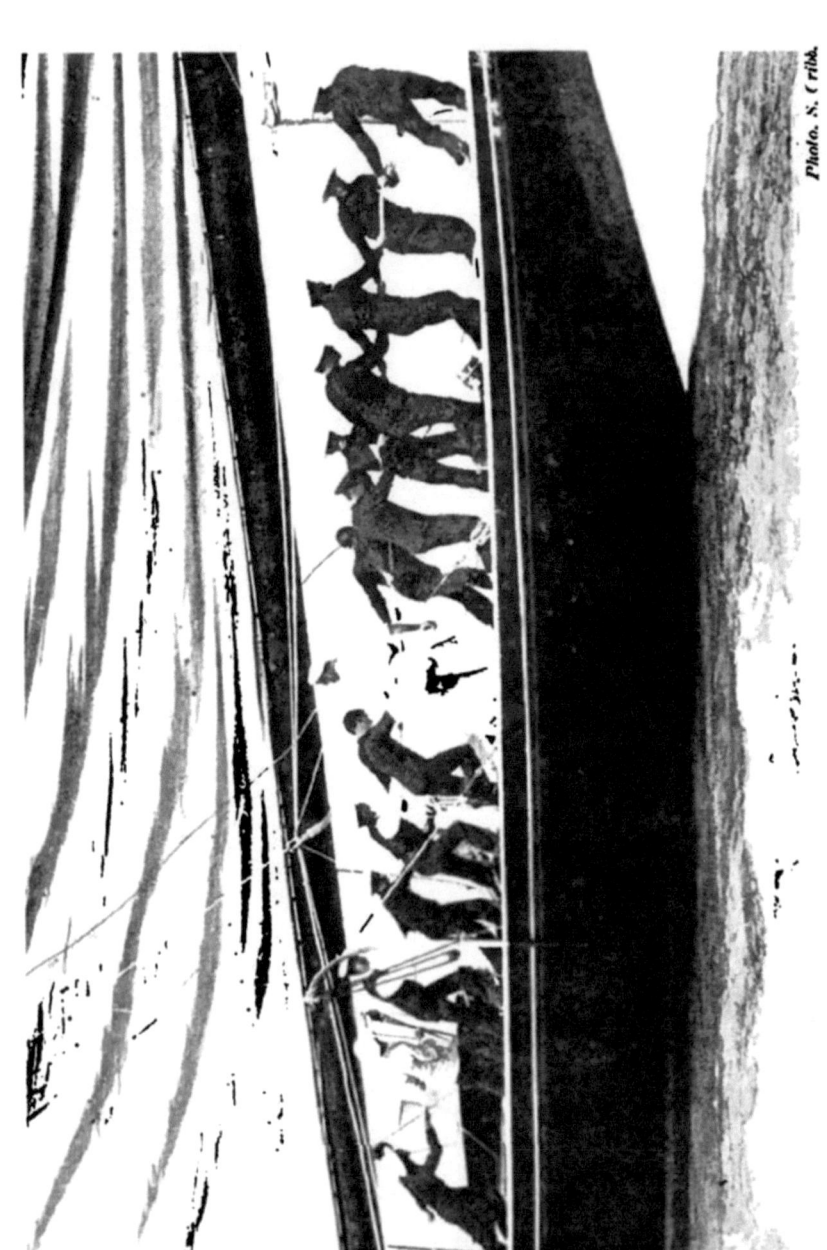

Fig. 119. King Edward VII's Cutter "Britannia," launched 1898, showing the mainsail being hoisted by fourteen of the crew.

Photo. S. Cribb.

p. 323.

have been perpetuated even in the newest royal yacht the *Alexandria*.

It is only with the nineteenth century that yachting really begins, but it was not till after the Crimean War that the sport began in earnest. At the beginning of the nineteenth century the cutters were built on the lines of the revenue cutters, which as we saw just now, owed much to Dutch influence. The reader who wishes to see what clumsy creatures they were has only to look at Turner's pictures (see, for example, the cutter in Fig. 71). In such a painting as Charles Brooking's *The Calm*, numbered 1475 in the National Gallery, we readily see the square topsails above the fore-and-aft mainsail and head-sails. Brooking lived from 1723 to 1759, but fifty years later the cutter had remained much the same. The spars these yachts carried were enormous, and they were built of such strength that they were up to the Government standard. Although the cutters were of large dimensions, sometimes having a tonnage of 150, yet they were very tubby, round creatures, their proportions being three beams in length and heavily ballasted after the mediæval manner with gravel, yet sometimes also with iron ore. But as match sailing became commoner, naturally a means was sought for making the cumbersome craft less heavy. The heavy ballast remained, but both timbers and planking were of less thickness. Hitherto of clinker build, this gradually gave way to carvel-work. One of the most famous yachts of the first quarter of the century was the *Arrow*, built clinker fashion in 1822 and still in existence.

The illustration in Fig. 111 represents the *Kestrel*, 202 tons, belonging to the Earl of Yarborough, Commodore of the Royal Yacht Squadron. In the early 'forties she was a well-known ship. She is rigged as a Hermaphrodite brig, that is to say she is brig-rigged on her foremast but schooner-rigged on her main. She also carries a tier of guns. The influence, indeed, of the Royal Navy on these early yachts is notable. The cutters were influenced by the Government revenue cutters and the bigger yachts by the Naval brigs. Fig. 112 also shows a yacht of this period. This is the *Xarifa* which belonged to the second Earl of Wilton. She is rigged as a topsail schooner and also carries guns. The rigging of yachts at this time was chiefly of hemp, but, as will be seen from the accompanying illustrations, the sails were very baggy.

In the 'fifties racing between yachts went rapidly ahead. The crack cutters of the south coast were the *Arrow*, 84 tons, the *Lulworth*, 82 tons, the *Louisa*, 180 tons, and the *Alarm* 193 tons. A general improvement was taking place. The old-fashioned gravel ballast was thrown out and lead was slowly but surely introduced in spite of the criticism that it would strain the ship and cause her to plunge badly in a seaway. Next, instead of inside the lead was put outside below the keel. Finally the tubby proportions vanished and yachts were given greater length, greater depth but narrower beam. Early in the 'fifties Thomas Wanhill of Poole introduced the raking sternpost. Instead of the Dutch-like bow the long clipper bow, now famous among the mercantile ships, was coming into popularity.

But a new force was to come from across the Atlantic which had far-reaching effects on the yachts of this country. Let us return once more to Massachusetts. The theory of the advantage possessed by a sharp entrance and hollow water-lines had been proved, in the case of the Gloucester fishing and pilot schooners, to be sound and correct. Then it was decided to build a yacht on similar but improved lines: so in 1851 was launched the famous *America*, costing £4000. She was sailed across to England and on August 22, 1851, was the winning yacht for the special cup offered by the Royal Yacht Squadron. In the race round the Isle of Wight she beat the pick of our cutters and schooners so handsomely as to make yachtsmen and yacht-builders, designers and sail-makers open their eyes in amazement. The cup was afterwards presented by the owners of *America* to the New York Yacht Club as a perpetual challenge trophy to be raced for by yachts of all nations. The reader is well aware that in spite of various plucky attempts we have not yet succeeded in bringing it back to the country where it was manufactured.

After the success of *America* a change was made in the old type of yacht. The *Alarm* which had been built in 1834 as a cutter of 193 tons, was in 1852, consequent on *America's* victory, lengthened 20 feet by the bow and converted into a schooner of 248 tons. The illustration in Fig. 113, which is reproduced by kind permission of the Royal Victoria Yacht Club, Ryde, shows the *Alarm* after she had been rigged after the manner of *America* with one head-sail, having its foot laced to a boom, with a fore-sail having gaff but no boom, and with a mainsail with both gaff and boom. As here seen she justified the alterations made in her and remained for many years the fastest schooner of the fleet. But not only in rig and design did *America* make a complete revolution. Hitherto our sails had been mere wind-bags, but the *America* had her sails made so as to lace to the spars, while ours had been loose-footed on the boom. The American yacht's canvas thus set flatter and she could hold a better wind than our craft. Henceforth English sailmakers adopted the new idea. Schooners at least took to the new shape at once but the cutters were a little time before they followed the lead thus given to them. It was to America, therefore, that the last existing relic of mediaevalism in British ships was banished off the face of the waters for ever.

In 1852 the famous cutter *Arrow*, for the same reason as had transformed the *Alarm*, was rebuilt. Her previous length when she was first built as far back as 1823 was only

3·35 times her beam. In 1852, also, Mr. William Fife of the famous " Fife of Fairlie " firm came into prominence with the *Cymba*. Sail-making in the hands of Lapthorn & Ratsey proceeded along scientific lines, and eventually cotton was used instead of flax. In the 'sixties, following the example set by the builders of the clipper-ships, iron frame-work was used in combination with wooden skin, and from the early 'seventies to the 'eighties the clipper-bow had attained such success on big ships that it became of great popularity on yachts. But during the 'sixties the old straight-stem cutters were at the height of their fame. The *Oimara*, seen in Fig. 114 with the long bowsprit of the period, was a famous racing craft of the south coast. Built in 1867 by Mr. William Steele of Messrs. Robert Steele & Co., Greenock, the well-known builder of clipper-ships, her tonnage was 163. She sailed a memorable race round the Isle of Wight in August of the following year against the American schooners *Sappho*, *Aline* and others. Going east about, *Oimara* led the fleet until the Needles were rounded, but running back to Cowes against the ebb tide, she was beaten by the schooners. This fine ship is still afloat in Poole harbour above the bridge, and is used as a houseboat.

The *Aline* just mentioned was another beauty of her day. Built by Messrs. Camper & Nicholson of Gosport in 1860, she was the first yacht to get away from the raking mast so well seen in the illustration of the *Alarm*. In the *Aline* the mast was stepped almost upright and she was also given a running bowsprit and jib. Another fast ship was the famous *Egeria*, 153-ton schooner, built by Wanhill at Poole. She was at her prime during the 'sixties, and beat *Aline* during the former's maiden race in 1865.

During the 'seventies and till the 'eighties, the tendency was to build yachts whose dimensions were still deeper, narrower and longer. Beam was thought deserving of little consideration and altogether undervalued until the

326

FIG. 199. THE "VICTORIA" II. OWNER OF THE BOAT — BRONZING

Photo, West & Son.

Fig. 121. The Auxiliary Ship-rigged Yacht "Valhalla."
1490 Tons. Built in 1892.

p. 397.

year 1886, when an entire change of feeling came. The illustration in Fig. 115 shows the wonderful old *Bloodhound*. She was built by Mr. William Fife of Fairlie in 1874 for the Marquis of Ailsa and was one of the famous class of 40-tonners which flourished during the 'seventies and into the 'eighties. During the six years she belonged to her first owner she won about £2500 worth of prizes, and afterwards changed hands. Last year, however, Lord Ailsa re-purchased her, and with new sails the old ship showed that her marvellous turn of speed had not deserted her. She did remarkably well during Cowes week until she had the misfortune to be sunk in collision with *L'Esperance*, and lay for some time at the entrance to Cowes fairway, a sad sight, with her masts showing above water and her crew at work salving what they could. She has since been raised, and this year is again racing with surprising success.

Few yachts, perhaps, are so well-known in name, at least, to the general reader, as the *Sunbeam*, in Fig. 116. Built in 1874, and owned by that enthusiastic yachtsman and experienced navigator Lord Brassey, the *Sunbeam* is an auxiliary topsailyard schooner. She was designed by Mr. St. Clare Byrne and is built of teak with iron frames. Her length over all is 170 feet; beam 27½ feet; depth 13¾ feet. Her displacement is 576 tons; her registered tonnage 227; her draught 13½ feet; while her sail area as now altered is 7950 square feet. She has cruised round the world, and been into almost every port where she could get. She raced across the Atlantic in 1905 to the Lizard, with the *Valhalla* among the competitors, although it was not to be expected that she would come in first against such an extreme type as the *Atlantic*. In her time she has covered as her best run under canvas, 299 knots from noon to noon, whilst her highest speed, also under sail alone, was 15 knots. She is still happily with us, and is a familiar sight at Cowes, where she fits out.

During the 'seventies, thanks to Mr. William Froude and others, experiments of the highest educative value were made to discover the laws which governed the resistance of water to bodies moving through it. This led to a scientific basis on which to model the lines of yachts' hulls. But suddenly and unexpectedly, from Maldon, on the Blackwater, in a remote corner of Essex, a Mr. E. H. Bentall, not a professional naval architect but an agricultural implement maker, who had received but little training in naval architecture, designed and had built the now famous yacht the *Jullanar*, in 1875. Since length means speed, he gave her much of this, whilst for stability she was given a fairly deep draught. But getting right away from existing conventions, he had the courage to dispense with the old-fashioned straight stem and stern, and cut away all dead-wood from both. And so the *Jullanar*, with her easy lines, and rigged as a yawl, came into being. She had a tonnage of 126 (Thames measurement); length over all 110½ feet; beam 16·6 feet; and a draught of 13½ feet. She immediately displayed such remarkable speed and was so successful as a racer that her lines considerably influenced the late Mr. G. L. Watson, the famous yacht architect of the nineteenth century, in designing the *Thistle*, although this ship did not come into being until 1887. The sketch in Fig. 117, showing the hull and rigging of the *Jullanar*, has been made from the fine little model in the South Kensington Museum.

Yacht-design has been considerably modified by contemporary existing measurement rules. Thus, when in the 'eighties the only taxed dimensions were, not length over all, but length on water-line and sail area, the temptation to introduce overhang both at bow and stern was irresistible. In *Jullanar* the germ of the idea existed, but it developed to its fullest extent during the 'nineties, and so by a curious fatality one becomes witness of still another revival, more strange and curious than all the others, the revival of that which was indeed one of the most characteristic features of the Egyptian craft in the early dynasties, the overhanging bow and stern. In 1893 was built the *Satanita*, in which this last-mentioned feature is well shown. (See Fig. 118.) This powerful beauty has on the

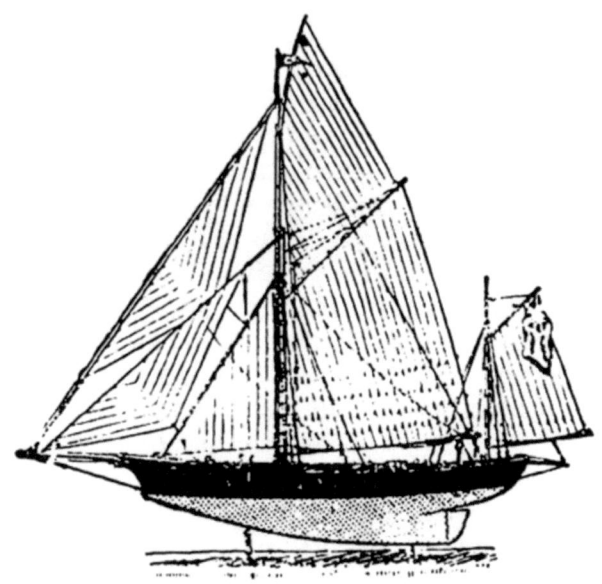

Fig. 117. The Yawl "Jullanar." Built in 1875.

water-line 97·7 feet, and an extreme beam of 24·7 feet, and a draught of 16·5 feet. Her sail area (Y.R.A.) was in her Solent days 9923 square feet. The beautifully-fitting sails seen in the accompanying illustration are in wonderful contrast to those hollow bags used in the pre-*America* days. In the same year was launched King Edward's (then Prince of Wales') *Britannia*, which with Captain Carter at her helm, won both fame and a considerable number of prizes during the 'nineties. Her length on the water-line is 87·8 feet; her extreme beam 23·66 feet; and draught 15 feet. The illustration in Fig. 119

of the counter of *Britannia* has been specially included to give the reader some idea of the weight of her mainsail, which, as will be noticed, is being hoisted by no less than fourteen hands on the halyard, including the ship's cook and steward. The year 1893 was made memorable by the launch also of the *Valkyrie*, one of the famous trio of yachts of the same name. She measured on the water-line 86·8 feet; her extreme beam was 22·33 feet. The illustration in Fig. 120 shows *Valkyrie I*. It was during this year that beam, being no longer taxed, was allowed to show its value, and ever since that time the tendency has continued for a more wholesome type of boat, instead of the vicious old plank-on-edge class of craft.

The illustration in Fig. 121 is of the *Valhalla*, which, like the *Sunbeam*, has auxiliary engines and is one of the largest and finest sailing yachts in the world. Under the ownership of the Earl of Crawford she has made lengthy voyages to distant countries, and was one of the fleet which raced in company with the *Sunbeam* from the U.S.A. to the Lizard for the German Emperor's Cup, obtaining third prize, and doing the passage across the Atlantic in 14 days 2 hours, using sail only. She was built in 1892, and was first rigged as a privateer of a hundred years ago with stun's'ls. She even had her ward-room, gun-room and armoury after the manner of the naval ships of a century ago. In the accompanying illus-tration she is seen with courses, topsails, t'gallants and royals. But when she came into the hands of Lord Crawford the stun's'ls were abolished, and she was given double topsails instead of single so as to facilitate her being worked with less labour. The old-fashioned deck arrangement below was also entirely changed. This handsome 1490-ton yacht has recently been sold, and left English waters to become an American training-ship.

Although American yachting existed long before the

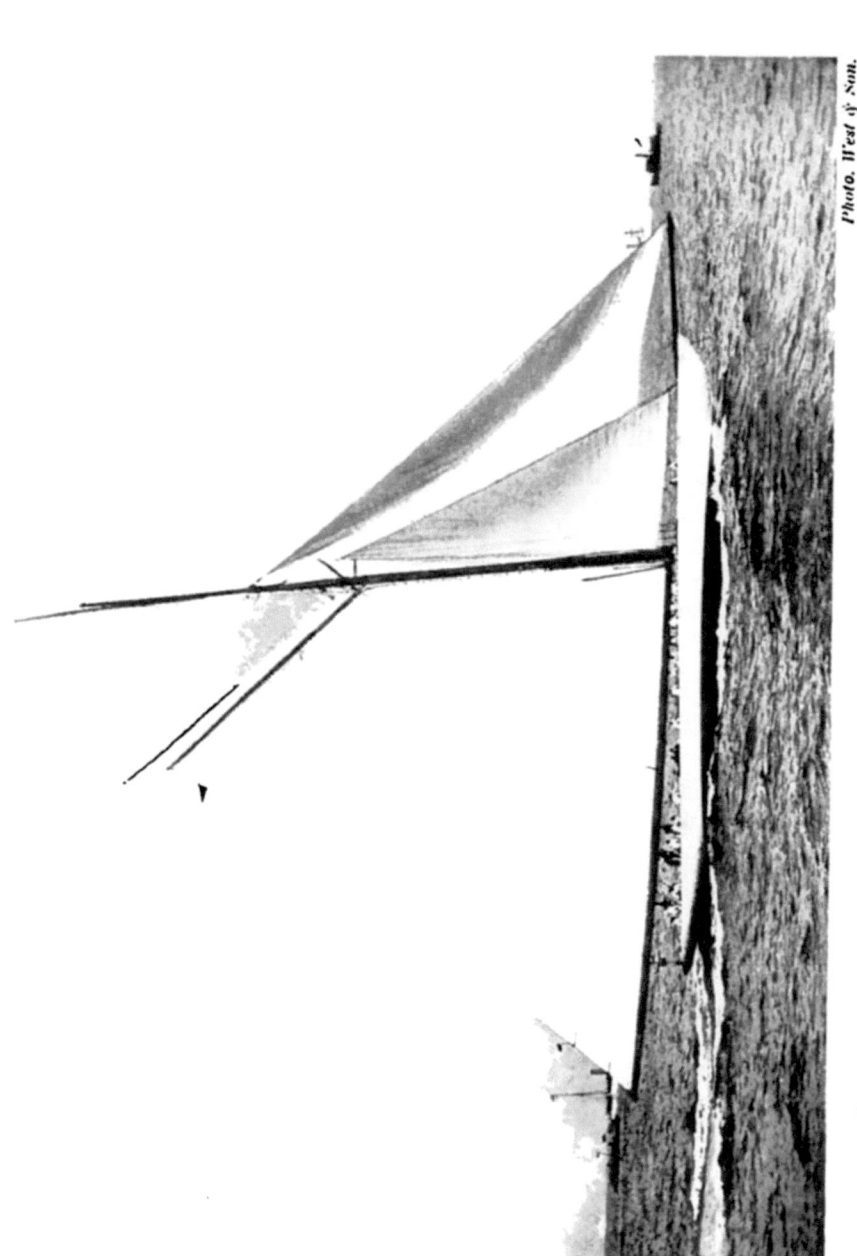

Photo. West & Son.

p. 330.

FIG. 122. THE AMERICAN CUP DEFENDER "COLUMBIA." LANCHED IN 1899.

Fig. 123. The Schooner-Yacht "Meteor."
Owned by His Majesty the German Emperor.

races for the America Cup, yet these contests have given an enormous fillip in the United States to the building of cutters as apart from their fast schooners. Such vessels, built to defend the Cup, as the *Defender*, launched in 1895, the *Columbia* in 1899 (see Fig. 122), the *Constitution* in 1901, and the *Reliance* in 1903, are about 90 feet on the load water-line, and carry about 13,500 square feet of canvas; though when *Reliance* beat *Shamrock III.*, the former carried over 16,000 square feet. But the most popular American large racing cutters are the 70-footers. In build the Americans have been accustomed to use lighter scantlings than we on this side of the Atlantic. *Meteor*, in Fig. 123, the well-known schooner belonging to the German Emperor, was the product of an American yard. The photograph here reproduced was taken while she was racing for the King's Cup inside the Isle of Wight.

Some sensation was caused in the Solent last summer by the arrival and success of the *Germania*, a remarkably fast and pretty schooner, notable as showing the ability to which German yacht designers and builders have now attained. That we can in England still build cruising as well as racing schooners is proved by two such different examples as the *Elizabeth* and the *Pampas*. The sail plan of the former will be found in Plan 5. Launched in 1906 from the yard of Messrs. White Brothers of Cowes from designs by Mr. H. W. White, her tonnage (Thames measurement) is 236, her length over all 132 feet, but on the water-line 93½ feet. Her draught is 12½ feet, and her sail area 7938 square feet. She is also fitted with a motor that can be run on either paraffin or petrol with a two-bladed propeller, giving a mean speed under motor alone of six miles per hour. The deck plan and longitudinal section showing motor installation will be found in Plans 6 and 7.

The *Pampas* is one of the most interesting yachts of 1908. In her will be found the very last word in schooner designing and building. The requirements were that she should be suitable to go to any part of the world in comfort and with speed. In order therefore that she might not be handicapped in the Doldrums she was fitted with a 60-horse-power motor giving a speed of six knots in smooth water. Designed by Mr. C. E. Nicholson, and built by Messrs. Camper & Nicholson for Señor Aaron de Anchorena, of Buenos Ayres, she has considerably more overhang than the *Elizabeth*, and has shown herself to be very fast under sail alone. The sail and rigging plan in Plan 8 will explain itself, whilst from the other plans the general internal arrangement of this most modern of yachts will be realised. She has between her two masts a sunken deck-house, a feature that has recently become very popular on sailing yachts. The two large cabins athwart the ship are fitted in satinwood, and other accommodation is in ivory white. Electric light and ventilating fans are also found on her, and she is classed twenty years A1 at Lloyd's.

To return to the English cutters, one of the most interesting of modern yachts is that seen in Fig. 124, which represents *White Heather II.* For size and sweet lines, with her bold bows and white graceful hull, her lofty mast and her mountain of canvas, she is an imposing sight if one comes across her on the Solent. She is at her best in a strong wind; in light winds she used to be no match for the latest *Shamrock*. But during the past winter *White Heather* has had some structural alterations made to improve her power in light winds.

An important step was taken in 1906, when an international conference was held to devise such an international rule as would be acceptable to the whole of yachting Europe. During the last fifteen years various rating rules had been in force at different times. It was now felt that something should be done to prevent the success of the racing-machine and skimming-dish type, and recent rating rules had indeed tended to produce a wholesome cruiser that was nevertheless good for racing. The conference therefore formulated a new rule based on that which had produced such recent healthy types as *Nyria;* but a premium was placed on freeboard and a check on clumsy overhangs, in order that a thoroughly healthy type of sea-going yacht might be evolved that should be good as well for cruising as for racing. Care was taken also to ensure the requisite strength in construction. The rule came into force on January 1, 1908. Under this rule, *Shamrock IV.,* seen in Fig. 125, was built, and during her maiden season last year she showed that in light weather there was nothing of her size to catch her. In spite of adverse criticisms the new rule has in it much that is likely to be an influence for good ; and since it is to be in force for ten years, it will certainly add to the prosperity of yachting by introducing to an extent hitherto unknown the element of international racing.

Shamrock, the fourth of that name owned by Sir Thomas Lipton, belongs to the 23-metre class. She was designed by Mr. William Fife and built by Messrs. William Fife & Son of Fairlie. She is of composite construction, her planking being of mahogany and her frames of steel. In yachting, as in the biggest sailing ships, wire rigging has now ousted the old-fashioned hemp. Runners, topping lifts, bobstay falls, outhauls, halyards—all are of wire. Racing boats and many cruisers now have rigging screws too, while the custom as to ballast is to bolt most of it outside the keel.

But our limit is at length reached. We have watched the primitive ship evolve from the tree ; we have seen how she has been changed and revived, degenerated and improved, made larger or smaller, tubbier or more graceful according as it has pleased the hand of man. Now that we have shown, however imperfectly, with however many

SAILING SHIPS

omissions, her noble and illustrious pedigree, her ancestry reaching back through the centuries into the first blush of the dawn of the world's creation, perhaps we shall regard her with an interest, a respect and affection at once greater and deeper because we have become better acquainted with the reasons that have caused each of these developments.

THE END.

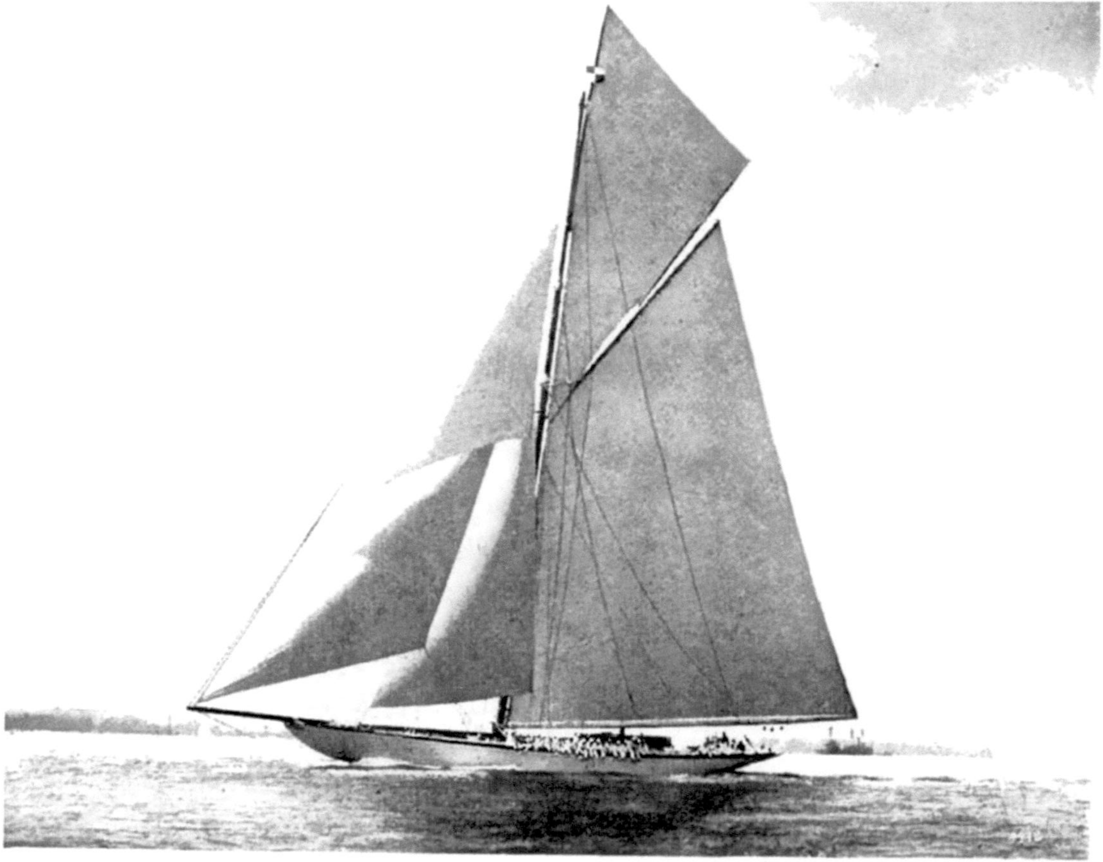

Photo. West & Son.

FIG. 123. "WHITE HEATHER II." 23-METRE CUTTER.

FIG. 125. "SHAMROCK IV," 23 MÈTRE CUTTER.
OWNED BY SIR THOMAS LIPTON. LAUNCHED 1908. *p.* 335.

GLOSSARY.

Braces. Ropes rove through blocks by which to control the yards of a square-rigged ship.

Brails. Ropes used for the purpose of shortening a ship's canvas, as in the case of the Phœnician and Roman ships, and to-day in the Thames barge.

Careen. To lay a ship over on to her side in order to be able to caulk her lower seams.

Carvel-build. The manner of building a vessel so that the planks are laid edge to edge, and not overlapping.

Caulk. To stop the seams of a ship with oakum, so as to prevent the water entering between the planking.

Clew. The lower corners of a squaresail, and the aftermost corner of a staysail.

Clinker-build. The manner of building a vessel so that the planks overlap each other. (Compare " carvel-build.")

Crank. An adjective applied to a ship when she is liable to capsize.

Davits. Short pieces, formerly of timber, now of iron, projecting over a vessel's side, for hoisting up the ship's anchors or boats.

Dhow. The term applied generally to the lateen-rigged ships of the East.

Freeboard. The amount of a ship's hull extending from the waterline to the gunwale.

Gaff. A spar used for extending the upper edge of a fore-and-aft rectangular sail—e.g., the mainsail of a cutter.

Goaring. An old English expression in use during Elizabethan times, applied when the lower corners of the sail extended much further out than the width of the canvas stretched along the yard.

Gooseneck. A piece of bent iron fitted to the end of a boom by which to connect the latter to the ship.

GLOSSARY

GUY. A rope attached to a spar for the purpose of steadying it.

GYBE. When a ship so alters her course in running free that the wind, instead of coming from one quarter, comes from the opposite quarter, the mainsail of a fore-and-after will have swung over, and be said to have gybed.

HALYARD. A rope or tackle used for hoisting or lowering sails and spars.

JETTISON. To lighten a ship by throwing goods overboard.

JIB-BOOM. The spar which continues further forward the projection of the bowsprit.

KEELSON. The piece of timber which is laid on the middle of the floor timbers over the keel.

LANYARD. A short piece of rope used for various purposes—*e.g.*, for making fast the shrouds to a ship's side.

LATEEN. A long triangular sail bent to a long yard, a characteristic sail of the Mediterranean and dhow-rigged craft. Also carried on the mizzen and bonaventure mizzen of mediæval full-rigged ships.

LEACH. The vertical edges of a sail.

LUG. A fore-and-aft sail hoisted on a yard, of which not more than about a third of its length is forward of the mast. In the dupping-lug the tack of the sail is made fast some distance forward of the mast, and because the sail must needs be set on the lee side of the mast it has to be dipped at each tack and hoisted afresh on the other side.

MIZZEN. The aftermost mast of a vessel having two or more masts; sometimes called a jigger. In the case of mediæval ships having four masts, the aftermost was called the bonaventure mizzen, and the one immediately forward of this the main mizzen.

PARRAL. A band for keeping the end of a yard to the mast; made in different ages of basket-work or rope—in the latter case running through a number of circular pieces of wood, to prevent friction in raising and lowering the yard or gaff.

PAVISSES. Shields of wood or other material placed round a ship's side for a protection against the enemy's missiles; used also in open boats for keeping out the spray.

PINTLE. The bolt by which a rudder is attached to the stern of a ship.

QUANT. A pole used extensively in Holland and East Anglia for the purpose of propelling a craft along shallow waterways. (Greek κοντός, Latin *contus*, a pole.)

GLOSSARY

Race. A rapid current of disturbed water caused by the unevenness of the bottom of the sea, frequently found off headlands—*e.g.*, St. Alban's Head, Portland Bill, &c.

Rocker. The curvature of a piece or pieces of wood in a vessel's structure.

Scuttle. To cause a ship to sink by making holes in her hull below the water-line.

Sheer. The curve of a vessel's hull from bow to stern, or *vice versâ*.

Spinnaker. A light, triangular-shaped sail set on the side opposite to that on which the mainsail extends, and used when running before the wind.

Sprit, Spritsail. (1) In full-rigged ships the *spritsail* was a square-sail set on a yard below the bowsprit ; now obsolete. (2) In fore-and-aft vessels the *sprit* is a spar used for stretching the peak of the sail, thus extending diagonally across the mast—as, for instance, in the case of a Thames barge (see Fig. 99).

Staysail. Usually triangular in shape, though in the seventeenth century sometimes rectangular, hoisted on a stay, between the masts or forward of the fore-mast.

Steeving. The angle which a ship's bowsprit makes with the horizon.

Stempost. The piece of timber to which the two sides of a ship's planking are united at the forward end.

Step. The block of wood into which the keel of a mast is fixed.

Strut-frame. A piece of timber used in shipbuilding for strengthening the vessel.

Topping-lifts. Ropes used for the support of the boom of a sail when the latter is stowed.

Truck. A small wooden cap at the summit of a mast.

Vang. A rope leading down from the end of a gaff to the deck. A characteristic of the Dutch sloops and Thames barge rig.

Wale. One of the planks of a ship.

BIBLIOGRAPHY.

ABBOT, WILLIAM J. American Merchant Ships and Sailors. 1902.
ABENHOLD, L. Die Historische Entwicklung der Schiffstypen. 1891.
BAIF, DE. (Lazarus Bayfius): Annotationes . . . de captivis et post-liminis reversis, in quibus tractatur de re navali. 1536.
BARNARD, F. P. (edited by). Companion to English History (Middle Ages). Article by M. Oppenheim on Shipping. 1902.
BASTON, T. Twenty-two Prints of several of the Capital Ships of his Majesties Royal Navy.
BEDFORD, Admiral F. G. D., R.N., C.B. Sailor's Handbook.
—— Sailor's Pocket-book.
—— Sailor's Ready Reference Book. 1890.
BERNOULLI, JEAN. Essay d'Une Nouvelle Théorie de la Manœuvre des Vaisseaux. 1724.
BIRCH, W. de. G. Catalogue of Seals in the Department of MSS. of the British Museum.
BLACKMORE, E. The British Mercantile Marine. 1897.
BOEHMER, GEORGE H. Annual Report of Regents of the Smithsonian Institution: Prehistoric Naval Architecture of the North of Europe. 1892.
BOFARULL Y. SANS, D. F. de. Antiqua Marina Catalana. 1898.
BRIDGE, Admiral Sir CYPRIAN A. G. (edited by). History of the Russian Fleet During the Reign of Peter the Great by a Contemporary Englishman (1724). 1899.
BRIGHT, WILLIAM, D.D. Chapters of Early English Church History.
BRITISH MUSEUM. A Guide to the Third and Fourth Egyptian Rooms. 1904.
—— Handbook to the Coins of Great Britain and Ireland in the British Museum. 1899.
BULLEN, F. T., F.R.G.S. A Sack of Shakings.
BURGESS, E. Fifty Photogravures of the Most Famous English and American Yachts. 1888.

BIBLIOGRAPHY

Cary-Elwes, Rev. D.   A Prehistoric Boat.   1903.

Chapman, Frederick Hennik af.   Architectura Navalis Mercatoria Navium Varii Generis.   1768.

—— A Treatise Concerning the True Method of Finding the Proper Area of the Sails for Ships.   1794.

Charnock, John.   History of Marine Architecture.   3 vols.   1800.

Clark, A. H.   History of Yachts 1600–1815.   1904.

Clowes, Sir W. Laird.   The Royal Navy.   1900.

Colasanti, Arduino.   Gentile da Fabriano.   1909.

Colin, Ambroise.   La Navigation Commerciale au XIX° Siècle.   1901.

Cook, A. B.   Article on Ships by, in A Companion to Greek Studies, edited by L. Whibley.   1905.

Cook, E. T.   A Popular Handbook to the National Gallery.   1901.

Corbett, J. S., LL.M. (edited by).   Papers Relating to the Navy during the Spanish War 1585–87.   1898.

Darenburg, Ch.   Dictionnaire des Antiquités Grecques et Romans.   1905.   (Article under Navis by Cecil Torr.)

Dassie, Le Sieur.   L'Architecture Navale, contenant la manière de construire les navires, galères et chaloupes.   1677.

Davis, T. M.   The Tomb of Hatshopsitu.   1906.

Du Chaillu, Paul B.   The Viking Age.   1889.   2 vols.

Duemichen, J.   The Fleet of an Egyptian Queen.   1868.

Egypt Exploration Fund.   The Temple of Deir El Bahari by Edouard Naville.

—— Publications of.

—— Reports.

Falconer's Marine Dictionary.

Folin, Marquis de.   Bateaux et Navires : Progrès de la Construction Navale à tous les Ages et dans tous les Pays.   1892.

Furtenbach, Joseph.   Architectura Navalis.   1629.

Gauckler, P.   Un Catalogue Figuré de la Batellerie Gréco-Romaine— La Mosaïque D'Althiburus (article in Monuments et Mémoires. Tome Douzieme).   1905.

Gosse, Edmund.   The Lost Tapestries of the House of Lords (article in Harper's Monthly Magazine, 1907).

Guglielmotti, P. Alberto.   Delle due Navi Romane.   1874.

—— Mercantorio Colonna alla Battaglia di Lepanto.   1887.

—— Storia della Marina Pontificia.   9 vols.   1886–93.

Gustafson, Gabriel.   Norges Oldtid.   1906.

Hakluyt, Richard.   The Principal Voyages of the English Nation. (Maclehose's and Dent's Editions).

BIBLIOGRAPHY

HAKLUYT SOCIETY, Publications of.

HAMMER, S. C. and HAAKON NYHUUS. Article on The Viking Ship found at Oseberg in The Century Magazine. Vol. 70. 1905.

HAYWARD, EDWARD. The Sizes and Lengths of Riggings for all His Majesties Ships and Frigates. 1660.

HOLMES, Sir GEORGE, C.V., K.C.V.O., C.B. Ancient and Modern Ships. Part I., Wooden Sailing Ships; Part II., The Era of Steam, Iron and Steel. 1900 and 1906.

HOLMES, T. RICE. Cæsar's Conquest of Gaul. 1899.

HULSIUS, LEVINUS. A True Account of the Three New Unheard of and Strange Journeys in Ships . . . in the years 1594, 1595, 1596. . . . 1612.

JAL, A. Archéologie Navale. 2 vols. 1840.

—— La Flotte de César.

JOCHELSON, W. The Jesup North Pacific Expedition : Vol. VI., Part II. The Koryak. 1908.

LANT, THOMAS. Sequitur celebritas et pompa funeris (of Sir Philip Sydney). 1587.

LAUGHTON, Professor Sir J.K., M.A., R.N., (edited by). The Naval Miscellany, Vol. I. 1902.

—— (edited by). State Papers Relating to the Defeat of the Spanish Armada anno 1558. 1894.

LESLIE, R. C. Old Sea Wings, Ways and Words in the Days of Oak and Hemp. 1890.

LEVI, CESARE AUGUSTO. Navi Venete da Codici Marini e Dipinti. 1892.

LINDSAY, W.S. History of Merchant Shipping and Commerce. 1874-6.

LLOYD'S Almanac.

—— Register of British Shipping.

MAGNÚSSON, EIRÍKR. Notes on Shipbuilding and Nautical Terms of Old in the North. 1906.

MALFATTI, V. Le Navi Romane del Lago di Nemi. 1905.

MANWAYRING, Sir HENRY. Seamen's Dictionary. 1644.

MARKHAM, Sir CLEMENTS R., C.B., F.R.S. Life of Captain Stephen Martin 1666-1740. 1895.

MASEFIELD, JOHN. On the Spanish Main. 1906.

MASPERO, GASTON CAMILLE CHARLES. The Dawn of Civilisation— Egypt. 1894.

MAU, AUGUST. Pompeji In Leben und Kunst. 1908.

MICHAELIS, A. A Century of Archæological Discoveries. 1908.

MOLMENTI, POMPEO and GUSTAV LUDWIG. The Life and Works of Vittorio Carpaccio. 1907.

BIBLIOGRAPHY

Musée Rétrospectif de la Classe 33. Matériel de la Navigation de Commerce à l'Exposition Universelle Internationale de 1900, à Paris. Rapport du Comité d'Installation.

Nares, Captain Sir G. S., R.N. Seamanship. 1897.

The National Review.

Naville, Edouard. The Tomb of Hatshopsitu. 1906.

—— The Temple of Deir-el-Bahari.

Navy Records Society. Publications of.

The Nineteenth Century and After.

Oppenheim. A History of the Administration of the Royal Navy; 1509-1660. 1896.

—— (edited by). Naval Accounts and Inventories of the reign of Henry VII. 1896.

—— (edited by). Naval Tracts of Sir William Monson. 6 vols. 1902.

Paris, Admiral Edmond. L'Art Naval à L'Exposition Universelle de Londres de 1862. 1863.

—— Souvenirs de Marine. 4 vols. 1882-6.

—— Le Musée de Marine du Louvre des Navires à Rames et à voiles. 1883.

Pepys' Diary.

Perrot, Georges, and Robert de la Steyrie. Un Manuscrit de la Bibliothèque de Philippe le Bon à Saint-Pétersbourg (article in Monuments et Mémoires). 1904.

Petrie, W. M. F. Gizeh and Rifeh. 1907.

Pritchett, R. T. Shipping and Craft. 1899.

Raleigh, Sir Walter. Judicious and Select Essays. 1650.

Robinson, Commander C.N., R.N. The British Fleet. 1894.

The Rudder.

Runciman, W. Windjammers and Sea Tramps. 1902.

Russell, W. Clark. The Ship: her Story. 1899.

Smith, Captain John. Seaman's Grammar. 1653.

—— An Accidence, or the pathway to experience necessary for all young seamen. 1626.

Smyth, H. Warington. Mast and Sail in Europe and Asia. 1906.

Spooner, Rev. W.A., M.A. The Histories of Tacitus. 1891.

Spont, Alfred. Letters and Papers Relating to the War with France 1512-1513. 1897.

Stephens, George. Old Northern Runic Monuments of Scandinavia and England. 4 vols. 1866-1901.

Stock, St. George, (edited by). Cæsar de Bello Gallico. 1898.

Sullivan, Sir Edward, Bart. Lord Brassey and others' Yachting. 2 vols. 1894-5.

BIBLIOGRAPHY

TANNER, J. R., M.A.   A Descriptive Catalogue of the Naval MSS. in the Pepysian Library at Magdalene College Cambridge.   2 vols. 1903.

—— Two Discourses of the Navy : 1638 and 1659 by John Hollond. 1896.

TODD, J., and WHALL, W. B.   Practical Seamanship for Use in the Mercantile Service.   1898.

TORR, CECIL.   Ancient Ships.   1894.

TRAILL, H. D., D.C.L., and J. S. MANN, M.A.   Social England. 1901.   Also articles in same by W. Laird Clowes.

THE VICTORIA COUNTY HISTORIES.

WEALE, W. H. JAMES.   Hans Memlinc.   1901.

WRIGHT, W. H. K.   Catalogue of the Exhibition of Armada and Elizabethan Relics.   1888.

The Yachtsman.

The Yachting Monthly.

The Yachting World.

YOUNG, FILSON.   Christopher Columbus and the New World of His Discovery containing a Note on the Navigation of Columbus's First Voyage, by the Earl of Dunraven.   2 vols.   1906.

INDEX

INDEX

INDEX

INDEX

INDEX

INDEX

350

INDEX

INDEX

INDEX

INDEX

INDEX

INDEX

INDEX

INDEX

INDEX

INDEX

INDEX

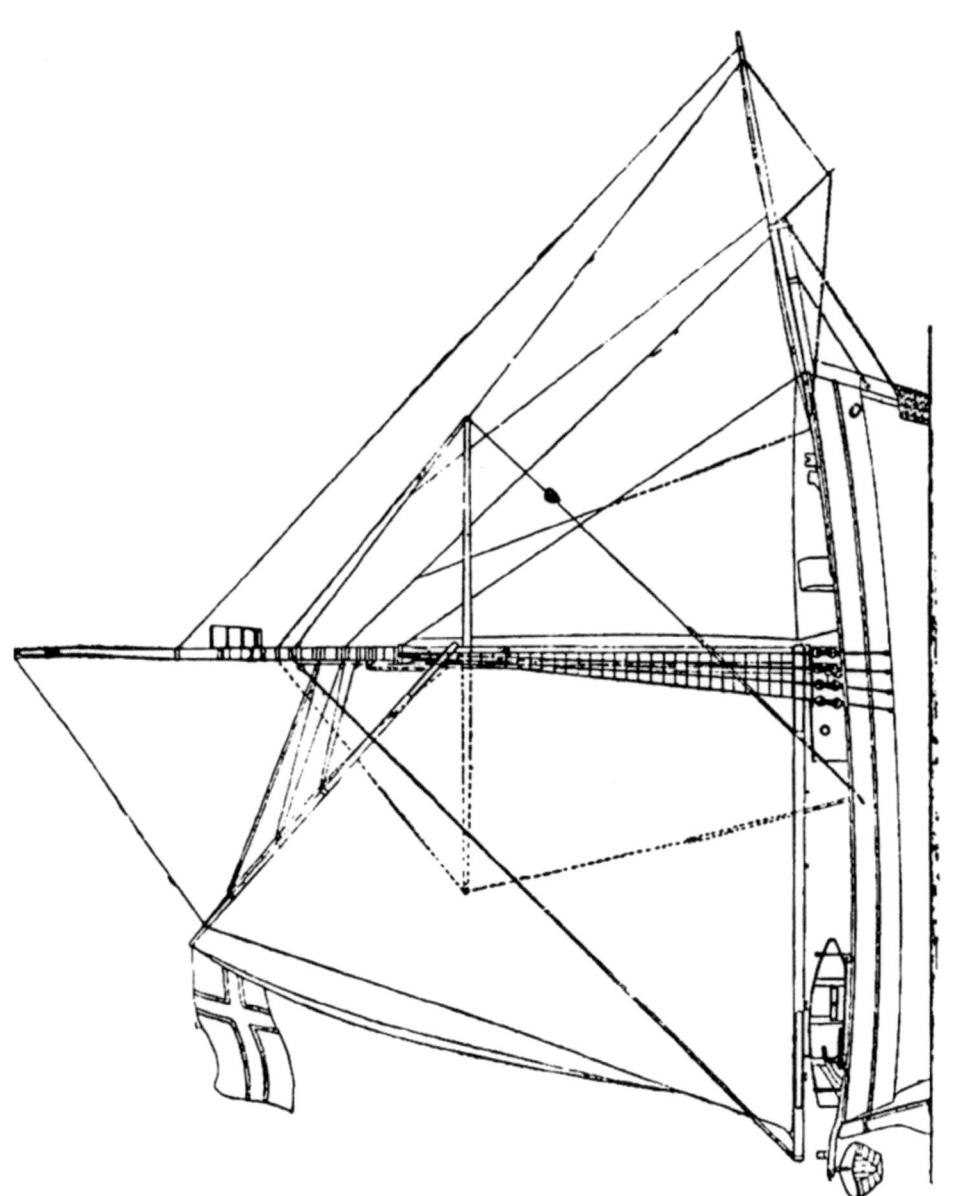

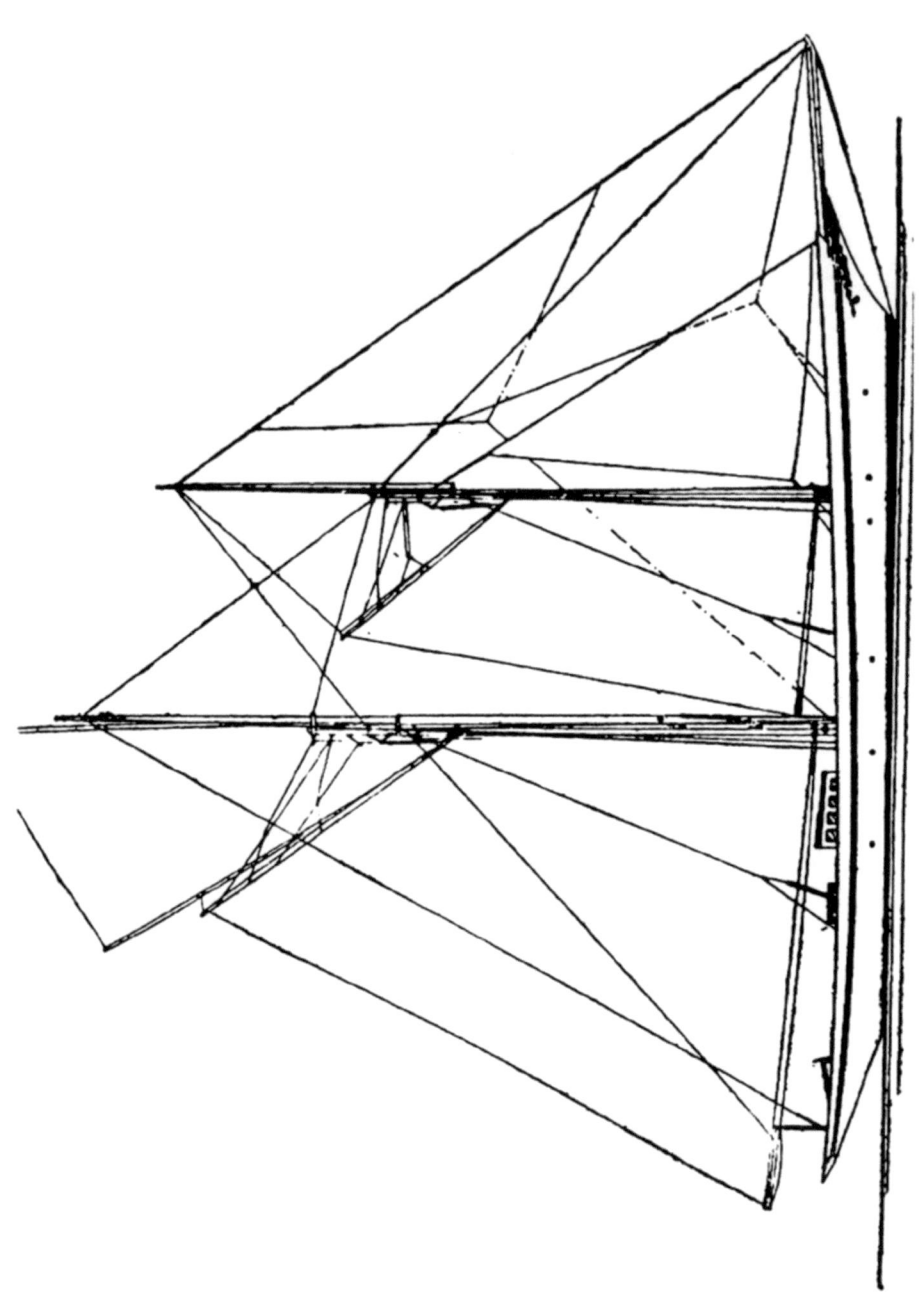